Avoid Stress and Fear for First Time Parents

The Latest on Pre- and Postnatal Development for Both Baby and Mom so You Can Adapt to Your New Role Easy and Without Feeling Overwhelmed

Harley Carr

Hello,

Even if you're not a fan of journaling or you don't have the time for it, many experts have confirmed the benefits of keeping a journal during pregnancy. Here are some of the reasons why you should start writing as soon as your baby bump begins to show.

1. **Reduce Stress**

   Finding an outlet for your thoughts during pregnancy, can help you find solutions to your pregnancy fears and manage the anxiety that comes from negative thoughts. It's an effective means to access your emotions and rid yourself of stress, which may affect the wellbeing of your baby

2. **Organize Yourself**

   We know how disoriented a pregnancy can make expecting mothers feel. It's no easy task getting everything ready for the little pink feet, maintaining a healthy lifestyle as well as managing your regular schedule. Apart from organizing your thoughts, journaling can also help to coordinate your duties, manage your time efficiently and ultimately make you a more productive mum-to-be.

3. **Track Your Progress**

   It is a lot of fun tracking your pregnancy and recording the way your baby bump has grown week by week. Journaling a pregnancy can also act as a confidence booster. Your journal will be an inventory of your achievements and successes during your pregnancy.

4. **Celebrate Your Happy Moments**

   How did you feel when you first found out that it was a boy or a girl? What was your first reaction when you saw the ultrasound image of your baby? Describe these positive emotions in your journal. At the end of each day, write down all the things that went smoothly and that you're proud of.

So, get your **"My Weekly Pregnancy Journal"** in PDF format for free by clicking the link below:

https://harleycarrparenting.com/from-baby-bump-all-the-way-to-babys-birthday

or

Print the document and start to make your own pregnancy Journal week by week.

This printable "My Weekly Pregnancy Journal" has 38 pages where you can track the fruit-like size of your baby from 4 weeks throughout 40 weeks.

Now, you can have your *own* "Weekly Pregnancy Journal " in just one click away!

Let´s get started …

Enjoy and Best Wishes to your Pregnancy Journey!

Harley Carr

© Copyright 2020 - All rights reserved.

The content contained within this book may not be reproduced, duplicated or transmitted without direct written permission from the author or the publisher.

Under no circumstances will any blame or legal responsibility be held against the publisher, or author, for any damages, reparation, or monetary loss due to the information contained within this book, either directly or indirectly.

Legal Notice:

This book is copyright protected. It is only for personal use. You cannot amend, distribute, sell, use, quote or paraphrase any part, or the content within this book, without the consent of the author or publisher.

Disclaimer Notice:

Please note the information contained within this document is for educational and entertainment purposes only. All effort has been executed to present accurate, up to date, reliable, complete information. No warranties of any kind are declared or implied. Readers acknowledge that the author is not engaging in the rendering of legal, financial, medical or professional advice. The content within this book has been derived from various sources. Please consult a licensed professional before attempting any techniques outlined in this book.

By reading this document, the reader agrees that under no circumstances is the author responsible for any losses, direct or indirect, that are incurred as a result of the use of information contained within this document, including, but not limited to, errors, omissions, or inaccuracies.

Table of Contents

_Toc55661860

Section 1: From Your Baby Bump To Your Baby's First Birthday 11

Introduction ___13

Part 1: Prenatal Development—The Nine-Month Journey ___21

Chapter 1: The First Trimester (1-3 Months) ___23

Chapter 2: The Second Trimester (4-6 Months) ___35

Chapter 3: The Third Trimester (7-9 Months) ___49

Part 2: Baby's First Year—Milestones and Mental Leaps ___61

Chapter 4: 1st Month-3rd Month ___63

Chapter 5: 4th Month-6th Month ___81

Chapter 6: 7th Month-9th Month ___99

Chapter 7: 10th Month-12th Month ___117

Chapter 8: 10 Mental Leaps in Your Baby's Life ___137

Conclusion ___149

References Section 1 ___153

Section 2: Pre- and Postnatal care for Both Baby and Mom ___157

Introduction ___161

Part 1: Prenatal Care ___167

Chapter 1: Finding the Right Maternity Care Provider and Check-Up Schedule ___171

Chapter 2: Healthy Options _____ 189

Chapter 3: Frequently Asked Questions About Safety During Pregnancy _____ 201

Make-Up Safety: Read the Label _____ 207

Chapter 4: Pregnancy Fears and Why You Shouldn't Worry _____ 217

Chapter 5: Late Term Pregnancy Comfort and Preparation _____ 229

Part Two: Postnatal Care _____ 239

Chapter 6: Taking Care of Yourself _____ 241

Chapter 7: Baby's First Days _____ 255

Chapter 8: Baby Essentials: Feeding _____ 269

Chapter 9: Baby Essentials: Clothing, Diapers, Bathing, & Skincare _____ 287

Chapter 10: Care Provider and Childcare _____ 303

Chapter 11: Check-Up Schedule and Vaccinations _____ 317

Chapter 12: Baby's Safety and Medical Emergency Concerns ____ 333

Conclusion _____ 347

References Section 2 _____ 351

Section 3: Smooth Transition to Parenthood for First Time Mothers and Fathers _____ *365*

Introduction _____ 369

Part 1: Adjusting to Parenthood _____ 373

Chapter 1: Becoming a Parent! What to Expect? _____ 375

Chapter 2: Adjusting to Changes _____ 387

Chapter 3: Parenting _____ 405

Chapter 4: Back to Work? _____ 417

Part 2: Time to Regain Your Strengths, Your Shape, And Yourself 429

Chapter 5: Workout and Exercise after Giving Birth _____ 431

Chapter 6: Benefits of Baby and Mom Exercise _____ 443

Chapter 7: Good Nutrition and Diet for New Moms _____ 455

Chapter 8: Your Intimate Relationship with Your Husband/Partner
_____ 469

Chapter 9: When to Have another Child? _____ 487

Conclusion _____ 495

References Section 3 _____ 501

Section 1: From Your Baby Bump To Your Baby´s First Birthday

Learn What Happens Before and After the Birth of Your Baby - So You Are Prepared and Confident During Pre and Postnatal Development

Introduction

Pregnancy is a fascinating experience that gives you an opportunity to learn something new almost every single day. While your body is changing from the inside out, there are several things that are happening that you are likely unaware of. A lot of mothers do not feel that they have enough knowledge or education on the various stages of development while their baby is still in the womb. While this isn't necessarily a problem, it can impact your confidence for when the baby is born. By knowing exactly what is going on during your given stage of pregnancy, you will feel better equipped to handle anything that comes your way as a parent.

Knowing how big your baby is each week can provide you with some insight as to how they are developing as well as why your body is feeling the way that it is. As pregnancy progresses, the body needs to literally shift internally in order to make room for the growing baby. As this happens, you will feel a wide variety of various symptoms. You might also be genuinely curious as to how big your baby is getting and how fast this process is taking place. One minute, you aren't showing at all and the next you have a bump that prevents you from being able to see your toes.

As your baby is growing inside the womb, you must wait patiently until the day that you finally get to deliver them in order to truly see them for the first time. Ultrasounds will hold you over until then, but there is nothing like being able to hold and see your baby with your own eyes for the first time. Once you give birth, all of your parenting worries and curiosities become intensified because you have your baby before you. If you felt like there were a lot of unanswered questions during your pregnancy, these are likely going to carry over into your baby's infant stage. This is why it is important to obtain this knowledge before the baby is born.

The main problem is that most parents do not know what the typical milestones are for their babies. They also do not realize that each baby is going to develop at a different rate of speed, and that is okay. Much like you are an individual with unique traits and your own personality, so is your baby. Though much tinier, your little human is going to develop at the rate that is natural to them. While there are some things that you can do to guide them toward the healthiest choices in life, most of what parenting involves is being able to accept the unpredictable and just go with the flow.

Real Solutions

Most pregnancy guides will simply state obvious facts that aren't hard to research on your own. This one is different because it will provide you with tried and true solutions that you can apply to your own life. Your baby will benefit from this useful information that you learn, and your confidence will continue to grow daily. From the instant of conception, you will learn all that you need to know regarding your baby's development. By the time you give birth, you will feel fully prepared and capable to be the best parent that you can be.

Some of the topics covered are:

- Week-by-week prenatal development
- Development of the senses
- Accurate gender identification
- What to expect in the first year of life (milestones)

You are going to feel knowledgeable and ready to guide your baby through each stage of development. What a child needs is a parent who takes action and has solutions. This is what this guide aims to provide you with. Though your solutions might need backup plans at times, it is better to have some ideas than to enter blindly. Parenting can be an unpredictable job, but it is one that can be very rewarding once you start to figure it out for yourself.

There will be no need to panic or wonder if you are doing the right thing because this guide is filled with real solutions to real problems that are faced by many daily. It is going to provide you with a way to track your baby's progress to ensure that everything is going well developmentally, cognitively, emotionally, and physically. By knowing what the standard rate of development is, you will be able to notice any patterns if something goes wrong. Instead of panicking and not knowing how to handle the problem, you will be able to get to your doctor quickly, providing your child with a faster solution.

My Story

My name is Harley Carr, and I'm a mother just like you. My three children mean the world to me, but raising them has provided me with just any many challenges as there were triumphs. With them currently aged 8, 5, and 3, I definitely have my hands full. The first year of a child's life is always one of the most chaotic for the mother. There are so many decisions to be made, ones that can shape the future of their lives forever. It is a lot of pressure when you truly think about it.

One of the biggest decisions I faced was whether to return to work or stay home with my newborn. My son, Jaden, was my first child. Luckily, I have a very supportive partner who told me that I should stay at home with the baby so that we could further bond. My partner knew how much I yearned to get out of the office and into the nursery. Since my pregnancy was filled with days of never-ending nausea and contractions that nearly made me pass out, he thought that I would benefit from just taking some time to be with the baby.

It was the best decision I ever made. I stayed at home with Jaden, and for his first year of life, I learned from all of our trials and tribulations. It was through this time with him that I decided I would breastfeed all of my children. Jaden was a very healthy baby, and he latched on right away—I felt so proud in that moment. He wasn't too fussy, but boy did he hate bath time. Through all of these experiences, I truly believe I became a better mother. I was as educated as possible, but there was still so much to learn. Jaden taught me everything else that I needed to know to raise him and his siblings.

Through all the diaper changes and baths given in the last 8 years, I feel that my knowledge can also help you. Whether you plan on becoming a stay-at-home mom or must return to the workforce shortly after delivery, you will be ready for the milestones to come. Instead of struggling, you can learn from my struggles. With the tips that I provide you and the methods that I share, not only will you feel prepared, but you will feel excited to guide your child through their first year of life.

The Benefits

There are countless parenting books to read, so you might be wondering, why this one? The answer is simple—you need a complete picture of how your baby is going to develop, and this book will provide you with one. I will cover the time spent inside the womb to the first year of your baby's active life, so you will know and understand exactly what is going on both physically and mentally. There is so much that can change every single week, from the time that you first find out you are pregnant to actually being a mother of a one-year-old. The progress never stops, so this means you need to keep up.

This book will actually allow you to feel that you are ahead of the game. Instead of struggling to catch up, you will be prepared and able to handle anything that comes your way. Being a great mom has nothing to do with getting everything right on the first try. It actually involves a lot of trial and error, which a lot of people do not realize is very normal for parenting the first year of a child's life. As long as you have good intentions with the desire to put in as much effort as possible, you are going to be great as a parent. Plus, if you have a supportive partner to help you, then your baby is going to have twice as much support throughout their life.

While it isn't possible to be worry-free parents at all times, having this knowledge will put you at ease in the times when you need it most. When a baby is crying but cannot tell you what is wrong, this can be one of the most intimidating moments of your entire life. Your natural instinct as a parent will likely kick in, trying to come up with solutions for your distressed baby, but there will be times when you just can't seem to figure it out. Don't forget to take care of yourself, to breathe. Your baby is going to be picking up on your energy, positive or negative.

This book will not only shed some light on the topics you normally wonder about, but it will also remind you that your approach and attitude are super important parts of parenting. The energy that you put out is going to be reflected right back at you. When your baby can sense that you are okay, they will also feel that they can be okay. Starting from the very beginning, you are that baby's entire support system. From developing in the womb to experiencing the first year of life, your baby will be relying on you to lead the way.

Why Is It Important?

Do you want to know that your baby is developing well?

Are you curious about what milestones you can expect?

Have you ever wondered what your baby is mentally capable of understanding?

All of these questions (and more) will be answered by the time you are finished with this guide. Not only will you have the answers that you need, but you will also have proven knowledge on the topics that will guide you toward making your own decisions as you explore the various joys of parenthood.

If you feel ready to become a great parent, don't delay in reading this guide. Though you might only be a few weeks pregnant, now is the perfect time to sit down and learn all that there is to know about your baby's developmental stages. As you progress, you can follow along in the book to see exactly where you stand and where your baby compares to the average statistics.

Any delays are only going to hold you back from becoming the best parent you can be and that will mean that you have to figure out the answers to important questions after your baby has already been born. You are going to learn that you have the ability to multitask like never before, yet it is still going to be easier to take care of a baby when you already have all of the knowledge stored in your memory. Waiting until the end of your pregnancy, or even after delivery, is only going to hinder your own progress.

No parent wants to feel unprepared, so you shouldn't put yourself in that situation. It can be confusing and very overwhelming to feel this way. Give yourself and your baby the advantage of a proper education. Read this guide several times if you need to, studying different sections if you feel that you need a refresher at any given time. This guide is much more than just information that you will benefit from. Think about it as a way for you to navigate through parenting while always being able to remain calm since the answers can be found as long as you keep on reading.

Part 1: Prenatal Development—The Nine-Month Journey

As you become familiar with the term prenatal development, you will realize that each trimester of your baby's life during your pregnancy is going to be different. There will be a lot of symptoms that you will feel externally, but your baby is also going to be experiencing many changes inside of the womb. Through all nine months of your pregnancy, you are going to be amazed at all that can happen in this amount of time. From a small embryo to a fully-developed infant, you are going to learn about each milestone along the way.

Chapter 1: The First Trimester (1-3 Months)

A lot changes within the first trimester of your pregnancy. Though you can't see it and you might not feel it very much, your baby is developing at a rapid rate of speed. During this time, you are likely preparing your own life for the arrival of your new bundle of joy. This can include a change in lifestyle, tightening up on finances, and planning a nursery design in your home. Prenatal development actually starts upon conception, and it does not end until your baby is born. Through these nine months, you are going to learn a lot about yourself and a lot about your baby.

The First Month

During your first month of pregnancy, your baby is a tiny embryo made up of cells. Though your baby is still microscopic, there are actually two layers of cells present, called the epiblast and the hypoblast. These cells are all going to develop into your baby's systems and parts that will continue growing throughout your pregnancy. Comparing its size to something you are used to seeing, your baby is no larger than a poppy seed at this point in the pregnancy. It is amazing, however, to think about how quickly they are developing at this stage.

When you first conceive your baby, a small ball of cells settles into your uterus. It will then split up into two groups, half forming your baby and the other half forming the placenta. As you may know, the placenta will begin to form once you are pregnant and it will house your baby like a protective barrier. In the beginning, the placenta starts out as a yolk sac. This sac is what produces blood for your baby, the embryo. As the placenta develops, it will also provide a way to remove waste and bring in nutrients. Think about it as your baby's lifeline, connected to you for support.

Though the embryo is tiny, it is still very powerful. During this time, the amniotic sac will also start to form. Think about this as a bag of water that surrounds the baby, providing it with proper fluids. It will later become incorporated into your baby's digestive tract. Eventually, the third layer of cells will emerge. The first is the inner layer that is known as the endoderm. This part becomes the digestive system, lungs, and liver. The mesoderm is the middle layer, and it becomes your baby's heart, bones, muscles, sex organs, and kidneys. The final layer is the ectoderm. This is what forms your baby's skin, eyes, hair, and nervous system.

Your Changes

Though the symptoms might be slight, you will notice some definite changes in the way that you feel. As soon as one week after conception, your body will know that some big changes are about to take place. Most of the time, you are going to be oblivious to all of this. Even those who are actively trying to get pregnant will typically not be able to confirm if they are indeed housing an embryo at this point or not. Some of the earliest pregnancy symptoms can mirror PMS symptoms. This can be confusing because experiencing PMS symptoms each month is likely a normal occurrence. The cramps that you feel won't likely faze you, and the mood swings will probably seem normal.

There might be some bloating, but that will likely be attributed to normal PMS behavior that you are used to each month. No matter if you are feeling anything in abundance or not at all, it is likely still too early to be able to rely on an at-home pregnancy test to deliver the news that you are waiting for. If you are pregnant, the fertilized egg and the uterus make contact within the very first week. This is when your baby will attach itself to your uterine lining. Though there is nothing to physically indicate to you that this is happening inside, a lot of women just seem to know when it is taking place.

If you notice some bleeding, this is normal. A lot of women are discouraged when they see bleeding because this is usually an indication of their period starting. Ironically, this bleeding can happen when the baby implants. It is known as implantation bleeding, and up to 25% of women experience it. The way to differentiate it from your period will be the timing and the color. This bleeding typically happens earlier than your period, and it will be a lot lighter in color. Whether it is pink, red, or brown, it should still be lighter than period blood.

Again, bloating can occur during this time, maybe even a little bit of abdominal pressure. Your breasts can also feel tender to the touch. Most of this is still normal for a lot of women when they are experiencing PMS. After the first 6-12 days of fertilization, your body will begin producing the hormone known as HCG. This is what at-home pregnancy tests can pick up on. HCG is what tells your body to produce progesterone and estrogen in order to nourish the cells until the placenta takes over (usually at around 8 weeks).

If you suspect you are pregnant, but it is too early for testing, the best thing you can do is take care of yourself. Be easy on yourself and get a lot of rest. Making sure that you are getting enough vitamin D is also essential. Take a prenatal vitamin if you haven't started already. Try to avoid toxic situations, like places where a lot of smoking will be taking place. Ingesting secondhand smoke puts your baby in great danger. As for eating, know that healthy fat is good fat. You and your baby are both going to need it as your baby continues to grow. Eat foods that are rich in omega fatty acids, like eggs and avocados.

If you need to get up and moving, go for a swim! Swimming is a great and safe low-impact way to exercise if you are pregnant or think you might be pregnant. It also allows for many cardiovascular benefits that will keep you healthy and in shape. Though your belly is going to grow, this does not mean that you need to sit around doing nothing all day. Being active is great for your body, your baby, and your mental health. Getting low-impact exercise into your schedule 3-4 times a week is a great thing. Go on walks, take a few dips in the pool, and do what makes you feel good as your body undergoes this first month of changes.

The Second Month

At this stage in your pregnancy, your baby should be around the size of a raspberry. This is a big difference from the cluster of cells that they were just a month earlier. Your baby's eyes are forming during this point, and though you won't know the color just yet, the retinas are well on their way to development. The same can be said for your baby's sex organs. Though it is still very early on in the pregnancy, your baby is currently developing in this way. In a few weeks' time, an ultrasound will be able to let you know if you are expecting a baby boy or baby girl.

It can be hard to estimate exactly how big your baby is during the second month, but most experts say that they can be anywhere from ½ inch to ¾ inch. The average growth rate is around a millimeter a day, which is astounding to think about. This growth is not only limited to height. It can also include growth spurts in various parts of your baby's body, like their limbs or back. If you were able to take a close-up look at your baby, you would see that they now have eyelids, lips, and a nose. Their hands and feet are still webbed, soon to be separated.

By the end of this week, your baby's systems and essential organs have begun to develop. In this tiny embryo, there is now a tiny heart, brain, liver, kidneys, and so on. They will continue to grow and develop quickly as you progress in your pregnancy. After the second month, a lot of mothers agree that time seems to go by very quickly and many developmental milestones are reached in short proximity to one another. Most doctors would agree that, during this stage, your baby starts looking more baby-like and less reptilian.

Their heartbeat is around 150-170 beats per minute. This is still about twice as fast as your own heart rate. While you might not be able to feel them just yet, your baby is able to make spontaneous movements. As your baby's growth progresses, so does the rate in which your amniotic fluid increases. This makes your womb bigger, making even more space for the growing baby that you have inside your belly. As your baby grows and grows, this space also becomes larger. This is why the size of your belly begins to show shortly after the second month of pregnancy. Typically, women have the infamous "baby bump" during their third month, but all women are different. You can have a perfectly healthy pregnancy, yet not be showing at all.

Your Changes

Even if you aren't showing just yet, your body is still likely feeling all of the impacts of having a growing baby inside of it. Your morning sickness might be hitting you pretty hard at this point. Though your baby is still tiny, remember that your uterus is still rapidly expanding to keep up with all of the growth that is taking place. Your uterus itself has likely expanded to the size of a large grapefruit by now. This is what can be causing your morning sickness and the feeling of tightness as you wear the clothes that used to fit you perfectly. It is thought that 75% of women experience morning sickness, so if you haven't at this point, then you can consider yourself lucky.

When you are expecting, it is thought that eating fruit not only provides you with essential nutrients that you need, but it can also be easy to eat for those times when you are feeling queasy. It can also keep your bathroom schedule regular. There is nothing worse than being pregnant, which already leads you to feel bloated, while also being constipated. A general rule of thumb to follow when it comes to eating fruit is the brighter, the better. This applies to vegetables as well. If the inside of the fruit or vegetable is particularly bright, this is a good indication that it contains a lot of nutrients.

Being fatigued is also pretty normal during your second month of pregnancy. Since your body is going through so many changes, it can be hard to adjust to this new lifestyle. You might find yourself getting tired more easily and needing more sleep throughout the day. Let your partner and your friends help you! Many pregnant women know that they are still capable of doing everything that they used to do before the pregnancy, but that doesn't mean that a little bit of help won't go a long way. Though you don't look very pregnant, your inner-body is still going through a lot. Do away with the heavy lifting and walking back and forth. Accept the help if it is offered.

You might notice an increase in vaginal discharge; this is normal, and it is happening due to the estrogen. Leukorrhea is a substance that is thin and milky. Your body produces it naturally when it is producing more estrogen. This happens because the estrogen increases blood flow to the pelvic region, and this stimulates your body's mucous membranes. Leukorrhea actually serves a purpose other than making you wash more laundry. It helps by keeping the birth canal area primed and free of infections. Leukorrhea contains a healthy type of bacteria, so don't worry about cleaning it up or washing it away. Just let it do its job. When you do wash your vagina, make sure that you aren't using any soaps that are heavily scented or filled with chemicals. This can cause an imbalance in the healthy bacteria of your vagina.

The Third Month

As big as a lime now, your baby is busy making white blood cells in order to fight off germs that are around them. In the last month, your baby's intestines were developing and becoming entangled with the umbilical cord space, but now they are migrating back into your baby's abdominal area. The pituitary gland is now developing at the base of your baby's brain. This means that hormones are now being produced, allowing them to have children of their own one day. It is fascinating to think that this stage happens when your baby is only in its third month of development.

Much bigger than last month, your baby can be around 2-2 ¼ inches in size now. They will weigh about half an ounce. This is a dramatic jump in size, so you can tell that your baby has done a lot of growing from month two to month three. During this week, a milestone occurs. This is when your baby's digestive system becomes fully operational. Most of their systems are now fully formed, so this means that your little one will now experience contractions as their muscles flex due to their fetal digestive system.

Of course, there is still plenty of time for growth and maturing, but the digestive system is obviously going to be a system that is very important for once your baby is born. Your little one will need to know what to do with food after you give birth and begin feeding them. As your baby is practicing these contractions and movements, this primes the body for the task of eventually digesting food on its own one day. These contractions allow for food to pass through the digestive tract. It is likely at this check-up that you will finally be able to hear your baby's heartbeat! It is an emotional and exciting time for all mothers. Hearing the sound of your baby's heart, still beating very rapidly, will often speed up your own heart rate.

Your Changes

You are in the last month of your first trimester, a milestone for the expecting mother! At this point, your uterus is still about the size of a large grapefruit. It will begin to migrate from the bottom of your pelvis to the center of your abdomen. This is why many women begin showing at this stage in the pregnancy. After this happens, you will likely experience the relief of the constant pressure on your bladder. Prior to your uterus migrating, all of that pressure was being placed directly on your bladder, causing you to feel the urge to urinate all the time. With this new arrangement in your body, you shouldn't feel the need to go as frequently.

Your baby bump may or may not be showing by now. It can differ depending on the size of the baby and the woman. Remember, all pregnancies are unique. Whether you are showing a little, a lot, or not at all, you are still carrying the great responsibility of growing a tiny human being inside of you. Your clothes should definitely begin to feel even tighter now. Instead of wearing your usual jeans and shirts, you might want to invest in some maternity clothing or at least clothing that is more loose-fitting. Many women like to buy normal clothing during this stage, simply sizing up. Do whatever you need to do to stay comfortable.

A new symptom might have found its way to you, and that is dizziness. A lot of pregnant women in their third-month report having dizzy spells. Progesterone is thought to be the cause of this. Since your blood vessels are relaxing and widening during your pregnancy, your baby is able to receive more blood flow. If you think about it, you are literally being drained and depleted on a daily basis. So make sure that you are staying hydrated. Drinking enough fluids is essential to avoiding these dizzy spells, or worse, fainting spells.

Your blood pressure might be a little bit lower, and some women can also experience dizziness from having low blood sugar. This can happen if you are not eating regularly, which only has one thing to blame--nausea. Even if you do not feel like eating, you need to keep yourself regularly nourished somehow. Try to opt for things that are plain and free of strong smells. This will keep you from feeling sick when you try to eat. As mentioned, fruit can be easy for a lot of pregnant women to eat, and fruit also provides plenty of nutrients per serving. If you do encounter a dizzy spell despite your efforts to eat a balanced diet, lie down or sit down with your head lowered between your knees. Take a few deep breaths as you loosen any tight clothing you might be wearing. This feeling of being constricted can add to your dizzy spells. Once you feel well enough to stand up again, try to eat a small snack and drink plenty of water.

While sex might be the last thing on your mind while you are pregnant, there are different levels of sexual desire that you can experience during these next few months. During the third month, a lot of women report that they feel as though their sex drive is low. Since you are feeling so bloated, and often so sick, it makes sense that you do not feel like having a lot of sex during this time. The hormones will also impact your desire or lack of desire to have sex. Most women agree that they are just not in the mood during their third month of pregnancy, while a small percentage actually state that their desire has increased.

Chapter 2: The Second Trimester (4-6 Months)

Once you reach your second trimester, you have likely experienced most of the pregnancy symptoms that you can expect from now on. As your belly continues to grow, your baby continues to develop even more rapidly than before. Many milestones are reached during this portion of your pregnancy, including the gender reveal (if you choose to find out)! It can be one of the most exciting parts of your pregnancy, other than the actual moment that you go into labor. This chapter will cover what you can expect as you navigate through your second trimester of pregnancy.

The Fourth Month

Your baby's eyes have now begun experiencing movement. These small, side-to-side movements can be triggered by light. Even though their eyes are still closed, and will remain closed for a while, they can still often perceive light. As you probably know, a lot of babies develop a thumb-sucking habit. What you likely didn't know is that this habit can start during the fourth month of pregnancy. Though it is still fairly early on in the developmental stages, your baby might have that thumb-sucking instinct while still in the womb. Though they cannot exactly begin sucking their thumbs just yet, they are able to make sucking motions.

About the size of an avocado now, your baby has grown tremendously since the prior month. With a range of about 4-5 inches in length, they can weigh around 3-4 ounces. Their tiny backbone is gaining some strength as their muscles continue to develop. At this point, your baby can straighten out their neck if they want to. Not only are these muscles getting stronger, but their facial muscles are also getting stronger by the day. Your baby can now make certain facial expressions, such as squinting and frowning. Through their eyes are still closed, you can imagine that your baby is still making these faces as they experience certain things inside the womb.

As your baby's face continues to develop and appear more human, their skin is still translucent. If you were able to see your baby, you would be able to see through their skin and take a look at their blood vessels that are just underneath. Because there is no baby fat yet, the skin remains translucent until this fat develops and creates pigment. Your baby won't be this way for long, though. In a few weeks' time, their skin is going to become thicker and less translucent.

Your baby now has tiny bones in their ears, which means that they can actually hear your voice. Though it might not be clear as to what they are hearing, talk to your baby often. They will get used to the sound of your voice, and by the time they are born, your voice will be one that is recognizable and familiar to your baby. A lot of expecting mothers start reading to their children during this stage of pregnancy. Whether or not your baby can hear you properly, it is still great to use your voice as much as you can and talk to your baby frequently.

Your Changes

Your uterus is now growing at around the same pace as your fetus—this is very fast! If you were ever trying to hide the fact that you are pregnant, it is likely going to be very hard for you to do so in the fourth month. Your belly should be showing by now, and this means that all of your clothing is going to fit differently. This part of your pregnancy should feel relatively calm when you compare it to your first trimester. The second trimester tends to be filled with less nausea, which comes as a big relief for all expecting mothers.

During this time, you will notice that you are gaining weight rapidly. A lot of women can find this difficult, even while knowing that it is because a baby is growing and developing inside of their womb. Know that as long as you are eating properly, all of the weight you are gaining is necessary in order to keep your baby healthy and developing properly. Try to avoid junk food, even if your cravings are telling you otherwise. A little bit of indulgence every once in a while is okay, but you should be focused on eating more nutritious foods instead.

As your stomach continues to swell, you might find it surprising when your nose begins to swell too. Your pregnancy hormones can cause a great deal of nasal congestion, and unfortunately, this is one of those symptoms that can just continue to get worse as your pregnancy goes on. For some relief, you can safely try to use saline solution or nasal strips. Having a humidifier in your room is also thought to be helpful to ease your breathing.

The moment that most are waiting for—you get to find out if you are having a boy or a girl. Getting your ultrasound photos is a big milestone, and even if you do not wish to reveal the gender just yet, these are your first photos of your little one that you will get to treasure forever. While you can remain grateful for this moment, it is likely going to be the best feeling that you will experience in your fourth month. As your belly grows, your breasts are also going to be growing. This happens because of the hormones telling them that a baby is on the way. Your breasts might begin producing milk relatively early on during your pregnancy, anxiously anticipating the baby's arrival.

In prior months, you have likely experienced some constipation or bathroom trouble. This might increase for a whole new reason during your fourth month of pregnancy. While hormones were to blame earlier, your expanding uterus is now another reason for why you might not be able to regularly make a bowel movement. To keep things running smoothly, try to increase the amount of liquid that you are drinking. The more liquid you drink, the better chance you have of being able to use the bathroom.

Naturally, a bigger belly means more weight for you to carry. This can begin to impact your back. During your early months of pregnancy, your belly likely wasn't big enough to cause much strain, but this can all change in your fourth month. Try getting a prenatal massage to ease the pain, or have your partner rub your back at night. Make sure that you are staying off your feet as much as you can because this can also help alleviate some of the pain you are feeling.

The Fifth Month

Your little one is moving their hands a lot this month. As mentioned, they might even be sucking their thumb by now! Aside from this, it is common for your baby's hands to drift to their face and start to feel around. If you have yet to feel any movement, this month should be a lot different for you. Your baby is now likely squirming and moving around a lot more, possibly even kicking and punching. While it can be a funny feeling, it is a reassuring action that shows you that your baby is developing in a healthy way. You can sometimes see this movement from the outside of your belly, little feet or fists pushing forward.

At this point, you will likely already know if you are having a boy or a girl (if you have opted to receive this information). Many parents enjoy doing gender reveal parties. This becomes possible by your doctor writing down the gender on a piece of paper. You can get very creative if you wish to have your own gender reveal party. The paper with the gender is then given to a bakery or party shop to make a cake or balloons with either pink or blue coloration inside. There are many other ways to announce the gender, but today, lots of parents enjoy hosting this event because it is also a surprise to them.

If you are carrying a girl, her uterus is fully formed at this point. She has a vaginal canal that is already starting to develop and she even has some primitive eggs forming in her tiny ovaries. For a little boy, his testicles are about to descend. Right now, they are still growing in his abdomen. Once the scrotum is finished developing, then the testicles will drop. This can all happen within a few week's time.

Your baby has grown a lot by now! They can weigh a whopping 10 ounces, a big jump from the month earlier. About the size of a sweet potato, they can measure around 6-7 inches in length. Naturally, this is why you are able to feel their movements a lot more in the fifth month. But your womb still has plenty of growing to do in order to accommodate your growing baby. Since there is still wiggle room, so to speak, your baby recognizes this and takes advantage of it frequently.

Your Changes

You are at the halfway point of your pregnancy! Believe it or not, there is not that much longer to go until you finally get to meet your little one in person. All of the symptoms that you are feeling now, especially the baby kicking, can make everything seem so much more real. A lot of mothers agree that, after this point, the time seems to fly by. Enjoy being pregnant while you can, even despite any challenging days that you might have. These little moments are unforgettable and one-of-a-kind. No matter how big or small your belly is, there is no doubt that you have a fast-developing baby inside.

At this point, your appetite has likely returned in full swing. Since nausea has likely subsided, you should feel ready and willing to eat just about anything. This can be a time when the intense cravings take over. While it is great to indulge in these cravings, you must make sure that you are also doing your best to keep a balanced diet. Also, don't forget to take your prenatal vitamin every day! It helps to keep track of what you eat each day. What would normally sustain you before you got pregnant is no longer going to be enough now that you are feeding two.

Your current wardrobe is likely stashed away and being replaced by loose-fitting clothing. Whether you have decided to buy a whole wardrobe of maternity clothing or simply size up from what you normally wear, you should be wearing things that allow you to feel comfortable and free of pressure. All pants should be pull-on, both for ease of access and your own personal comfort. Flowy dresses are also a great option for a woman in her fifth month of pregnancy. Invest in some comfortable shoes, as well. If your feet get swollen, wearing shoes that are tight can cause you aches and pains.

If you notice that your nails are stronger and your hair is healthier than ever, you can thank those pregnancy hormones. This happens because the hormones trigger a surge of circulation that is felt throughout your entire body. Extra nutrients are then distributed to the cells. Don't get too attached to these benefits, though, because your hair and nails will likely return to normal after delivery. A lot of women love this part of being pregnant. It is a chance to feel great about yourself when you are mainly feeling bloated and immobile.

You might be experiencing some heartburn or indigestion; this is normal. If this happens to you frequently after eating, try chewing a piece of sugarless gum after each meal. This will increase your saliva production which will then neutralize your gastric acids. It also helps to get those fluids back into your stomach where they are needed. Headaches are also a common symptom at this stage in your pregnancy. These headaches are typically triggered by hot conditions. If you are in a room that is overheated or too stuffy, you might just need to step out for some fresh air to avoid getting a headache. Dress in layers if you need to. This will allow you to avoid overheating if you do not have the option to step outside. Beware of the dizzy spells, as well. Unfortunately, they can still pop up when you least expect them.

The Sixth Month

You now have a pomegranate-sized baby! This little one is not so little anymore, measuring at almost 12 inches. At this point, they can weigh over 1 pound. Your baby is putting on weight, and this is a great sign of healthy development. This means that fat and muscle are continuing to develop, both essential to becoming a healthy newborn. There is also additional weight because of their growing organs and bones. Each week, they keep getting bigger to fit the size of your baby's body. If you were able to see your baby right now, there is a good chance you'd know what they would look like. Their tiny face is nearly fully formed, and they have eyelashes, eyebrows, and hair. However, the hair is still free of pigment, so it would appear white. Their skin is still fairly see-through, but that won't be the case for much longer.

Many sounds can be heard by your baby now. Make sure that you are still talking to them, reading to them, and singing to them when you can. Not only is your voice a lot clearer to them, but they can also hear the sound of your lungs breathing, your heart beating, and even sounds that you pass by on the street. It is important that you and your partner both keep talking to your baby so that they will be familiar with your voices by the time you deliver. This is one way that you can start bonding even before the baby is born.

Since your baby is even bigger now, your belly button has likely been pushed forward to become an outie. Whether you started with an innie or an outie, it is common for most pregnant women to temporarily have an outie during this point in the pregnancy due to the baby's growth. Your swelling uterus is what causes this to happen. After you give birth, your belly button will go back to what it looked like before. You might also notice some stretch marks forming, not only on your belly but on your thighs too. So many pregnant women go through this, and you can think about them as your badges of honor. Your body is literally changing in order to bring life into this world, so know that it is doing its best. Rubbing shea butter on your stretch marks can help to fade them if they start to bother you.

As the weeks' progress, you should feel your baby lower and lower in your abdomen. Do not confuse this with the final "drop," though. Your baby will eventually drop before you go into labor. The feeling of your baby getting lower is simply happening because of the growth that is taking place inside of your uterus. This is when you are going to be extra thankful for clothing that does not push on your belly. While it might not be painful, it can become uncomfortable, especially if you need to be sitting down for long periods of time.

Your Changes

A unique pregnancy symptom you might be experiencing at this point is carpal tunnel syndrome. It is normal to have a feeling of numbness in your wrists and fingers, even if you aren't using them more than you usually do. While repetitive motion can contribute to this symptom, it is typically triggered by the swelling that you experience while pregnant. Fluids can tend to accumulate in your lower body, therefore not reaching your upper body as much as they used to. You can feel some relief from the carpal tunnel by avoiding sleeping on your hands or using your arms to prop your pillow up. Nighttime is a way for your body to reset the circulation because you will be lying down. It can also help to just shake everything out every so often. If you do work in some kind of an office setting that requires typing or writing, take breaks frequently.

Another unique symptom that you might experience is red and itchy palms. This one also has little to do with the activities that you participate in throughout the day. Much like all of the other pregnancy symptoms, you can blame your hormones for this one, as well. This is a fairly mundane symptom, but it is one that you should definitely keep an eye on. In rare cases, it can be an indication of a pregnancy complication known as cholestasis of pregnancy. This is more common in the third trimester, but you shouldn't rule anything out. If your palms start to bother you to the point where you are in constant pain, or if you notice that the symptoms just won't go away, contact your doctor for a consultation.

There are a plethora of other random symptoms that you might be feeling, too. The sixth month tends to be one where the most obscure symptoms will pop up, sometimes surprising you. Your mouth might be producing additional saliva, and you might also notice a metallic taste. Skin tags (small, soft skin growths) can appear out of nowhere, and your vision might even temporarily change. These are all normal symptoms that must be dealt with during pregnancy, but know that they won't last forever. The best way to get relief is simply by taking it easy. While you might be an energetic person by nature, try not to do too much. Even if you feel up to it at the moment, your body will face repercussions in the future.

Constipation can become an issue again. You should be very keen on dealing with it by now. As stated before, you need to keep drinking plenty of water to keep everything in your digestive system moving. This is the easiest and best thing that you can do for yourself if you are feeling constipated all the time. Drinking prune juice can also help because it will soften your stool. While taking actual laxatives isn't typically recommended, using nature's laxatives can work just as well.

Chapter 3: The Third Trimester (7-9 Months)

You are in the final stretch, quite literally! Your pregnancy is nearing its end, and for some women, delivery does come early. While you are feeling your baby gets even bigger and watching yourself grow, a lot of planning happens in the third trimester. From making a birth plan to decorating the nursery, you are going to be pretty busy. It is usually in the third trimester that a lot of women decide to have a baby shower. Of course, that is a personal decision, but it is a fun way to celebrate with your loved ones a final time before the baby arrives.

The Seventh Month

You are carrying a baby that is roughly the size of an entire head of lettuce now. At 15 inches long and over 2 pounds, you should be feeling your baby a lot during the seventh month. Your baby can now experience REM (rapid eye movement) sleep. This means that your baby is likely having dreams! It is exciting to think about what they might be dreaming about while they are waiting to come into this world. Brain wave activity has been measured in studies showing that your baby actually does go through different cycles of sleep. These are the same cycles that you go through when you are sleeping.

Before this point, their eyes have been closed while they were developing. Now, they are able to open their eyes and blink. The eyelashes are fully formed, as well. Before, your baby could squint and frown. Now, there is a chance that they are sticking their tongue out on a regular basis. Many doctors can't explain why babies do this in the womb, but it is likely because they can now feel that they have a tongue that has developed. They also might be tasting the amniotic fluid.

Your baby is dropping lower now, getting into a position that will be suitable for birth. If all is going as planned, their head should begin moving downward. This process can happen at different rates for different women. Some babies never get into the "correct" position, but this does not mean that a natural birth isn't possible. You can deliver feet-first, and there is also the option of having a C-section. Know that while you are making your birth plan, so much can change once you go into labor. Make sure that you are willing to be flexible with the plan because you might have no choice once your baby is ready to come out.

Aside from blinking and making faces, your baby is now also likely sucking a lot more. They can also get the hiccups! This can be felt by you, and it is adorable, to say the least. This is also a time when your baby is going to practice taking deeper breaths, preparing for what breathing will be like in the outside world. They know exactly what they need to do in order to prepare for delivery, just as your body seems to know exactly what to do.

While you might be feeling more uncomfortable as your size is increasing, so is your baby. The space that your baby calls home is not growing as much as it used to in the past. This is why they might be moving around a lot more, eager to explore. All of the kicking, punching, and squirming can be attributed to curiosity. Your baby wants to see exactly how much room they have to move around inside of the womb.

Your Changes

In the seventh month, you have probably experienced your fair share of sciatica. This is what is known as the tingling leg pain that you feel. This is the kind of symptom that might keep you up at night because it prohibits you from fully relaxing. Your feet can also get swollen, and your back might be aching more than usual. While you are noticing these symptoms all day and all night, they can often feel more intense at night when your body needs to relax. A lot of this discomfort comes from the fact that your baby is now so big that they might be putting pressure on your sciatic nerve. This is located in the lower part of your spine.

Another symptom of the position that your baby is currently in can be shooting, sharp pain that stems from the sciatic nerve. It can be felt from your butt, all the way down the backs of your legs. This is a more intense version of sciatica that many pregnant women do experience. Relief is hard to find for this symptom, but if your baby shifts positions, this can take some of the pressure off of your nerve and temporarily relieve you of the discomfort. Otherwise, try to stay off your feet as much as possible. In order to remedy most other symptoms, proper rest and relaxation are what you will need to make your sciatica feel better too.

You might find that your skin is more sensitive than usual. Even if you have never experienced sensitive skin before, your pregnancy can tend to bring this out. Some parts of your body might become easily irritated, red, itchy, and dry. Make sure that you are moisturizing daily with a fragrance-free moisturizer that was designed for sensitive skin. This will keep your skin calm and will keep you free of pain. Your most sensitive spot is naturally going to be the skin on your belly. Because, of all the stretching that it is doing, this skin can become irritated very easily. Certain fabrics might even trigger the irritation. Make sure that your clothing is made of breathable material.

Bloating and gas are common symptoms that you will continue to experience as you progress into your third trimester. Your uterus is putting pressure on your rectum, and you might not be able to help it when that gas must be released. Your sluggish digestive system is also playing a role in the amount of bloating and gas that you are experiencing. Though you might have a perfectly fine appetite, try to change the way you eat your meals. Instead of having 3 large meals, break this up into 6 small ones that you can eat throughout the day. This will make it easier on your digestive system, and it can help you feel full longer. The same rule still applies—eat a balanced diet.

The Eighth Month

You are now carrying a child that is comparable to the size of a cantaloupe. At 16-17 inches long and about 3-4 pounds, your baby is almost fully developed! At this point, your baby's major organs are all fully formed except for the lungs. Since your baby is still inhaling amniotic fluid, their lungs are still in a practice stage. Once they are born, they will learn how to transition to breathing air. If you were to deliver your baby this week, chances are that you would give birth to a baby who is healthy and ready to take on the world. As mentioned, some women do go into labor early, so be ready! The baby's skin is no longer translucent, as a pigment has now surfaced. You would be able to see a very clear image of what your baby is going to look like if you were able to look inside the womb.

Your baby has been practicing a lot of things in the last few weeks. They know that it is almost time to meet you and enter the world. Swallowing more frequently and breathing deeply are just two of the functions they have practiced lately. Your baby's digestive system is now fully ready to begin working once they are born. In anticipation of the birth, you can expect your baby to be very active at this point. There will be plenty of kicking and squirming for you to feel. These are your last few weeks of pregnancy, so enjoy them and the feelings that they bring.

Most babies have settled into their birthing position by now. This is a curled position, known as fetal position, with the head down and bottom-up. Your baby will fit better through the birth canal if they are able to get into this position, but sometimes this does not happen. As mentioned, it is okay if your baby is in a breech position (feet down, head up). 5% of babies do end up in this position. There is still time for them to flip over before delivery, but if that does not change, then your doctor will tell you what your best options are for having the easiest delivery possible.

Since sleep cycles have been discovered, your baby should be sleeping at regular intervals now. They probably have a sleep schedule that mirrors your own. This means, if you are up and active, the baby is likely going to be awake. Once you go to sleep, this should calm them down. This is an ideal cycle, but it doesn't always end up syncing up perfectly. There are still many nights when your baby will likely keep you awake because they just aren't ready to go to sleep yet. There isn't much you can do to change this, but it will give you insight into how great a sleeper your baby may or may not be after they are born.

Your Changes

In preparation for delivery, your body might be sending you some signals that are known as Braxton Hicks contractions. This occurs when you feel your uterus tightening, but what differentiates them from labor contractions is that they are just practicing for when your water actually breaks and you begin to experience regular contractions. If there isn't a pattern to the contractions, and if they aren't lasting for a very long time, then they are likely just Braxton Hicks contractions. They typically last 15-30 seconds, but some women have reported them lasting for up to 2 minutes. Another way to tell them apart from true labor contractions is by moving around. If you change positions, the Braxton Hicks contractions will likely stop or at least lessen in severity.

Since there is so much additional weight for your body to carry, you are likely going to experience an increase in leg cramping/spasming, especially right before bedtime. This can happen in your calves, and doctors aren't sure about exactly what causes the sensation. The most likely cause is simply the sudden shift from your legs holding all of that additional weight to now lying down and attempting to redistribute the way that it carries the weight. With the permission of your doctor, you might need to incorporate more calcium or magnesium into your daily vitamin routine to help your legs feel better.

It is something that isn't frequently discussed, but yes, pregnant women often get hemorrhoids. These are actually varicose veins in the rectum that are swollen, and they can be very uncomfortable. If you are in pain when you sit down, you might need to rely on some ice packs to help relieve the urge to keep shifting in your seat. Warm baths can also help if you are at home and experiencing hemorrhoids. Another option is the use of witch hazel to soothe the pain. It is a great and natural solution that can be applied directly to your anus. Though it might be embarrassing to experience such a problem, know that this is all a normal part of your pregnancy. This is an indication that your baby is growing big and strong, so your body must make quick adjustments in order to accommodate this.

Your breasts are likely bigger than they have ever been by this point. You might experience colostrum, which is a term that indicates leaky breasts. Colostrum is a yellowish fluid that is sort of like the precursor to breast milk. While there is nothing that you can do to stop the leaking, you can wear breast pads inside your bra to create a buffer for the leak. This is also a very normal part of being into your third trimester, and you can think about it in a positive way knowing that, if you decide to breastfeed, these are the very first nutrients your baby will receive after being born.

The Ninth Month

You are officially in your last month of pregnancy! Your baby is as large as a bundle of kale by now, likely weighing around 6 pounds or more. They are about 18-19 inches in length. During these last few weeks, your baby's hearing is going to be incredibly sharp. From hearing your voice to the music you play, your baby is definitely going to be listening closely. Another big change that happens sometime during the ninth month is the "drop." This is when your baby shifts positions, moving downward toward your pelvis. This is an indication that your little one is almost ready to come out into the world.

This is finally a point where your baby is going to slow down on growth and development. All of the development that has happened in the womb has led you to this stage in your pregnancy. Most of the rest of it will take place after the baby is born. However, during this time, your baby's bones are still not quite fused together yet. This is normal, and this is going to assist with your baby's head maneuvering through the birth canal during delivery. During the first few years of your baby's life, their bones will become harder and stronger.

Most of your baby's systems have reached their final stage of maturity, as they are done with their in-womb development. The only system that needs to catch up once your baby is born is the digestive system. This one takes longer because your baby is used to being fed directly through the umbilical cord.

After birth, your baby will either be drinking your breastmilk or formula and given the chance to learn how to digest and process food on their own. A fully functional digestive system can take up to 1-2 years to mature. This is why your baby is still going to be spitting up after feeding for a while, but don't worry, this is all perfectly normal when it comes to the behaviors of a newborn.

There is no doubt about it, your baby looks like an infant in this final stage. They will have skin that has a slight pink tinge to it with chubby arms and legs. Their tiny facial features are fully formed, giving you a glimpse at a part of yourself and a part of your partner. All of their fingers and toes should have separated, and their little heart is working effectively. Your baby is now a tiny human, and it is only a matter of time before you finally get to meet one another.

Your Changes

Your back is likely going to be aching more than ever in these final weeks—it's normal. Since your baby is basically fully grown, this is a lot of extra weight for you to carry around as you try to remain mobile in your last few moments of pregnancy. Your walk has likely turned into a waddle because your baby has dropped. There is nothing wrong with this walk, as it is actually normal for your body to adopt a new method since the connective tissue in your body is softening in preparation for your delivery. Embrace your walk, and know that you have a healthy baby to look forward to meeting very soon.

While your joint flexibility has increased more than ever, there also comes a downside. You are likely experiencing a lot more pelvic pain than usual. Since your baby's head is lower in your pelvis than ever before and your uterus is as heavy as can be, this will cause the soreness that you feel. When you walk around, you are likely to feel it more. It is a good idea to stay off your feet as much as possible in these last few weeks. Though it can be tempting to walk around because walking can often induce labor, you need to be smart about how much time you are actually spending on your feet.

If you do not feel that your baby has dropped, this isn't a bad thing. Some babies actually do not drop before labor. Though most will drop within the ninth month of pregnancy, some babies stay in the same position until it is finally time for delivery. If your baby is insistent on staying put, then you are likely to feel pressure on your uterus. It might be uncomfortable for you to enjoy a meal, even if you are starving. This pressure can make it feel like there is no more room for food inside your stomach, even though there really is enough room.

Ironically, you will feel your baby moving around less during this final month of pregnancy. This happens because their space to move around is now limited because of how big they are. Instead of kicking and jabbing, you might only be able to feel squirming. You are also going to experience a lot of gas and burping during this time, and you will find that it feels so good to let it all out. When you eat, try not to eat too quickly. This will push more air into your body, therefore creating more gas for you to have to pass.

Heartburn and indigestion should also be familiar to you in the ninth month. Your stomach is getting pushed around by your uterus, as mentioned, so you might not be able to eat as much as your appetite feels like you can handle. Try eating smaller meals so that you can still enjoy your food without too much trouble digesting it. Remember, all of this pressure will soon be gone once you give birth to your little one.

Part 2: Baby's First Year— Milestones and Mental Leaps

In this part of the guide, you are going to learn everything that you need to know regarding your newborn baby. From feedings to first steps, you are going to experience all of these joys with your little one. You will find that they are going to look up to you, so you need to remember that you are their main role model in life. Behavior is mirrored at this age, so to ensure that your baby is learning as much as possible, you need to lead by example. As your infant gets closer to becoming a toddler, there are many milestones to look forward to that will be sure to delight and surprise you.

Chapter 4: 1st Month-3rd Month

Congratulations! You now have a bundle of joy in your life that you have worked so hard to carry for the past 9 months. In the first 3 months of your baby's life, so many changes will happen developmentally. Not only are you getting to know your little one's personality, but you will also be able to see them accomplish many milestones and allow your heart to swell with pride as you do. From what you can expect to what is about to happen next, this is a very exciting time for both the baby and the parents. It is a fast-paced period of growth and discovery.

First Month

Milestones

Achieved Milestones

- Eye-tracking
- Gripping an object placed into the hand
- Notices faces and people within close range
- Making throaty noises
- Crying subsides when held by a caregiver
- Has reflexes
- Stops crying to notice a sound/voice
- Moving limbs in symmetry
- Can recognize mother's breast

Emerging Milestones

- Eye-tracking from side to side
- Attempts to swipe or hit objects
- Noticing hands and legs
- Ability to briefly hold objects
- Making cooing sounds
- Crying subsides at sight of caregiver
- Can lift head slightly during tummy time
- Will respond to caregiver's voice with cooing and throaty sounds
- Will learn that hands and legs are bodily extensions
- Knows the difference between a mother's breast and bottle

Development

Cognitive: By one month of age, your baby should be expecting regular feedings. This means that, if not fed during certain intervals of time, you will notice additional fussing or crying. Your baby will be able to look at and acknowledge people, either by simply using their eyes or potentially making noises when they notice someone new enters the room. They will be able to tell the difference between a soft item and a hard item; textures will likely be very interesting to them. If you eat something that changes the taste of your breast milk, your baby will have a reaction to this. If you notice a puckered expression or a refusal to eat, this might be an indication that your one-month-old is telling you that the taste of the milk has changed.

Physical: Though the movements will remain jerky for a little while, your baby should be thrusting their arms and legs. While this is an exploration, it also serves as a way to strengthen the muscles. You will also notice more symmetrical limb movement from your little one. As they figure out that certain limbs are parts of their own body, you will start to see this symmetrical movement. Your baby might also be putting their hand into their mouth a lot. After this discovery, a lot of babies will even begin gnawing on their tiny fingers or fist. Since they still cannot hold their head up on their own, it will fall backward if unsupported. Make sure that you are holding your baby with proper neck support at all times.

Social/Emotional: Since your baby cannot talk yet, crying is the main form of communication. If they are content, they will happily stay in a certain spot or position. When they need something, however, the crying will begin. There are different cries for different reasons. For example, a cry for hunger might sound different than a cry for a dirty diaper. As your baby learns to recognize the faces they see around them, they will also be able to provide eye contact. This helps them with their focus, but it is also a way for them to connect with the individual in front of them. Your baby is going to be very eager for these connections at this age. This is great because they will likely be meeting a lot of new people in their first month of life!

Is Your Baby Healthy?

Your baby is likely to weigh around 9 pounds, on average. Since birth, it is normal for an infant to gain around 1½-2 lbs. In terms of length, you should also see a difference here. Most babies grow around 1½-2 inches, as well. Know that these are just the average estimates, and if your baby is not growing exactly as indicated, this does not necessarily mean that they are unhealthy. During your first check-up with the doctor, official measurements will be taken. These will be compared to the ones taken at birth, and then your doctor will be able to refer to a growth chart.

Pay attention to the way your baby's senses are working. Do they respond to loud noises? Look at bright lights or colors? Can they recognize the sound of your voice and the feeling when you hold them? This, along with regular feeding, is how you can form an indication of your baby's health from home. As long as you notice normal development and your baby is willing to eat, then it should all be going pretty well. Of course, your first doctor's visit will be able to provide you with more concrete insight as to what your baby is actually experiencing and how they are developing.

Keep an eye on your baby's eyes, nose, and ears. They can all provide you with hints that something might be wrong, depending on how they look. If your baby's eyes appear glassy or bloodshot, along with a stuffy nose, they might have developed a cold. Their ears also might feel tender to the touch, indicating a possible ear infection. Babies have very fragile immune systems, so if you notice these symptoms, it is a good idea to get to the doctor right away. While adults can typically heal on their own from a common cold, it can feel a lot more severe to a newborn baby.

Even if you cannot see any external symptoms, yet your baby won't stop crying no matter how hard you try to soothe them, it is also a good idea to take your baby to the doctor. There could be things happening internally that you wouldn't know about unless the doctor takes a look. Inconsolable crying, for whatever reason, should not last for hours at a time. Some babies are able to be soothed easier than others, but crying for hours at a time is a sign that a trip to the doctor might be necessary.

How To Help Development

The best way to help your baby's developmental progress is by creating a routine. This will allow your baby to feel comfortable and familiar as to what is going on each day. Stick to a feeding schedule that fits with your lifestyle. Do your best to create a sleep schedule, as well. It can be very hard for certain infants to regulate their sleeping schedules within the first month, but it is worth a try. Babies typically sleep for most of the day during their first month of life, and when nighttime comes, they are wide awake. This is why it is important that you create a schedule that you can alter. Keep your baby engaged and social during the day so that they are tired by the time it gets dark out.

Introduce your baby to as many new people as you can. This likely won't be very hard, as a lot of people will probably be dying to meet your little one anyway. Your baby is going to know yourself and your partner as their primary caregivers, but it is great for their social development to meet and be handled by other people. This can be confusing or interesting to your baby and don't be surprised if they immediately burst out in tears after leaving mommy's arms. Babies attach very quickly, but there are certain levels of attachment that are healthy, as well as levels that can become unhealthy. You will want to build your trust with your baby, showing them that they will return to you, even after being held by a new person.

Talk to your baby using real words and sentences. While it can be tempting to coo at your little one, it is actually going to help their development more if they hear you speaking properly. This is how they are going to make sense of language and communication. If you start talking to them from a very young age, they will also be more likely to begin mimicking the sounds that you make. This is the first stage of being able to speak and communicate effectively. Your baby will likely be fascinated as you talk to them in your native tongue, unable to take their eyes off you.

Second Month

Milestones

Achieved Milestones:

- Can raise head 45 degrees during tummy time
- Holds head straight when sitting in a supported position
- Can support partial weight on elbows
- Virtually follows objects in an arc formation
- Searches for sounds by turning head
- Recognizes faces
- Coos and grunts
- Smiles at familiar people
- Becomes fussy when bored

Emerging Milestones:

- Ability to raise head 90 degrees during tummy time
- Raising the head and looking up while sitting in a supported position
- Can place complete weight on elbows and forearms
- Follows objects within 180 degrees of their line of sight
- Recognizes faces, voices, and objects
- Squealing and babbling

- Smiling spontaneously at people
- Trying to imitate voices and tones

Development

Cognitive: Your baby will now be paying close attention to the faces that they see. Instead of staring at a face as though they are in a haze, they are tracking individual details of each face in front of them. Your baby will now have better coordination between hearing and brain function. They are going to look for the sound by turning their head in order to determine where the noise is coming from. As mentioned, different cries can determine different feelings. By now, you will know that your two-month-old has several cries that vary depending on what they want or need. There will be a hunger cry, a cry for when a diaper is soiled, a cry for when they are feeling antsy, and so on.

Physical: When you hold your baby up with support, their head should be able to stay straight fairly easily. These muscles develop very quickly for newborns, especially since they are so eager to look around at all there is to see and hear. You might also notice your baby trying to push up onto their elbows or forearms during tummy time. This is getting your baby one step closer to the scooting/crawling stage. Now, when your baby moves their limbs, the movements aren't as jerky as they used to be. The movements should appear smoother and more purposeful. Hand-eye coordination will also improve significantly. When your baby wants to grab something, they will likely be able to grab it on the first try if it is within reaching distance.

Social/Emotional: Smiling is the biggest milestone of the month. Your baby will likely be flashing many smiles at the sight of familiar or friendly faces. If you ask your baby questions, you will likely get a response in the form of gurgles or cooing. Self-soothing is something that you might also notice that your baby is doing. This can be anything from bringing their hands to their mouth while they are crying to sucking their thumb for comfort. Boredom also becomes something that your two-month-old can experience. This can cause them to become fussy or grumpy. This is actually another significant milestone because it shows you that your baby is developing unique emotions. They might be playing with a toy one minute and then throwing it on the ground and crying the next minute because they grew bored with the activity.

Is Your Baby Healthy?

There are a few signs that you can look for if you are concerned about your baby's developmental progress. One of the biggest signs to look for is if your baby cannot hold their head up, even despite pushing themselves up on their forearms during tummy time. The same level of concern is valid if your baby is struggling to keep their head straight while you are helping them sit in a supported position. Watch your baby's eyes. Do they respond to stimuli that are in front or to the side of them? Your baby should be moving their eyes a significant amount, and if they don't, this could indicate possible cognitive issues.

Most 2-month-olds will frequently put their hands in their mouths, as mentioned. This is both a self-soothing technique, as well as an exploration of their body. If your baby isn't bringing their hands up, this could be another indication that something is wrong or developing at a slower pace. A quiet baby can seem like a great thing, but a baby who never coos or smiles can be a cause for concern. In the first few months of your baby's life, their personality should be shining through. If you notice little response from your little one, it would be worth bringing it up with your doctor.

Of course, the best time to discuss any of your concerns is during your baby's two-month check-up. Even if you think the issue is minor, your doctor will be able to put you at ease and explain to you exactly how well your baby is developing. There are also certain screening tests that you will be offered to check for developmental disorders. Though they aren't mandatory, a lot of parents do opt for infant screening in order to catch any issues at an early stage. Listen to your maternal instinct. You are likely having these worries for a good reason, and remember, there is no such thing as asking too many questions when it comes to your baby's health and wellness.

How To Help Development

To help your baby continue on the right path, make sure to include plenty of tummy time in your daily routine. Not only does tummy time strengthen neck muscles so your baby can hold their head up on their own, but it actually strengthens muscles throughout the entire body. This is an ideal way to stimulate your baby's physical growth, according to pediatricians. You can have 3-5 sessions of tummy time daily, each lasting for around 5 minutes. Most babies really enjoy this time because it provides them with a new perspective and a feeling of independence. Don't forget to put some brightly colored toys in front of them on the ground for them to interact with.

Play with distance more. Encourage your baby to look for you from across the room by using your voice and waving your arms. This is an interactive game that is fun for an infant, and it also improves their cognitive ability to focus on things and to recognize things. You can begin to do this with toys, as well, showing your baby a brightly colored toy from afar and seeing if you can get a reaction. Experiment with different sounds. Your baby should be very reactive to high-pitched and low-pitched noises, along with the sound of your voice, which should be most comforting.

As your baby's social skills are developing daily, continue to let them meet with plenty of other people. It is likely that you are still going to be getting a lot of visitors who are eager to meet the little one. Try to get the whole family involved with playtime, showing your baby that it can be fun to interact in a group setting. This can often be very exciting for a two-month-old, and it will usually elicit a great response in return. Seeing so many people that your baby loves in one place is genuinely exciting. This is also a great way to improve your baby's memory. If they see family members in this setting daily, they will begin to remember their faces.

While you might want to jump for joy during every tiny milestone, know that this is only the beginning. You do need to allow your baby to explore and discover on their own. Providing positive reinforcement is a great thing, and you should continue providing it. Try not to guide your little one so much to the developmental stages that you feel they should be reaching. They will get there when the time is right, and they will know what they need to do to get there on their own when they are ready.

Third Month

Milestones

Achieved Milestones:

- Regularly lifts head to 45 degrees during tummy time

- Pushes legs down when held vertically
- Bringing hands to mouth
- Grasping objects that are close
- Shaking objects that are held
- Tracking moving objects/people
- Being quiet or reserved around strangers
- Strong back muscles from tummy time
- Can imitate certain actions
- Supports entire body weight on arms

Emerging Milestones:

- Moving head 90 degrees
- Bearing weight on feet when held on the ground
- Bringing hands together
- Attempts to grab objects beyond their reach
- Hitting an object to a surface during playtime
- Moving head to track objects/people all around
- Becoming anxious in the presence of strangers
- Rolling over in one direction

Development

Cognitive: When your baby sees you from across the room, they might express joy or excitement because they recognize that you are headed their way. If they hear something of interest, they will be able to turn their head in order to locate where the sound is coming from. This is an indication that your baby's brain is able to locate sources, which is a great sign. No matter if the sound causes joy, fear, or curiosity, your baby will likely still be interested in locating it. You should be able to have "conversations" with your baby now. Though they cannot respond with words, they will still respond with chortles, grunts, cooing, and more. You will also notice more imitation this month, with both sounds and actions.

Physical: You should feel that your baby's head is very steady during feeding and while being held in your arms. With all of the tummy time that your baby is having, this is causing their muscles to develop rapidly which is a great thing. A big physical milestone is the desire to stand when placed feet-first onto a surface. If your baby has this instinct already, then you can expect them to be walking sooner than you think. When your baby is on their back, you might notice that they are kicking and stretching more. This is an exploration of movement, and it is also a small milestone. Overall, your baby should be sleeping about an hour less than they did last month. The average infant sleeps for 16 hours, so you can expect your three-month-old to sleep around 15 hours.

Social/Emotional: Smiling is one of the most important social responses that your baby can have toward people. Since communication is limited, a smile is worth a thousand words. You might also hear your baby bust out in the giggles this month! Laughter is a beautiful sound, and your baby will become amused very easily. While your baby can be very friendly and bubbly toward familiar people, you might notice a reserved version of their personality when they are introduced to strangers. This shows that they are aware that the person is new. It is actually a good sign, and once you show your baby that this new person can be trusted, they will open up and start acting more bubbly again.

Is Your Baby Healthy?

Similar signs last month can also apply this month. As stated, a quiet baby is not necessarily a bad thing, but a baby who never laughs, smiles, or gurgles can be a cause for concern. Your baby should be making some noise every day aside from crying. If they still aren't doing that at this stage, mention the behavior to your doctor. This can be a serious sign of a developmental delay. Sometimes, this progress can be made up with the help of more interactive play and experiences. Other times, the delay is a sign of a learning disability.

If your baby's head is still bobbing back and forth seemingly uncontrollably, this is not a good sign. By the third month, your baby should have a very strong head, neck, and back muscles. Even despite tummy time, if your little one isn't able to control their head on their own, this could be an indication of some kind of physical developmental delay. Also, make sure that your baby can support their own head when you first pick them up. Though it is still necessary to assist them with a little bit of neck support, they should be able to maintain initial control over their head when being picked up.

Not being able to hold onto an object is another sign of a developmental delay in a three-month-old. By now, your baby should be holding onto objects, possibly even banging them on surfaces in front of them. If you notice that your baby cannot even grasp an object for a long period of time, mention this to your doctor. You will also need to pay attention to their grip. By now, your baby should be able to grip fairly hard. An abnormally loose grip can mean that there is a delay.

If an object or a person is moving within your baby's field of vision, no matter what is happening, your baby should be responsive to this either by looking or making a verbal response. When your baby simply does not react, then this is likely an indication that there is some kind of a developmental delay occurring. It is a good idea to keep a checklist to ensure that your baby is on track each month. You can reference it each month, looking at the progress that is being made.

How To Help Development

Interact with your baby as much as possible. It might seem silly, but explain what you are doing as you carry your baby around the house. You already know that hearing words and sentences being spoken can encourage learning and imitation, so make sure that you regularly narrate activities that you do together because you never know what your baby might understand, even from such a young age. Show them that you are listening to their responses, as well. If they respond to you or "talk" to you, it helps to show your baby that you will reply because this will prepare them for how to have an actual conversation.

Select activities that will promote tracking, like playing with toy cars that have the ability to move all-around your baby. You can also utilize toys that are placed on strings and have a wide range of mobility. These are the kind of activities that can make sure your baby is right on track with their tracking abilities. Use sounds to get your baby's attention. Making silly sounds should cause your baby to respond, and this can often be a fun game to play together. A three-month-old is going to have great listening ability, so it is up to you to get them to listen.

Along with these tips, also ensure that you are maintaining a regular schedule. This includes your feeding schedule, playtime, tummy time, socialization, and sleeping. In order to avoid developmental delays, having your baby on a routine shows them their first sense of regularity. If they are confused and wondering what is going to happen next each day, then they are less likely going to be developing and learning because their routine doesn't have enough structure to it. The self-discipline that it takes on your behalf is what will regulate your little one's schedule, and you will both feel thankful for it. Everyone is happier when they are able to get enough rest and have a sense of familiarity. If a baby's routine is disrupted, it is very easy to see the consequences. You will experience a lot more fussiness, and your baby will be expressing how they do not enjoy what is happening. Noticing a spike in fussy behavior could be an indication that a routine has been disrupted.

Chapter 5: 4th Month-6th Month

Your little one should now be as playful as ever. Each day, they are likely to surprise you by their willingness to explore and their curious mind. Being a parent to a baby who is under one year old can be filled with many different celebrations, as well as pitfalls. Your baby might not allow you to get any sleep at night, but that charming smile and adorable giggle are enough to make up for it. As your little one enters the second trimester of life, they will be babbling and, eventually, trying different solid foods to see which ones they enjoy most. Have fun during this time because your baby will give you many candid reactions that you will never forget.

Fourth Month

Milestones

Achieved Milestones:

- Responds to basic sounds and words
- Regularly supports the body with arms during tummy time
- Smiles and laughs while looking at faces
- Regularly tracks objects
- Can sit upright with support
- Makes basic movements during tummy time
- Holds toys with both hands

- Has different cries for different feelings
- Pays close attention to new faces and objects

Emerging Milestones:

- Will respond to their own name
- Rolls over from tummy onto the back
- Responds differently to different facial expressions
- Can track objects that are further away
- Can sit without support for short periods of time
- Crawls when placed on tummy
- Can pass toys from one hand to the other
- Makes different sounds for different feelings
- Supports weight on both legs while standing with support
- Shows curiosity when seeing new people and objects

Development

Cognitive: Your baby is starting to understand cause and effect. For example, when you put your baby into a feeding position, you will notice that their mouth automatically opens. Your little one also has a better memory now, remembering different people and objects that they might only see every once in a while. Understanding affection, your baby should be responsive to your hugs and kisses. This is especially true when the affection is given by the primary caregiver. Sadness is a feeling that your baby should regularly be expressing. When you leave the room, your baby might cry to show you that they are sad. This crying should subside as you return. Sadness isn't the only reason why your little one will cry. They will give you different tones for different feelings.

Physical: One of the biggest changes that you will notice is that your baby can now hold their head up on their own when they are in your arms! As you pick your baby up from a lying down position, their neck muscles should be strong enough to keep their head in place. Your baby has balance while in an assisted position. No more wobbling and falling over because your baby has strong lower back muscles, now. While speech isn't happening just yet, it is developing rapidly. Infants find it easy to say words with M, D, and B. You will typically notice their babbling beginning with these letters. Another big physical development is your baby's ability to roll over! Tummy time can be turned into tummy and back time.

Social/Emotional: Imitation should be happening frequently. From expressions to sounds, your baby will be very curious about other human behaviors. They will show a preference toward familiar people—for example, those that they see on a regular basis. This is an example of how your baby is telling you when they are comfortable. And strangers don't always elicit a shy response. Your baby might like to stare at a newcomer or try to get their attention by playing coy. Babies who are particularly social love meeting new people everywhere you go. This can make a standard trip to the grocery store extra long because of your baby's social tendencies. Don't be surprised if your baby actually starts crying when the new person approaches. This can be overwhelming for some.

Is Your Baby Healthy?

When your baby cannot move their eyes in a coordinated way by this point, this is abnormal. There might be a little bit of lag due to the ocular muscles still developing, but a response that takes longer than a few seconds might be a cause for concern. Much like last month, a lack of smiling at all means that there is likely something that is not connecting cognitively for your baby. This can also be a sign of social detachment, which can become a big problem if it is not addressed early on in your little one's life.

Having a wobbly neck by the fourth month is not normal, either. Because of all the tummy time and muscle formation, your baby should be lifting their head on their own regularly. If you notice any struggles, bring this up with your doctor. This can be a sign of a deficiency. Having stiff arms, hands, and legs is also abnormal. Babies are generally very flexible, so if you see that your baby is having trouble moving their limbs or bringing their hands to their mouth, this could be another sign of a deficiency.

It is unusual for any four-month-old to be silent. At this point, your baby should be babbling nonstop. If your baby has never made any noises or attempted to make any noises, this is an indication of either a speech or hearing problem. If you notice something like this, it is important to take your baby to the doctor right away.

Remember that a developmental delay, at this stage, does not necessarily indicate a permanent problem. Picking up on these signs early in your child's life will give you the chance to help them catch up. With a plan that is made by your doctor, you will be able to determine an appropriate line of action to take. Some babies develop slower than others, while some need special therapy in order to catch up. No matter what the case is, by noticing these little things, you are doing your best as a parent to give your child a wonderful life. While you don't have control over these delays, you have control over how you take action and find solutions for them.

How To Help Development

Talk to your baby all the time. This is something that has been stated from the beginning, but your baby is so close to forming words at this point. Though they might not understand everything that you are trying to express, your tone and volume will give them many context clues to pay attention to. If you do notice your baby saying something simple, such as "mama" or "dada," encourage this by repeating it. They will feel encouraged when they hear you saying the exact same thing back to them. Of course, this is a huge milestone in your baby's life, and it might even bring tears to your eyes when you hear them speak for the first time.

When a person walks in the room whom your baby is familiar with, refer to them by name. This will create even more familiarity. Now that your baby is getting so close to speaking, their ever-expanding memory will make a note of each person's name that you teach them. Pretty soon, they will be able to recognize their grandparents, siblings, and other loved ones by name. You can do the same thing with toys, objects, and food. It is never too early to teach your baby these things. When they are able to learn what everything is called, their vocabulary will be full of knowledge and information on how to ask for what they want and express how they are feeling.

Read books to your baby often! Picture books that contain bright illustrations are the best for capturing your baby's attention. Not only will this help your baby cognitively, but it will also help their physical development (by being in a seated position) and their vision. Now is the time to become a little bit more active during play sessions. Truly engage with your baby and play with toys that move or have moving parts. You will want to encourage them to explore how things work and how there are plenty of other cause and effect lessons for them to learn. Along with this, tummy time should still be a regular occurrence. You can place objects just beyond their reach to encourage crawling. You'll find that your baby will try harder to reach for the item, maybe even scooting.

Fifth Month

Milestones

Achieved Milestones:

- Sitting with slight support
- Regularly rolling over from back to tummy
- Responding to sounds
- Making a few consonant sounds
- Tongue growing more sensitive to tastes
- Showing curiosity toward stationary objects
- Communicates in response to basic expressions
- Flexes legs during tummy time
- Tests cause and effect
- Recognizes familiar faces regularly

Emerging Milestones:

- Sitting without support
- Rolling over from back to tummy and vice versa
- Responding to their name
- Making sounds with more consonants
- Learning to taste solid foods
- Tracking moving objects
- Uses sounds and expressions in conjunction
- Uses knowledge of cause and effect for more complex actions

- Tries to communicate with known people

Development

Cognitive: You will find that your baby is more captivated than ever before. By tracking objects and people, you will notice your baby observing before expressing a reaction. This is the most simple display of thinking before acting. Just as easily as your baby can become fascinated, they can also become distracted. Since their vision has improved immensely in the last few months, they are going to notice shiny, colorful, or interesting things. You might find that your baby is playing one minute and then staring at something else that has caught their eye the next. On the topic of colors, your baby should begin to start showing preferences for certain colors. This is another indication that they recognize the differences between colors. By now, your baby also has a mini vocabulary full of repetitive, mono-consonant sounds.

Physical: It is unlikely that anything will slip from your baby's hands unless they intentionally drop it. Your baby's muscles and grip should be very strong now. They will pick up objects when they want to, potentially even reaching out of their way to pick things up. Make sure that everything around your home is fully babyproofed! During tummy time, your baby will support themselves on their elbows while also lifting their chest off the ground. This is the precursor to being able to crawl. Paired with upcoming leg movements, your little one is almost mobile. Your baby is going to have a lot more say in what they want to do with their body. From sitting to rolling from their tummy to their back, they will go where they want to go.

Social/Emotional: You should clearly be able to read your baby's emotions on their face. Along with smiling, your baby should also be frowning, showing an indication of being surprised, making curious glances, and crying when they are feeling fearful or unsure. There might be some heightened anxiety when it comes to strangers, but as long as you make the introduction seem less intimidating and more joyful, your baby will start to feel more comfortable around new people. Your attitude and energy are the main things that your baby will learn from. You are setting an example for them to follow the actions that you choose. You'll learn that this is a common pattern when it comes to parenthood. You will have to utilize it often.

Is Your Baby Healthy?

Even when you are not directly addressing your baby, if you are nearby, they should turn their head to look over at you. If you notice that your baby doesn't seem to respond to the sound of your voice unless you are in front of them, this could be due to some sort of hearing impairment. You can test your baby's hearing by walking over to different parts of the room and saying their name to see what their reaction is. Also, make sure that your baby is reacting to you. Your baby should feel keen on giving you love and excitable expressions. If your baby is showing no reaction at all, this is definitely abnormal and should be brought up with your doctor.

At this age, body control is a very big milestone that should have already been accomplished. If your baby is stiff or appears very wobbly, then something is likely wrong with their muscle development. This can also be an indicator of certain autism spectrum disorders. While you cannot diagnose these things yourself, it is important that you bring them to your doctor's attention right away. The sooner the issue is addressed, the sooner you will have an answer and a solution. While it can be scary to find that your baby is behind with their development, it is much better to get a concrete answer than to worry over something that is potentially going to pass.

As stated, your baby should be a babbling machine. From cooing to expressing mono-consonant sounds, your five-month-old should be on the verge of talking any day now. This is why it is unusual if your baby is particularly quiet, and it could be the first indication of a speech impediment. It isn't realistic to expect your baby to be saying full words or sentences, but you should know that your baby is getting closer and closer to this point. While it can be unsettling to discover that your baby is extra quiet, the good news is that speech therapy can often correct these things. The earlier that you discover there is a problem, the better chance there will be for your baby to catch up on the developmental spectrum. Again, this isn't something that you can diagnose by yourself, but your doctor can provide you with more insight.

How To Help Development

Increase the amount of tummy time that you are giving your baby. A fun way to engage them is by placing all of their favorite toys around them during tummy time. You will watch as your baby giggles and rolls around, trying to get to each one of their treasured items. This is a great way to promote movement and even more muscle development. Keep speaking to your baby, as well. Even if you do not think that your baby is listening, they are. Subconsciously, your baby is receiving all of this information from you, and once they are able to process it, they are going to be talking up a storm. Explain what you are doing, as you are doing it. Point to places and things and say their names. This is going to give your baby a headstart on building up a fantastic vocabulary.

Make reading a regular occurrence, as well. Reading bedtime stories is a great way to bond with your little one. Basic stories with lots of colorful pictures will keep your baby engaged and then get them feeling sleepy enough for nighttime. Some books come with textured pages and are more interactive. These are also great to introduce to your five-month-old. The more senses you can work on, the better. Try to encourage your baby to explore each book, even if they aren't meant to be touched for textural purposes. Allow them to feel the paper and the cover of the book. If they try to put it into their mouth, gently guide them away from it and show them that it is for reading, not eating.

When you notice that your baby is putting toys in their mouth, this is likely pretty adorable and you shouldn't have a reason to stop them. However, there are potential dangers present when you allow your baby to put everything into their mouth. For example, if you are playing outside, you don't want your baby to pick up a handful of rocks and try to eat them. Teach them what is mouth-appropriate and what is off-limits. You don't have to be hard on your baby with a mean tone, and always remember to use positive reinforcement. This means that you need to focus on when they do something great and then gently guide them to a better action when they are doing something incorrectly.

Sixth Month

Milestones

Achieved Milestones:

- Can eat select fruits and vegetables
- Sits without any support
- Can use all fingers to hold objects
- Regularly practices basic cause and effect
- Makes simple vowel and consonant sounds

- Rolls in both directions
- Stretches often to reach for objects
- Sleeps for several hours through the night
- Better color, vision, and depth perception

Emerging Milestones:

- Can eat more fruits and vegetables
- Learns to get into the sitting position on their own
- Can use finger and thumb to hold items in a pincer grasp
- Can utilize cause and effect for complex actions
- Communicates through gestures and faces
- Will start to make more complex sounds
- Will roll into various positions like sitting and crawling
- Will start crawling to reach and grasp objects
- Will have even more sleep through the night with fewer feedings
- Can identify a wider range of colors and depth perception

Development

Cognitive: Your reactions will now be tested by your six-month-old in the form of cause and effect. If they throw a toy, they will be able to gauge the results by your reaction and by no longer being able to play with it. More curious than ever, your little one is starting to put these concepts together in a way that makes sense. You will notice a more vocal baby as well! Your little one should be able to make basic sounds, such as "ah" and "eh." You will also notice more imitation. This is due to the rapid rate of brain development that is happening. Even if your baby cannot speak or fully understand sentences, they should be responsive to their own name. Calling their name should cause a turn of the head.

Physical: At six months, your baby has great depth perception and color vision. They will be able to tell the difference between two different shades of the same color, and might even begin to show a preference. Their hand-eye coordination will also be improved. They will be able to hold objects, observe them, and then choose to perform an action if necessary. At six months old, your baby's back muscles are strong. They should be able to sit up without any support. You will also notice an improvement in their neck muscles. When you pick them up, their head won't fall back as easily as it used to. Another perk to these newly developed muscles is the ability to roll over in either direction, whether on the tummy or back.

Social/Emotional: A big social milestone is the ability to respond to others' emotions. If you are upset, you can expect your baby to appear concerned or upset as well. If you show them joy and elation, they will likely mirror this response. They should also be making unique vocal noises to indicate different requests. For example, a hungry noise should sound different than general fussing noise. Your baby should be inclined to play with you when you engage them. There is often nothing that an infant loves more than getting interactive with a primary caregiver. Keep playing with your baby, and encourage family group play. This will allow for even more socialization. Infants associate familiar faces with warmth, comfort, and food, so this is why your baby is so keen on you.

Is Your Baby Healthy?

If your baby tends to stay either stiff or droopy, this is abnormal for this developmental stage of life. Their muscles should be helping them greatly by now, not hindering them. If you notice this kind of abnormality in the way that their muscles are forming, this could be an early indication of some kind of physical developmental delay. Make sure that this stiffness or droopiness isn't causing them any pain if you do notice it, and tell your doctor about the issue right away.

A quiet baby can be relatively normal, depending on their personality, but a silent baby brings up a cause for concern. Differentiate if your baby is being quiet by choice or because they do not know how to begin communicating. Not responding to any sounds or noises, not even their name is another red flag. This can indicate that something isn't processing mentally, or perhaps there is a hearing impairment that is preventing them from responding.

At six months old, your baby should visually respond to you when you enter the room. By their giving you a smile or expressing a vocal sound, you should be able to tell that your baby can recognize you. It is abnormal for a baby to go without any reaction whatsoever after seeing a parent or another familiar face walk into the room. They should typically be responsive to new people walking in. A lack of reaction can indicate that they have early vision problems or perhaps some sort of cognitive delay.

Babies can be clumsy and rough when they play with their toys, but there is a difference between this and having poor motor skills. Pay attention to your baby's ability to grip objects. If your baby is given a selection of toys in front of them, they should be able to deliberately pick up the toy that they want and play with it without issues. If they cannot avoid dropping objects or just seem to be unable to reach for objects, this might be an early indication of a problem. Test your baby's motor skills by directly handing them toys and then observing what they do with them. If the object immediately falls, then you can assume something is probably wrong with their grip.

How To Help Development

Help your baby develop by including conversations into play sessions. As you are playing, explain what is happening and what each object is. Your baby will become familiar with these terms, and they will get an understanding of how everything relates. When they do begin speaking, they will already have these words in their vocabulary, which will put them ahead. Plenty of parents love to baby-talk their little ones, and it can be hard to resist, but they will not learn how to speak properly unless you speak to them first. All of the knowledge that they get at the beginning of their life is coming directly from you and the activities that you provide them.

Do some more outdoor exploration! Put your baby in the stroller and take frequent walks around your neighborhood, possibly visit some parks. This is another way to expand your baby's experiences in an educational and fun way. Point out various objects and name them so your baby understands what they are seeing. It can be a lot for a little one to process, and it might even leave them feeling worn out by the time you get back home. They will likely love this change in scenery, though. With so much to look at, your baby won't get bored.

At this point, your baby can be introduced to some solid foods. This is a huge milestone! Be careful when you introduce new foods to your baby because you aren't going to be sure about what they are allergic to if they are allergic to anything. Make sure that everything you give them is cut up into small pieces in order to avoid a choking hazard, as well. It helps to make a note each time you let your baby try something new for both the purpose of learning their preferences and also ensuring that they do not have any food allergies. You are now at a point where you can share meals with your baby, and this is a very exciting milestone for both the parent and the child. A balanced diet is still very important, so don't go crazy with junk food. Your baby might be delighted at the little taste of a cookie, but you still need to ensure that the food you are giving them is nourishing.

Chapter 6: 7th Month-9th Month

This time period is known as the third trimester of the first year of life. Your baby has done a lot of physical and mental growth in the last few months. Compared to what they were able to do merely a few months ago, looking back on their progress should amaze you. As a parent, you have every right to feel proud of your baby and what they have learned so far. This is only the beginning because, in these next few months, the learning is only going to be expedited.

Seventh Month

Milestones

Achieved Milestones:

- Uses voice to express emotions
- Can understand the word "no"
- Can discover partially hidden objects
- Develops raking grasp
- Responds to their own name
- Can place weight on arms during tummy time
- Continues to test cause and effect
- Can identify vocal tones
- Explores objects by using hands and mouth

Emerging Milestones:

- Can make simple consonant sounds
- Understands one-word instructions
- Can completely uncover hidden objects
- Develops a pincer grasp
- Can remember the names of certain objects
- Attempts to lift the body with arms during tummy time
- Can remember the results of certain actions
- Improved ability in judging distances
- Uses hands more to manipulate objects

Development

Cognitive: If you place a favorite toy under a blanket, your baby should understand that the toy is now partially hidden. It can become a fun game of hide-and-seek as they attempt to uncover their toy. Every new object that they are given is typically going to be examined visually, as well as with their hands and mouth. Babies love to put everything in their mouths! This is a phase that you need to watch carefully, as they can often end up eating things they aren't supposed to. If you place your baby in front of a mirror, they should understand that they are seeing themselves in the mirror. This activity can provide endless hours of fun as your baby explores new facial expressions and gestures.

Physical: When you hold your baby, any weight that is placed on their legs should immediately be followed by their leg muscles kicking in as if they were about to stand on their own.

This is a great sign when you notice your baby can attempt to put weight on their legs and feet. This means that walking is going to happen soon! Their raking grasp is now their preferred method of handling objects. It involves picking up items using all of their fingers, but their grip should remain solid. Since your baby has the complete ability to see all colors now, you might find them fascinated on a daily basis by the objects that they see around them. Allowing them to play with colorful toys and read colorful picture books will also enhance this curiosity.

Social/Emotional: When you tell your baby no, you should be doing this with a stern tone. You don't need to be particularly mean or authoritative, but your baby is going to acknowledge that this means they are doing something wrong. Immediately provide them with a corrected behavior that they can perform so they can understand what you want from them. This is an example of positive reinforcement, which works very well on infants. Your parenting style is up to your own preferences, but positive reinforcement tends to produce great results. At this point, building up a social circle is important. Try to get your baby involved in as many social interactions as possible. Playgroups can be a great option for you.

Is Your Baby Healthy?

The main warning sign to look for in the seventh month of your baby's life is the inability to bring their hands to their mouth. Not only is this a norm for babies of this age, but it is also an essential skill that is necessary for being able to eat. If you notice that your baby never explores this option, then you can try to show them that it is a possibility by bringing their hand up to their mouth for them. You can do this during feeding time as well as playtime. See how they react to this, and if there is still no response, you might need to discuss this with your doctor. This is an essential activity for a baby of this age to accomplish, so the sooner your baby is able to do it, the faster your baby will develop.

A lost gaze while looking around can also be concerning. Most seven-month-olds are very attentive and curious, no matter where they are or what there is to see. Staring off blankly into space can indicate some sort of a cognitive delay. Perhaps your baby just isn't processing their surroundings. You can also test this by standing beside or behind your baby and making various noises to get their attention. Call out their name, and see if you can get them to appear interested. Even the most simple gesture of returning your smile is a sign that your baby is able to process what is happening, and then react appropriately based on how they are feeling.

The same as last month, if your baby's body appears either stiff or floppy, this can mean that there is something wrong. If your baby is having tummy time, they should have the ability to roll around and move their limbs freely. The same can be said if your baby is on their back. If there isn't any movement at all or any attempt at movement, there is likely something that is preventing your baby's mobility from developing. By now, they should have plenty of muscles developed in order to assist them with this movement.

A modulation in voice is important for a seven-month-old. This is how they are able to express different emotions to you and let you know what they need. If your baby can make sounds, but they all seem monotone, this can be an issue that you should bring up to your doctor.

How To Help Development

Assist your baby in doing sit-ups. This is going to work on the development of their essential core muscles. Placing your baby into a vertical position, you can then help them up into a half-seated position. Gently placing them back down, you can do this several times to encourage them to lift their bodies up on their own. You can also encourage self-feeding. When you place your baby's food in front of them and they are hungry, they are going to make an effort to grab the food and eat it. By taking a step back and allowing them some independence, you will help them realize that they no longer need to rely on you to get fed.

At seven-months-old, you should still be providing your little one with plenty of tummy time. You can do this at least three times each day with a minimum of five minutes per session. If you notice that your baby keeps lifting their body weight onto their arms, this is a great sign! Your little one will soon be crawling all-around your home. You can place toys all-around your baby during tummy time to also encourage more reaching, a fun and interactive form of playtime.

As mentioned, social time is very important for an infant of this age. If you cannot get involved in a playgroup, try to find some friends who have children around the same age. Getting to interact with other babies will boost their social development, and it is the fastest way to get them to learn how to be social without your direct guidance.

Be selective with the toys that you get for your baby. There are certain toys that are meant to enhance comprehension skills, and these are the ones that will be best for this developmental stage. Any toys that are interactive or require a bit of a puzzle are going to be great for your little one's brain development. It will also lessen the chances of your baby getting bored or growing tired of the toys they usually play with. A challenge can be fun for a baby. You can be interactive with them at first, showing them what the objective is. They will likely catch on super quickly. Babies learn through imitation, so when they see you playing with the toy, they will want to mirror your action.

Eighth Month

Milestones

Achieved Milestones:

- Can support weight on both legs when placed upright
- Tracks moving objects
- Can manipulate objects by passing them between hands
- Can speak simple words starting with M, D, and B
- Understands basic repetitive instructions
- Develops a pincer grasp
- Displays separation anxiety
- Can easily get into a crawling position
- Understands the purpose of personal objects

Emerging Milestones:

- Can stand when holding onto support
- Tries to catch moving objects
- Develops finer control of each finger
- Improves on the range of spoken words
- Can understand a wider range of instructions
- Uses the correct noun when addressing parents ("mama" vs. "dada")
- Can use the entire hand to grasp objects
- Appears more at ease about separation

- Understands the purpose of other household objects

Development

Cognitive: Your baby might be talking now! Though the words and syllables spoken will be fairly simple, they are getting one step closer to full communication. A permanent state of curiosity is normal for an eight-month-old. They love to see how things work and like to know what you are doing. When you provide them with basic instructions, such as to put something down, they should be able to listen to you and obey. If an object is dropped in front of them, they should have no trouble keeping track of its path, and they also might reach out in an attempt to grab it. Pointing is also a new milestone that has probably been achieved. If they see something of interest, they might point to it while vocally exclaiming.

Physical: If a sound is heard from any direction, near or far, you can expect your baby to physically turn toward that sound. They should display an interest in wanting to know where it came from. Another new physical development is the mastering of the pincer grasp. This is the grasp that allows them to hold objects between their index finger and thumb. As you can imagine, this is a very useful grasp that can assist with eating and picking up smaller items. Though they might not have any teeth yet, you will notice your baby-making chewing motions with their jaw—this is a great development!

Coordination is another big improvement. From passing things back and forth between hands to being able to stand with support, you will notice a lot of progress.

Social/Emotional: If your little one needs to spend time away from you, they might start to display signs of separation anxiety. This means that they might be extra fussy until they are able to see your face again. This behavior is normal at this age because you have bonded so much. Because of this, there might also be a newfound shyness when it comes to meeting strangers and accepting new people into their life. Try to encourage them as much as possible by being friendly with the individual as well. They should learn to mirror your behavior. Empathy is also something that will be learned by now. If they see or hear another infant crying, they might start crying too. This shows that your baby is developmentally on track in social situations.

Is Your Baby Healthy?

At an age where your baby should be standing with support, it is very concerning if your baby cannot sit up with or without support. When you try to prop your baby up and there is no sense of muscle control, this is an indication that they likely do not have enough muscle mass to hold themselves up. While this can be corrected, it is important to discuss it with your doctor in order to develop a plan. This will also ensure that there isn't a more serious developmental issue happening.

Plenty of babies can develop neuromuscular disorders, and if they are caught early enough, there are ways that you can assist them.

Your baby should be delighted to see a familiar face, but if it appears that they cannot recognize people who should be very familiar by now, then a cognitive issue might be taking place. This is especially alarming if your baby appears to not be able to recognize your own face. Babies who do not recognize familiar faces have delays in development, and this can lead to a socially detached attitude as a result of their shortcomings. If you notice that your baby does seem drawn especially inward, this needs to be discussed with your doctor right away. There is a difference between having a shy personality and not being able to recognize faces that should definitely be familiar by now.

As time goes on, a silent baby is a big sign that something is wrong. An eight-month-old should definitely be babbling away at all times and using their vocal cords often. Even if no words are being spoken yet, attempts should be made. If you find that your baby is just quiet, then there is likely something that is preventing them from being able to make noises. Experiment with their ability to vocalize by showing them a range of their favorite objects and foods. Your baby might appear visually excited, but if there is still no ability to make any noise, then there is likely a problem occurring internally. There are many instances when speech therapy can help your little one find their voice, so don't become overly concerned until you discuss the issue with your doctor. They will be able to come up with a proper treatment plan.

How To Help Development

Have plenty of interactive play sessions! This can be done one-on-one or in a group setting. No matter what toys you are playing with or what games you are playing, talk to your baby while this is happening. This is going to both stimulate their interest in the play session as well as encourage them to be more expressive. All around, you should notice that your baby wants to be more expressive with their body as well as the sounds that they are able to make. You might even experience some high-pitched squeals of delight as your baby experiments with their vocal range.

When you are referring to individuals and objects, refer to them by name. This is going to give your baby a better sense of what everything is and who they are interacting with. When they start talking, they will already know these words which will take out a bit of the frustration that babies can experience when they are trying to find the right words to describe things. Your baby is never too young to learn about object-noun association, so don't let their age hold you back from teaching them.

Make reading a regular activity. Whether you are reading throughout the day or before bedtime, reading to your baby is an excellent way to expand their mind. Not only do they get to see intriguing images in picture books, but they also get to listen to you reading them the story. Having these multiple stimuli is very helpful to a developing baby, and it can make them quite happy to sit down and have these reading sessions with you.

Try to play games that encourage crawling. During tummy time, place some objects in front of your baby, just beyond their reach. This might cause some frustration, but it will also encourage them to get up and moving in order to reach their toys. Make sure that you are giving them plenty of positive praise and encouragement as they try to hold their weight up and get to these objects. The more that you do this during tummy time, the more your baby will realize that they have to take action in order to get what they want. It is a big lesson to learn in a fun way.

Ninth Month

Milestones

Achieved Milestones:

- Crawls for short distances and then sits
- Stands with support regularly
- Can say "mama" and "dada"
- Understands the word no
- Copies simple gestures

- Holds and drops objects at will
- Has favorite toys
- Moves objects from one hand to the other
- Gets nervous around new people

Emerging Milestones:

- Can crawl faster at longer distances
- Can take a step with support
- Will speak more basic syllable words
- Can interpret simple words such as "yes" and "come here"
- Will pass you an object when requested
- Will have favorite toys and people
- Can put objects into a container
- Gets nervous or shy around strangers

Development

Cognitive: Understanding the word "no" is a very big milestone. This is the beginning of your obedience training, and when your baby can correctly respond to this, you should feel very proud. Not only does this indicate that your baby trusts you and respects you, but this is also going to keep them safe. When your baby sees something interesting or unique, they will continue to use their fingers to point even more than before. They might also be pointing to indicate that they want you to bring them this object. Another way babies might use pointing is to show you that they recognize a favorite or familiar person entering the room. Pointing can lead to a very positive response from your baby, and you should encourage it.

Physical: The pincer grasp should be getting stronger, as your baby attempts to grip things strongly between these two fingers. You might even feel a cheeky pinch on your skin when your baby realizes that the grasp can be used to get your attention. An infant who is now likely crawling will also return to a sitting position on their own frequently. This position should be strong and balanced, with no wobbling. Their leg muscles are also stronger than ever, and they should be standing with assistance a lot at this age. While their upper body might be a little bit wobbly, it will soon catch up as your baby learns how to walk! This is a very exciting time in physical development for both the parents and the child.

Social/Emotional: At nine months old, it is normal for your baby to be particularly attached to you. After all, you spend the most time together. This can result in a clingy phase where your baby seems to show no interest in being held by other people or socializing with new people. This is only a temporary phase, but a lot of parents secretly enjoy it because it just shows how strong your bond is with your baby. This being said, your baby might appear more nervous around strangers than usual. As long as you keep introducing them to new people and encouraging interaction, your baby should grow out of this shyness. Be patient with your little one during this time because it is new for them as well. This behavior should never be punished or scolded because this could send a confusing message to your child.

Is Your Baby Healthy?

Nine-months-old is a very monumental age. You should have experienced many milestones by now. As a parent, trust in your ability to determine when something seems wrong with your child because you are usually correct. If your baby has not mastered sitting or crawling by now, this is definitely something that you should be concerned about. While most nine-month-olds are preparing to take their first steps, your baby is considered to be very behind developmentally if they cannot sit down or crawl without assistance. Know that this is not your fault, nor your baby's fault. Sometimes, these developmental delays just happen. There are often links to the delays in the form of disorders or defects, but with your doctor's help, you will be able to help your baby manage them.

Make sure that your baby is practicing standing up as much as possible. It is okay if they do not feel comfortable doing this on their own so much, but with your assistance, they should be okay to stand up for moderate periods of time. If this seems difficult or impossible for your baby, then there is likely something wrong. By now, your nine-month-old's leg muscles should be more than strong enough to hold up their entire body weight. If it appears that the muscles are underdeveloped, bring this up to your doctor at your next appointment.

Handgrip is a very important aspect of development. It has been discussed a lot throughout this guide, and it should be stressed that your nine-month-old should have a variety of different grips by now. From grabbing objects with their entire hand to using select fingers, there should be no issues with the strength of their grip. As they get older, the weaker their grip is, the more of a problem this presents. If your baby cannot hold onto anything, they are going to struggle as they enter the standing/walking stage and the stage where they are able to feed themselves. Keep an eye on this, and ensure that your little one has enough grip strength to perform basic necessary actions. You might need to work with your baby on certain games or activities that promote holding onto objects. Throwing a ball back and forth is one example of a game that will allow your baby to practice gripping. Feeding them finger foods often is another way to help.

How To Help Development

The best way to encourage your baby to develop is to encourage all different types of playtime. Play one-on-one with your baby, allow them to entertain themselves, find other infants for them to interact with and have regular family play sessions. Use games and toys while you play. Also try the alternative—playing with only the imagination. The more that your baby gets to experience in these final months of infanthood are going to shape them tremendously. They will turn your baby into a smart and well-rounded toddler who is ready to take on the world.

All parents want what is best for their children. While you might be feeling particularly protective over your little one, especially if they are in a clingy stage, you need to allow them to explore new places. Take them on short trips, even if only 10 minutes away from home. Show them the grocery store and the mall. These different journeys might seem very mundane to you, but to your baby, they are all going to be learning experiences. From the sights they will see to the people they might interact with, outings are a very great part of contributing to your baby's development.

Read plenty of books to your baby. You can continue to read picture books, but also try reading books that require your baby to rely solely on their imagination. You'll probably find it harder to keep them engaged with a book that doesn't have brightly colored pictures, but they will listen if you keep your tone interesting and the mood lively. Allow them to feel the textures of a book, the pages, and covers. Show them that books are special and that it is not okay to tear books. You might have to rely on your use of the word "no" here.

Continue to have conversations with your baby. You don't have to tell them your life story, but do talk about meaningful and simple things, like feelings and what is going on today. They will begin to understand more complex words and sentence structures. Pretty soon, they'll be responding to you in full sentences! This is why it is important to start early; your baby understands more than you think. You will be able to gauge their feelings by their level of vocal expression and enthusiasm when you speak to them.

Chapter 7: 10th Month-12th Month

These are the final stages of infanthood—your baby's last three months until they turn one year old. Many parents wonder where the time has gone during these last few months. While it certainly does move quickly, your baby is still going to be teaching you new things every single day, even as a toddler. This is the final transition between infant to young baby, and you will learn about all of the final milestones that will be reached during this time. As you become familiarized with what to expect, remember to also enjoy what is happening at the moment. Your baby's milestones should fill you with pride because you helped them reach every single one.

Tenth Month

Milestones

Achieved Milestones:

- Crawls and pulls to stand
- Understands some words
- Moves from tummy to sitting position
- Understands requests
- Imitates basic actions
- Searches for hidden objects
- Reacts to scary or distressing situations
- Has some teeth

Emerging Milestones:

- Walking with support (cruising)
- Understands and speaks simple words
- Can sit from standing position
- Repeats activities after observation
- Remembers the location of objects by memory
- Can have around eight teeth by their first birthday

Development

Cognitive: Object permanence is one of the biggest cognitive milestones reached by this age. This means that your baby realizes that objects continue to exist, even when hidden under blankets or other objects. When their toy disappears behind a wall in the next room, they should not throw a fit thinking that their toy is now gone forever. Because of this, your baby should feel slightly less anxious when you have to walk out of the room. They should have an understanding that you are always going to come back to them.

Another benefit of having object permanence comes with the enhanced ability to search for hidden items. Hide-and-seek games will likely become a favorite for your baby. Without upsetting them, you will now be able to hide all of their favorite toys and then watch the joyous reactions as they are all found. Your baby should now also take initiative when you hand them a picture book. While it might be hard to flip through the pages, they should be engaged as to what is going on in the book. A lot of books that are designed for babies come with hard, chew-proof pages. These are essential for your developing 10-month-old.

Physical: It is likely that you've had to barricade nearly every room in your house by now. Your baby should be crawling all over the place! Let them crawl, and let them continue to build these essential muscles in their body. Another new physical development that you might have noticed is boredom with tummy time. Instead of throwing a fit, your baby can now simply switch from being on their tummy to being in a sitting position. Of course, this puts them at an advantage to either pull up into a standing position or to begin crawling. It is a much more independent experience than it used to be.

An exciting part about your baby standing is the instances in which they feel comfortable enough to attempt to take some steps. This is one thing that you cannot rush. Your baby will feel physically ready to do this, and you need to make sure that you have your camera ready! Those first steps happen after a whole lot of exploration and a rush of bravery. They might be wobbly, but they will improve over time.

Social/Emotional: Your baby likely knows now that waving can be used as a gesture to indicate that someone is either coming or going. Waving hello and goodbye should be a regular habit by now, and it is one that forms by you waving to your baby on a regular basis. Make sure to indicate whether you are coming or going by choosing the appropriate "hello" or "bye-bye" in order for your baby to fully understand the concept. You might even find them waving at strangers during your outings, another brave step toward socialization.

Along with all of the social progress that is made this month, there comes a great deal of anxiety. Sometimes, it is normal for your baby to go through this overly-anxious phase. They might be particularly wary of strangers and unwilling for you to leave them for long periods of time. This is definitely something that they will grow out of, and you must continue working with your baby to show them that they can trust both you and the people around you. This can take a great deal of patience on your behalf.

Is Your Baby Healthy?

Your baby having some teeth is likely going to be one of the biggest changes that you will experience this month. Having some teeth assists your baby with eating, and shows that their overall development is going well. If your baby has absolutely no teeth and no indication of teeth coming in by now, then you might need to discuss this with your doctor. The average 10-month-old has at least a few teeth emerging from their gums. The potential of having a dental problem might be a setback for your baby as you try to introduce more finger foods into their diet. This problem can also eventually lead to a nourishment issue, preventing your baby from getting all of the proper vitamins and nutrients needed for a growing infant.

Dental health is very important. A lot of people underestimate this for both themselves and their children. It is best to stay on top of your baby's dental health from an early age instead of worrying about fixing it with painful and expensive surgeries later on in life. Of course, fixing dental problems as soon as you notice them also means that your baby won't have to live in pain or with uncomfortable symptoms. You will know if this is happening if your baby is reluctant to eat or refuses to allow you to open their mouth to look at their gums/teeth.

Failure to recognize people who are definitely familiar faces in your baby's life becomes even more alarming at this age. This is a clear indication that your baby either has vision problems or cognitive difficulties. For the former, this can typically be corrected fairly easily if it is a routine case of poor vision. Some babies have this gene, and they do need to wear glasses. It is not uncommon to see an infant or toddler wearing glasses, so don't feel ashamed if this is what it comes down to for your little one. Of course, the latter is a bigger problem that needs to be diagnosed by a doctor. It is impossible to tell if there are truly cognitive issues going on unless given a proper examination.

Being unable to stand, even with a lot of support, is a problem. But being unable to crawl is an even bigger issue. As you know, your baby should be well into their crawling phase by now. In fact, it is usually hard to *not* get your baby to crawl due to their constant bursts of energy and curiosity. If your baby does not show interest in crawling, you need to determine if it is physically possible to do so. When you put them into a crawling position, does it seem like they are experiencing any pain? They will likely move out of the position or move awkwardly if there is any pain being caused.

Try to assist your baby as much as you can, but know that you should not have to be assisting them very much at this age. Their independence should definitely be kicking in by now, and if it isn't, then you need to monitor them for potential delays and difficulties. No matter what, a 10-month-old should go through daily periods of being very active. If they are unusually calm or immobile, then you need to have a conversation with your doctor right away to discuss the potential problems that need to be handled.

How To Help Development

Give your baby space! Having enough space to move around is going to encourage more movement. If you can, section off certain areas of your house that allow your baby ample crawling space. Make sure they also have things to hold onto in case they want to experiment with supported standing and taking some steps. The area should be flat and level, and it should ideally be soft in case of any falls. If you have hardwood flooring, this can be slippery. You might need to put a pair of slip-free socks on your baby or place some blankets down on the floor to prevent them from getting hurt. Try not to layer too many blankets because this can also pose a potential risk of tripping your baby. One single, large blanket should do the trick. Rugs also work very well.

Get your baby at least one toy that calls for some pushing action. These toys are usually in the form of cars that have handles on the backs to give your baby a chance to stand with support. By walking forward, still utilizing this support, your baby will make the car go forward. This is an excellent way for them to develop additional muscle strength and to get them one step closer to walking on their own. Let them have regular time with this walking toy each day. The more you let them practice, the quicker they will develop the necessary skills.

At this point, you should not be baby talking to your 10-month-old. There is a difference between expressing verbal affection and baby talking. When you are affectionate, you can use your tone and attitude to show your baby your love. There is no need for any "goo-goo" or "ga ga" to do so. This will only become a setback. Use full sentences and speak properly, no matter what you are saying to your baby. Try to encourage meaningful conversations daily. Your baby is going to comprehend these things, and though the words might not be there just yet, they should respond to you in the best way that they currently know-how.

Introduce your little one to new foods. Try to offer your baby a little bit of whatever you are eating during meal times. This will expand their palette while also giving them opportunities to practice feeding themselves. You should have a set of infant utensils for them to use when the foods are not finger foods. Be aware that you should not introduce too many new foods at once for food allergy purposes. Do this with one food at a time, and if your baby has an allergic reaction, you will be able to easily narrow down which food caused the reaction.

To improve your baby's nurturing abilities, play games that encourage your baby to show their nurturing side. You can do this by playing with baby dolls and showing your baby how to take care of a younger child. Though it seems early to explore these skills, they are very important for the future. Surprisingly, a 10-month-old is very capable of having these nurturing abilities and should enjoy displaying them. You can also do things like hand your baby a comb and ask them to brush your hair. Though this is a more simple display of nurturing, it still falls into the same category. Being a great caretaker is an important skill for every individual to have.

Eleventh Month

Milestones

Achieved Milestones:

- Can stand without support

- Walks with support
- Follows basic instructions
- Manipulates objects through nimble fingers
- Knows the names of their toys
- Repeats easy and small words
- Has a wider range of foods eaten
- Can spot a familiar face in a group of strangers
- Displays frustration by babbling

Emerging Milestones:

- Will take steps without support
- Can understand complex instructions and commands
- Will develop sharp finger control with a wide range of motion
- Will remember relations to relatives
- Can remember the names of household objects
- Will repeat complex words
- Gets vocal about frustration

Development

Cognitive: Your little one should now be able to identify people by hearing the mention of their name! This means that if your baby has a grandparent who is active in their life, hearing "grandpa" will surely cause a reaction. Your baby is going to understand who this person is and what you are saying about this person. Playing with toys also changes during this month. Your little one will find new uses for toys, advancing in the way they play. They should be particularly keen on building and destroying. This shows them how things are made and what it takes to put them back together. It is a great developmental tool for them to utilize, so encourage this kind of play if you notice it. Alternatively, your baby might also be ready for precise and gentle playtime. This can include objects that are more fragile or difficult to play with, such as puzzles.

Physical: Your baby should become great at utilizing their fingers. Instead of awkwardly bending them to try and grasp their utensils, you might notice a more purposeful grip than before. The same can be seen in the way that they pick up their toys and other objects that you place in front of them. By 11-months-old. it is average for your baby to have around four teeth. This typically includes upper and lower central incisors. With these new additions, your baby is able to eat harder food items. Teething is bound to become an issue, so make sure that you have some pain-relief toys handy. A frozen teething ring feels great on your baby's sore gums. You might notice some additional fussiness due to teething, and this is normal; it will subside soon.

Social/Emotional: If your baby is around a group of strangers, they will be able to spot familiar faces in the crowd. You might even get a verbal calling out of the person's name or title as your baby realizes that they know someone. This is the month where they begin to break out of their shy phase and social anxiety. Encourage them to spend time with familiar people often. This will allow them to continue on a great path to having excellent social skills. Tantrums are another social change that you might notice, so get ready! When your baby is this smart, yet cannot express their feelings with words, they might begin to throw more tantrums. You might also notice additional babbling when they are frustrated. This is all leading up to their big milestone of turning one year old.

Is Your Baby Healthy?

A flourishing vocabulary is the sign of a healthy 11-month-old. Your baby should be on the verge of being able to tell *you* a story, so the lack of uttering even a single real word is concerning. Speech therapy might be necessary in order to get your baby caught up on the milestones that they should have reached by now. Another possibility is that there is a cognitive issue preventing them from being able to process the words that they know and turn them into vocal sounds. Consult your doctor for an opinion on the next step you should take if your baby appears to be incapable of speech.

There is a difference between having a defiant child and a child who does not understand basic instructions. An 11-month-old should be able to hand you an item at your request. If it appears that your baby does not understand your request, or ignores you, this isn't necessarily a sign that you have an unruly child. Your baby might be experiencing a cognitive delay that is preventing them from fully grasping this concept. It is another reason why you should always be conversing with your baby and explaining what things are. Talk to your doctor if you feel that your baby is developmentally behind in this area.

If your baby has poor or delayed senses, this is going to serve as a red flag to you. When you call your baby's name from behind them, this should cause an immediate reaction. Your baby's head and body will turn in unison as soon as they realize that they are being called. If you notice any type of lag between your baby hearing their name and then their reaction to being called, this could be an indication of some issues impacting their ability to fully utilize their senses. The same conclusion can be made if your baby sees an object falling and has a slight delay when trying to reach out to grab it.

With all of the encouragement that your baby has been given, standing should be mastered by now. Though they might not be able to stand on their own, a supported standing position should be regular and normal. If you notice that your baby still cannot support their own body weight, even given plenty of support, this is an indication of a physical developmental delay. Perhaps their muscles are not strong enough to make them feel secure enough to attempt a supported standing position. Discuss this with your doctor if it appears concerning.

How To Help Development

Though it seems early and it might be hard for you, encourage independence. Let your little one feed themselves and attempt to put on their own socks and shoes. This is how they are going to learn! While you will always be there to help them throughout their childhood, and even into adulthood, you need to let them learn how to do things on their own. You might notice bouts of frustration, but let your baby see if they can work through them on their own. If you notice true distress, you can insert your help and show your baby how it's done.

When you tell your baby bedtime stories, experiment with making up your own stories. Use their name, and names of familiar people, to create characters for your story. Try to keep your baby engaged by using simple situations and environments that they will understand, but tell the story directly to them as if you are a narrator. This is a different way to encourage the use of imagination, and it will help your baby explore these new elements of creativity.

Continue utilizing positive reinforcement whenever you can. If your baby does something great, let them know! A reward does not always have to be given, but praise and attention can amount to the same thing in certain cases. Your baby is never going to know right from wrong if you do not make an effort to address the differences. In positive reinforcement, punishment is not encouraged unless absolutely necessary. When possible, correct your baby instead of immediately punishing them. By showing them an alternative solution to good behavior, they will learn a lot faster with a clear mindset. If they are punished or scolded frequently, they might not realize why they are being punished in the first place.

Keep allowing your little one to socialize with other children frequently. As your baby grows older, they are going to be reaching a stage where they crave interaction with other children their own age. While interacting with you is very beneficial, there is something about interacting with other children that will teach them different social lessons. They will have to learn how to share and how to communicate with a limited vocabulary. As they play with others, you will also get to take a look at their natural temperament. Some babies are calm while others are more high-strung, and this is normal. Learn how to work with your baby's unique temperament in various social situations.

Twelfth Month

Milestones

Achieved Milestones:

- Pulling up to stand
- Taking some steps alone
- Speaking simple, single words

- Imitates actions and gestures
- Mimics sounds
- Remembers last-known location of objects
- Uses index finger to point and poke

Emerging Milestones:

- Gets into a standing position without support
- Walks for longer distances alone
- Can speak using simple phrases
- Remembers gestures and performs them on their own
- Can understand complex instructions and requests
- Remembers sounds and their sources
- Can grasp and lift objects
- Develops good hand-eye-feet coordination

Development

Cognitive: If your baby knows that their toys are normally stored in a toy box, they will automatically go to the toy box when they are ready for playtime. The associations will be made with other items around the house. For example, your baby might know that the shampoo is located in the bathroom and will be able to bring it to you upon request. They will also have a much stronger noun and object association. This means you can show your baby a bowl of fruit, and they should be able to identify which fruit you are requesting them to hand to you. These concepts should be very strong and easily understood by a 12-month-old. Imitating actions and gestures will also be very popular this month, so be careful how you present yourself! Your little one will want to be just like you.

Physical: Letting go is one of the most exciting physical developments that your 12-month-old can display. This means that they are comfortable and balanced enough to stand, unsupported, and take a few steps on their own. While they might be unsteady, these steps mark a very big milestone that officially shows you that you no longer have an infant. This is the beginning of the toddler stage, and it only continues to get faster from here. Your little one is likely going to have three pairs of teeth by now, able to eat a wide variety of foods and have a strong bite. Due to their improved vision, your 12-month-old will also have great coordination improvements. They will be able to better judge distance, as well. The index finger will be one of your baby's main tools to poke, point, and prod.

Social/Emotional: If your baby sees something that they interpret as scary, they will cry or scream. Being able to sense fear and have a personal understanding of what is scary is a huge social milestone to accomplish. This shows that your baby knows how to listen to their gut instinct. This is the age when your baby will try testing your limits. While they clearly know the difference between right and wrong, they might push your buttons to see what kind of reaction you will display. Your patience will be put to the test, but know that you are in charge! Remain firm with your positive reinforcement parenting strategy, but also know that there are certain instances when you are going to need to reprimand your little one. You will have to use your best judgment as a parent.

Is Your Baby Healthy?

There are several red flags that you can look for when determining if your 12-month-old is healthy and on the correct developmental path. One of the biggest signs to look for is their ability to sit, crawl, and stand. If they are having difficulties with any of these tasks, then they are likely developmentally behind their peers. A 12-month-old baby should have plenty of strength to get into all of these positions unsupported. If you do help them into the position, they should be able to remain in it in a sturdy fashion. While they might not be walking regularly just yet, taking a few steps is a great sign that their body is allowing for this next stage of development. A 12-month-old who is developmentally behind won't even be able to let go during a supported standing position.

The amount of talking and babbling that your child is able to do will always be a determining factor regarding their overall health. If your baby still cannot manage to form words or associate words for certain objects, then a cognitive delay is highly likely. At this age, you should be able to communicate with your baby with them having an understanding of what is being said. In turn, they should also be able to communicate back to you. Whether they use words, sounds, or expressions, communication should definitely be happening on a regular basis.

A baby who doesn't or cannot use their fingers properly would be a concern at this age. Babies at this age should be able to feed themselves if you place finger foods in front of them. With the help of infant utensils, they should also be able to have enough hand-eye coordination to use those. If your baby still doesn't seem to take any initiative when you place food in front of them, it might be due to the fact that they do not know how to eat. Some babies might display a lot of joy and excitement when given food, yet if they do not begin eating it, there might be a delay preventing them from knowing what to do next.

Overall, you need to look for any signs of independence. Your baby is one now, and this is a huge milestone! Babies at this age love to babble about things that they care about, express their feelings, try new foods, show you their favorite toys, and spend time with their loved ones. If your little one is abnormally quiet or slow, lacking enthusiasm, then you should bring this up with your doctor. There should be many ways that your baby is becoming more independent by now.

How To Help Development

Play games that encourage your baby to learn new skills! The telephone game is a favorite. Using a toy phone, pick it up and pretend that you are on a call. Your baby is likely very used to you speaking on the phone normally. They might have even tried to grab a hold of your phone before. After your conversation, pass the toy phone to your baby and tell them that someone would like to talk to them. Encourage them to speak into the receiver and have a "conversation."

Teaching your baby about sounds and where they come from is important. Allow your little one to experiment with music. Whether you get them toy instruments or simply allow them to bang on pots and pans with wooden spoons, you will likely receive a response of delight when your baby realizes that they can control what noises come from which actions.

Building with blocks is also a great mind-booster. Your baby will have to determine which pieces fit together, and through their own creativity, they will be able to build a tower of their choosing. The colors and shapes are also great for their visual and mental stimulation. Make sure that you get the blocks that are pinch-free and big enough to not become a choking hazard. Always encourage your baby when they show you their finished masterpieces.

Chapter 8: 10 Mental Leaps in Your Baby's Life

A mental leap refers to a milestone that your baby experiences mentally. Many of these mental leaps can be seen throughout the first year of life, and it becomes a joy to experience them with your baby. This chapter is going to explore the various mental leaps you can expect to see and what you can do to encourage them all. While your baby is supposed to go through these mental leaps naturally, it always helps to have a primary caregiver who is one step ahead and encouraging them. If you know that a particular leap is coming up, you can guide your baby in the right direction. As much as you would like to lead them directly into each mental leap, know that you can only do so much. Your guidance is all it takes, and then your baby will be able to figure out the rest naturally.

Mental Leap 1

This week is known as the week of changing sensations, and the name certainly suits the feelings that your one-month-old is likely having. During this first month, you have watched your baby grow faster than you could have imagined. Your baby's vision is still in soft focus right now, and you might notice a few curious gazes as they look around while trying to make sense of the world. The new sensations that your baby experiences during this first mental leap have to do with their metabolism. Since your baby relied on the umbilical cord for nutrition, they must now learn how to digest their own food. This is a very big change, so don't be surprised if your baby spits up a lot of breastmilk in the first month; it is normal.

Another way that your baby is utilizing their senses more comes from the way that they are able to remain more alert when they are awake. If they sense movement or hear noises, you might notice that they are looking around and listening to what is going on. This is a big observational phase in your baby's life, but it is a great sign that their senses are all developing as they should be. Your baby already had all of these senses present inside of the womb, but they now have a reason to use them. In the outside world, there are many more stimuli present. If your baby ever looks bewildered, it is likely that they are simply experiencing a sense from a different perspective for the first time. This is a mental leap that you might not be able to notice right away, but your baby definitely feels it.

Mental Leap 2

At around eight weeks, your baby is going to begin experiencing the world in a new way. They will begin to recognize patterns, and the things that are happening around them will start to make more sense. For example, if you put them into a feeding position, they will automatically open their mouth because they know that this means food is coming. It takes these little steps to make the bigger picture of what exactly is happening in your baby's life. At this age, your little one might make the first discovery of their hands and feet. If this happens, you can expect a lot of kicking and punching, just as they used to do in the womb.

Lights and shadows will also be of interest. Since your baby's vision is improving daily, they will better be able to see these things. You might notice your baby staring at details for longer periods of time. If you take them on an outing, they might be fascinated by the way that the grocery store is set up, with so many objects on display to observe. Your baby might start to make a few sounds at this age. You will notice some grunting and basic vowel sounds coming from your little one's mouth. When they discover their voice, they will probably experiment with it a lot. Babies this age love to see how loud they can get and what noises they can create. You might even notice some fits of giggling.

Mental Leap 3

At 12 weeks, your baby's movements should be smoother and more intentional. There will be less jerking and jumping. They are realizing exactly what they can do with their body and what it takes to move it. Though this milestone won't be reached overnight, you should notice it gradually during this mental leap. This tends to be what parents notice most at this point in their baby's development. It can be very exciting to see that your baby is experiencing more physical progress because this shows that they are discovering something new about themselves every single day.

Because of this physical leap, they will also typically experience a new cognitive leap— the ability to acknowledge exactly where sounds are coming from. Whether these noises are happening around them or nearby, your baby will be less startled by these noises and more curious. This all becomes a part of the organization that your baby is starting to develop. Events and situations will seem more purposeful and less random as they continually realize where they stem from. With this sense of a constant flow being present, your baby is beginning to mentally process where they belong in the world. Show your baby new things, slowly. Changes that are too sudden can still appear very overwhelming to an infant at this age. Introduce basic objects, perhaps some toys. New faces are also going to be interesting to your baby. The more that you can show your baby, the faster it will help them reach their next mental leap.

Mental Leap 4

Your baby now has an enhanced sense of familiar events. For example, adults know that if a ball is bounced, it is going to come back up. Babies are easily distracted and fascinated by these seemingly simple events because they have yet to fully grasp this concept. During this mental leap, your baby is going to piece some of these things together. Events become more predictable, and this is a soothing feeling to an infant who is still trying to figure out exactly how the world works. This is why a baby might cry when you leave the room; they are only beginning to find out about object permanence and concepts that are similar.

With this newfound discovery, your baby is likely feeling more confident than ever. They might begin to experiment with certain outcomes. For example, if they throw a toy down, they will wonder if it is going to come back or remain out of reach until you hand it back to them. Your baby is going to figure this concept out very quickly, and you should definitely feel very proud of your little one for making this discovery. Continue teaching them these valuable lessons, and console them when they appear to be crying in confusion. Show them that the toy will be returned to them and that you will come back into the room. While not all things are so certain, you can reinforce the concepts that are more concrete, as mentioned above.

Mental Leap 5

This mental leap marks a time of bravery! Your baby will continue to attempt to experiment with cause and effect. Watching closely, you'll notice that your baby will feel more confident with themselves and the events going on around them. Exploring their hands and feet should be a regular occurrence. They might also begin biting various objects, even if they are not edible. Babies learn best by having first-hand experiences, so allow your little one to undergo these various tasks that involve trial and error. Certain things might make them irrationally upset, but they will become less fussy the more they are able to learn.

Your baby should be around the age where they begin crawling, or at least getting into a crawling position. Mobility is a huge mental leap that happens around this time! The coordination of their arms and legs becomes very apparent, even when they are having tummy time or lying down on their back in the crib. Another significant mental leap that your baby will have is the concept of distance. This creates a radical change in perception, one that adults often take for granted. If your baby sees that a toy is out of reach, they will do what they can to indicate that they want it. They might grunt, make other noises, or attempt to reach for it. Around six months old now, your baby should be developing a unique personality that truly makes them an individual.

Mental Leap 6

At nine months old, your baby should experience yet another mental leap. This one makes your baby quite observational. When they are on the floor, they might pick up small objects and hold them tightly for examination. This tends to happen a lot when you begin feeding your baby finger foods. You might notice that a little bit of playtime happens during meals because these small pieces are going to be very intriguing to your baby. Though, they will also simultaneously understand that this is food and they can eat it. You might have to watch them closely during meals to make sure they are getting nourishment as well as entertainment. Don't be surprised if they tend to get messier; it's a fun stage!

At the same time, your baby will begin to categorize frequently. While they might be squishing their bananas and crumpling their spinach leaves, they will still realize that both of these items are food items. The same can be said for their toys, familiar people in their lives, and places that are frequented. By becoming more keen on categorization, this will help further develop all of their other senses. They will be touching more, tasting more, and hearing more. The entire world will appear even more vibrant and exuberant than it once was, and when your baby is in a good mood, you will know it. There is nothing better than the sight of a delighted nine-month-old! Get ready for even more vocal noises, too. Your baby should love attempting to put words together.

Mental Leap 7

You are now the parent of a vivacious 11-month-old, very close to the milestone of turning one! Babies are great at making messes, and they can also be great at cleaning them up if you teach them early. You might notice that mess-making is at its peak during this mental leap. Anything that you give your baby, you can expect it to be returned disassembled or changed in some way. This is how your baby is learning exactly what objects are made of and how they work. Toys that enhance these skills are essential for this mental leap. Giving your baby a productive way to make messes is going to be best for them and best for the parents who will have to do some reorganization at the end of each play session.

At this age, your baby will realize that they have to take steps in order to reach their goals. This can apply both figuratively and literally. If they want to get to a certain toy that is in the toybox, they might have to take out some of the other toys before they are able to reach the one that they desire. This is a great skill to have, and it is definitely one that is going to serve its purpose all throughout the rest of your baby's life. If your baby is hungry, they will know that in order to get fed, they will need to indicate to you that they want food. This can be done by asking for the food by name or potentially even rub their tummy.

Mental Leap 8

Your baby's first birthday is a significant leap on its own. This year signifies that babyhood is about to come to an end. Soon, you will be a parent to a walking, talking toddler. In a lot of ways, your baby is still going to be your baby. They will be reliant on you for basic care, but their independence should be on full display at all times. Children this age can be very resilient, insisting that they do things on their own (or at least, attempt to before you step in to help). Give your baby this time to discover what they are capable of. If you never take that step back, they will never know their true potential.

In this mental leap, your baby will realize that certain tasks require some level of decision-making. Though your baby is not in charge of how they are being raised and cared for, they will still exercise their decision-making rights when possible. They might make very careful selections regarding what toys they choose to play with or what books they request you to read before bedtime. You will definitely notice that your little one now has their very own set of likes and dislikes. These preferences make them individuals. Be proud of how far you have come; you've raised a well-rounded little human! Nonetheless, your baby should still be very keen on getting your opinions and knowing what you think about their actions.

Mental Leap 9

This mental leap happens when your baby is around 16 months old, and there are so many changes to look forward to. Assuming you have allowed your baby to play outside a great deal, their love and appreciation of nature should be shining through. Your child will realize that the outdoor contains so many possibilities that are not present in indoor spaces. They will likely be delighted to spend time underneath trees or on a walk in the stroller to look at flowers. Allow as much outdoor exploration as you can. Keeping your baby curious about the world will encourage them to try new things.

Their vocabulary should be quite impressive by this point. You might hear them saying words or phrases that you didn't even realize they know! Continue having meaningful and educational conversations with your baby. They might begin asking "why?" a lot, and this is a great expression of curiosity. Show them that you have the patience to answer all of their questions and explain all of their wonders. Imitation will also be a big mental leap. Be careful what you say and do because your baby is watching you closely. You are their biggest role model. Another change you might notice is your baby's ability to be dramatic, which can be quite hilarious. They might also become more demanding. Encourage these parts of their personality within reason, but also teach them about the proper way to behave.

Mental Leap 10

18 months old now, your baby will have a sense of flexibility and accountability for the way they react to certain situations. They will realize that they can be honest and kind or demanding and aggressive. These are all facets of their personality, and by having this awareness, you have the ability

to shape your little one into a mindful individual. You might have to discipline your child a lot during this mental leap because they will be so eager to show you all of these different sides of themselves. You must teach them that there is a time and a place for everything, but they also need to be observant of the rules that you have set in place from the beginning.

Your baby will now be able to handle the concept of systems. When you go to the grocery store, they should understand that there are people who work there and other people who are shopping there like you. If they attend a playgroup, they will form an association that this is a system of people who are familiar and friendly. Of course, there is also a system that is made up of family members—your baby's support system. Family and loved ones should be very trusted individuals in your little one's life. They will often prefer these people and have the most trust for them. Strong family relationships are beneficial to having a well-rounded toddler.

Conclusion

The joys of parenthood are apparent in each section of this guide. While babies can be unpredictable, there are certain milestones that you can prepare yourself for as a parent. Even if you don't know exactly what you are doing, your baby doesn't need to know that. They are going to be relying on you for guidance and support for the rest of their lives, especially as they are growing from an infant to a toddler. Try your best to have a confident approach to parenting, and you are bound to have a successful relationship with your baby.

From the moment that you find out you are expecting, you are likely going to feel elated and proud. It is during this moment when it truly sinks in that you are going to be a parent. Even if the baby is still only a few cells that are mingling together, they will be developing at a rapid rate of speed. Before you know it, you will be giving birth to your baby and learning about all of their unique habits and traits. From the way that they smile to their favorite foods, your tiny human is going to see you as their biggest role model. Because imitation is the sincerest form of flattery, be careful of what you say and do! Your baby is always going to be paying attention to you for guidance and examples.

Celebrate all of their milestones, and show them at any chance you get that you are proud of them. Babies love to be acknowledged in this way, and they require a lot of attention in order to build up their own self-confidence. A baby who is praised and raised with a positive reinforcement style of parenting is going to be a happy child. As soon as your baby is able to understand the concept, creating a reward system will help with general obedience. It will give your baby incentive to be on their best behavior in order to make you proud.

If you do happen to encounter any developmental delays or issues along the way, never panic. Your doctor is there to help you through them. They should be a professional you can trust, and they will be able to come up with a structured solution that you can follow to make sure that your baby is living their best life possible. Even if the developmental issues are permanent or uncertain, put some trust in your doctor that they are doing everything possible in order to make your baby feel better. The best thing you can do is pay close attention to each milestone and ensure that your baby is on track with their abilities and skills.

All children are different. It would be foolish to assume that your baby is going to wake up one morning with the perfect ability to communicate in full sentences, so understand that their development might be happening at a different rate for a perfectly normal reason. Again, your doctor can provide you with some clarity if you are unsure about this. You cannot compare your baby to other children their age because of this varied rate of development. As long as your baby does not appear to be in any pain or struggling, then you can keep them engaged in an effort to build their skills and abilities.

The number one thing to remember is to have fun! Your baby isn't going to stay little forever, and they won't always be so dependent on their caregivers. Enjoy this bonding time that you get to have with one another. Play with your baby frequently, talk to your baby in meaningful ways, and show your baby as many new experiences as you can. These are the true joys of parenthood. Though there can be challenging times, know that you will be able to work through them. No rough phases last forever, even the fussiest babies do calm down as they grow up. Believe that you are doing what is best for your little one, and give them all of the love that you have. When you parent them this way, they will mirror your actions and give you plenty of love in return.

References Section 1

Garoo, R. (2019a, September 10). 2-Month-Old's Developmental Milestones: A Complete Guide. Retrieved from https://www.momjunction.com/articles/babys-second-month-development-guide_00101929/

Garoo, R. (2019b, September 10). 3-Month-Old Baby Developmental Milestones - A Complete Guide. Retrieved from https://www.momjunction.com/articles/babys-third-month-a-development-guide_00102426/

Garoo, R. (2019c, September 10). 4-Month-Old Baby Developmental Milestones - A Complete Guide. Retrieved from https://www.momjunction.com/articles/babys-4th-month-a-development-guide_00104153/

Garoo, R. (2019d, September 10). 5-Month-Old Baby's Developmental Milestones - A Complete Guide. Retrieved from https://www.momjunction.com/articles/babys-5th-month-a-development-guide_00103315/

Garoo, R. (2019e, September 10). 6-Month-Old's Developmental Milestones - A Complete Guide. Retrieved from https://www.momjunction.com/articles/babys-6th-month-a-development-guide_00103340/

Garoo, R. (2019f, September 10). 7-Month-Old's Developmental Milestones: A Complete Guide. Retrieved from https://www.momjunction.com/articles/babys-7th-month-a-development-guide_00103344/

Garoo, R. (2019g, September 10). 8-Month-Old's Developmental Milestones: A Complete Guide. Retrieved from https://www.momjunction.com/articles/babys-8th-month-a-development-guide_00102825/

Garoo, R. (2019h, September 10). 9-Month-Old's Developmental Milestones - A Complete Guide. Retrieved from https://www.momjunction.com/articles/babys-9th-month-a-development-guide_00103235/

Garoo, R. (2019i, September 10). 10-Month-Old Baby Developmental Milestones - A Complete Guide. Retrieved from https://www.momjunction.com/articles/babys-10th-month-a-development-guide_00103241/

Garoo, R. (2019j, September 10). 11-Month-Old Baby's Developmental Milestones - A Complete Guide.

Retrieved from https://www.momjunction.com/articles/babys-11th-month-a-development-guide_00103429/

Garoo, R. (2019k, September 10). 12-Month-Old's Developmental Milestones: A Complete Guide. Retrieved from https://www.momjunction.com/articles/babys-12th-month-a-development-guide_00101960/

Garoo, R. (2019l, September 10). A Guide to One-Month-Old Babies' Milestones. Retrieved from https://www.momjunction.com/articles/babys-first-month-development-guide_00101911/

Higuera, V. (2014, June 12). Prenatal Development. Retrieved from https://www.healthline.com/health/prenatal-development

Mental Leap 1 - Wonder Week 5. (2019). Retrieved from https://www.thewonderweeks.com/mental-leap-1/

Mental Leap 2 - Wonder Week 8. (2019). Retrieved from https://www.thewonderweeks.com/mental-leap-2/

Mental Leap 3 - Wonder Week 12. (2019). Retrieved from https://www.thewonderweeks.com/mental-leap-3/

Mental Leap 4 - The World of Events - Wonder Week 19. (2019). Retrieved from https://www.thewonderweeks.com/mental-leap-4/

Mental Leap 5 - Wonder Week 26. (2019). Retrieved from https://www.thewonderweeks.com/mental-leap-5/

Mental Leap 6 - Wonder Week 37. (2019). Retrieved from https://www.thewonderweeks.com/mental-leap-6/

Mental Leap 7 - Wonder Week 46. (2019). Retrieved from https://www.thewonderweeks.com/mental-leap-7/

Mental Leap 8 - Wonder Week 55. (2019). Retrieved from https://www.thewonderweeks.com/mental-leap-8/

Mental Leap 9 - Wonder Week 64. (2019). Retrieved from https://www.thewonderweeks.com/mental-leap-9/

Mental Leap 10 - Wonder Week 75. (2019). Retrieved from https://www.thewonderweeks.com/mental-leap-10/

The Bump. (2017, June 19). 1 Month Old Baby. Retrieved from https://www.thebump.com/baby-month-by-month/1-month-old-baby

WhattoExpect. (2019b, October 8). 4 Weeks Pregnant Symptoms - Week 4 Pregnancy Signs, Cramping, Baby Development, and More. Retrieved from https://www.whattoexpect.com/pregnancy/week-by-week/week-4.aspx

Section 2: Pre- and Postnatal care for Both Baby and Mom

A Practical and Step-by-Step Manual on How to Care of Your Baby and Yourself Starting from the Conception Up To the End of Your Baby´s First Year

Giving birth isn't exactly a vacation. Delivery of your baby is a time when you will likely be staying away from home for at least 24 hours to between 2 to 4 days (Caesarian delivery) and sometimes longer.

Do yourself a favor and have your bag packed before the of the 36th week of your pregnancy. In this way, you won't have to give it an extra thought until those contractions start coming full force. Being prepared reduces stress at the time of delivery. In labor just grab your prepared bag and leave for the Hospital.

You've probably read over a bunch of packing lists that seem beyond comprehensive. You don't need to bring everything and the kitchen sink.

Know what to pack in your Pregnancy Hospital Bag with **"My Hospital Bag Checklist"**

Receive a list of the most important items **to pack in your hospital bag for labor**, the practical things you will actually need during your stay in the Hospital.

Get your **"My Hospital Bag Checklist"** in PDF format by entering the link below or scanning the QR code below:

https://harleycarrparenting.com/pre-and-postnatal-care-for-both-baby-and-mom-book/

or

Print the document and start to pack as early as 36 weeks.

Let´s get started ...

Enjoy and Best Wishes to your pregnancy journey!

Harley Carr

Introduction

If you're looking at this book, it means you're either pregnant, planning to become pregnant, or you know someone who needs some help with their pregnancy. Either way, congratulations are in order. Having a baby is a remarkable, unforgettable, and euphoric experience like no other, though it's filled with many ups and downs. The first time a couple sits down to have the baby chat is the very moment when you feel closest to each other — as though you've left your present reality and reached an alternative realm, together. However, it doesn't matter how you feel in that moment; you need to approach pregnancy and parenthood in a logical manner.

It doesn't matter if your parenthood journey was planned or unexpected, or whether you're entering this world for the first time or you're having a second or third child — the best future you can give your entire family lies within good planning, knowledge, and understanding. As much as your entire body and soul are filled with a new, unique sense of happiness, you'll probably also feel some dread lurking beneath the surface. If you've had a child before, you know what that feeling is: it's the nagging fear of an unknown future, filled with worry, fear, and expectations. Any expectant parent becomes nervous, insecure, and starts doubting their own abilities. For a parent who has been through this before, you start questioning all your previous decisions and whether you did things right the first time. As a first time parent, your entire stomach has just become home to a kaleidoscope of butterflies.

You're filled with questions about taking care of your baby, yourself, or your wife, if you're the partner. These questions start rushing through your mind at the speed of light. How can you ensure your baby's safety and health in the womb, or the health of the expectant mother? How can you do your best to give yourself and your baby all that's needed? How will the delivery go, and will your baby be healthy after birth? What can you do to look after your newborn baby? How do you get through the first day? What about all the days thereafter? What do you do to successfully raise your baby for the first year and give them the best start in life?

Now, stop asking yourself a thousand questions before your mind explodes. First, acknowledge that you're taking the first step here. No matter what you do in life, you can't achieve anything without knowing how. When you started working, you didn't know exactly what to do. You had all these company policies and manuals to help you gather knowledge. You might even have attended a few training programs.

However, it doesn't matter if you have children already. A parent knows one thing for sure: every pregnancy and every baby will be different. I'm going to help first-time parents learn about all they need to prepare for. New parents will learn how to do things differently, prepare for a different journey, and even find out the reasons behind many things that need to be done.

I'm going to cover topics that will help any expectant parents understand and prepare for the prenatal and postnatal journey ahead. These topics include:

- Choosing the care provider that best suits you and your baby;
- What to expect during pregnancy check-ups;
- Nutrition, vitamins, and medical treatment during pregnancy;
- The truth behind common pregnancy myths;
- Scientific evidence pertaining to common vices, their impact, and how to overcome them;
- How to sleep when you're expecting;
- How to prepare for your baby's arrival;
- The critical first day and what to expect;
- Choosing your postnatal care provider;
- Common concerns about your baby's first-year check-ups;
- Vaccinations: why, are they necessary, and what can happen;
- Recuperating from labor or a C-section;
- Breastfeeding and bottle feeding: nutrition, common concerns, and solid food introduction;
- Bathing, diapers, clothing, and skincare;

- Need-to-know basics about your new baby's hygiene;
- Baby ailments and what to do;
- What is really an emergency;
- Creating a safe environment for your baby.

There will also be other topics. As a mother, I've tried to cover all the basic concerns you may have. My intention with this book is for you to gain confidence by learning useful information about the importance of prenatal and postnatal care up to the first year of your baby's life.

Let me start by introducing myself. I'm Harley Carr, a mother of three children aged three, five, and eight. Raising three kids is a challenging role, to say the least. I've been through a lot of challenges and difficulties during their first years of life, especially deciding whether I'll go back to work or stay at home to take care of my newborn. I chose to stay at home and became a full-time mom, and the rest is history. All of my kids were breastfed and, now that they're older, I can see the benefits of breastfeeding. I've been changing diapers for the last eight years, but I have no regrets. With the help of my partner, I've been able to survive the first year of each of my three children's lives.

In this book, I will share my insights and tips about how to manage challenges and difficulties during your baby's first year, and how to cope with the struggles of being a parent to embrace the life of parenthood. Even though I'm a mother of three, no child or pregnancy is identical. Therefore, I've meticulously searched for helpful information that pertains to this journey and I'll share any ideas that I've personally tried and tested. In addition, I've ensured that it's all the latest information, because times change and so do solutions to parenting problems.

This book will offer frank advice to help any expectant parents to become confident parents who can take care of their baby from conception until the age of 12 months. You'll learn to enter pregnancy with a healthy outlook, to cope with a newborn baby, track your baby's monthly progress, and a lot more. When you find out you're pregnant, it's difficult to distinguish unfounded concerns from reality; however, with this book, you'll learn to bridge this gap.

Enough procrastinating! Ask yourself the following questions:

- Are you prepared to learn everything, good and bad, about pregnancy?
- Are you curious about recovering from your C-section or vaginal birth?
- Do you want to learn how to take care of your newborn?
- Is introducing solid food to your baby important to you?
- Do you want to provide your baby with everything they deserve?

- Is your baby's health your number one priority?
- Do you have any doubts about your current knowledge?

Honestly, I could go on and on. The fact of the matter is, you probably only have a few months to prepare. The time will pass before you can blink, because time stands still for no person. The sooner you prepare, the faster you'll be free from prenatal and postnatal stress. What's that? You're only 12 weeks pregnant? I actually giggled there for a moment, because it doesn't matter — you need to start now. As much as I believe and encourage that you and your partner enjoy every moment, you also need to approach this with confidence, knowledge, and the tools needed to help you overcome any problems that may come your way.

Are you feeling amped now? Are you ready to go? Then say no more and continue reading this informative guide.

Part 1: Prenatal Care

Prenatal care — a foreign word, at first. If you're expecting, or even planning a pregnancy, prenatal care is essential. Half of all pregnancies are unplanned in America. I should tell you about my first pregnancy — it was an unplanned accident, but it was also a happy challenge.

I was working at the time and started feeling off. I would feel tired for no reason, and I suffered from nausea and headaches. My light bulb finally lit up when I started urinating a little more than usual and noticed my breasts had become tender. I'd been with my husband for a few years, but we hadn't discussed a baby yet.

I thought I'd test myself quietly and let him know if my suspicion was right. I was one of those women who bought three pee sticks from the drug store because I was a skeptic. I didn't have enough privacy at home, so I tested at work. All three sticks showed positive. I'm not sure why, but I refused to believe it. I went into a state of denial. I went home that night and never said a word to my darling husband.

The following day at work, I started throwing up viciously. My colleagues were concerned and called my doctor to make an appointment. My husband left work and drove me to the clinic, but I went into the doctor's office alone. I explained the three positive results I'd gotten the previous day and told my doctor that I thought they were wrong. My doctor convinced me to do a blood test and said my results would come back the next day.

I couldn't go back to work the next morning because I was suffering from such terrible nausea. However, I was feeling better later that day, and my husband took me out for lunch. As we were preparing to leave, my phone rang — it was my doctor. My husband made his way to the car before he could realize I was on the phone.

I assume my doctor didn't know how I would handle the news, because I was so clearly in denial about it. He asked me, "How would you feel about being pregnant and how would you feel if you weren't?" I was taken aback by his question but told him that I was fine either way. My doctor cleared his throat and said, "You're definitely pregnant."

The restaurant started spinning around me as the words came from my phone's speaker and I told my doctor thanks before hanging up. I made my way to the car and my husband could see that I was upset — my face was swollen and my eyes were red. When I got in the car, my husband took my hand and asked what was wrong. Somehow, I managed to tell him that I was pregnant. I remember there being an eerie silence for a few moments before he pulled me closer and kissed me gently. We hadn't planned the pregnancy, but it was welcomed with open arms.

It doesn't matter if your pregnancy is planned or not — prenatal care is essential. This is the health care needed during your pregnancy; the care that ensures both you and your unborn baby are as healthy as you can be. It's crucial that you start prenatal care as soon as you suspect pregnancy. If you aren't expecting and you're planning to become pregnant, you can start preparing your body for pregnancy before you conceive.

Preconception health can benefit you and ensure that you have fewer complications. You can prepare your body with the correct foods and vitamins, and you can quit bad habits that can harm your baby. Birth and spinal defects occur during the early stages of pregnancy, and can even happen before you know you're pregnant. Speak to your doctor about planning your pregnancy.

If you're pregnant or have any suspicion that you may be, call your doctor and start prenatal care as early as possible. Mothers who skip prenatal care are three times more likely to have a baby with low birth weight and five times more likely to have their baby die than a woman who gets prenatal care.

Your doctor can advise you on how to give your baby a healthy start in life by caring for your baby while they're in your womb. Doctors can also detect and treat health problems early on. Early treatment can cure many serious problems and prevent others.

Your doctor can also advise you on medication, treatment, habits, food, and nutrients that will ensure both you and your unborn baby are healthy. Personalized healthcare is the best option here. Something that helps other women might not work for you. Your doctor can advise you of physical exercise you may need, ways to control stress, and keep you from getting sick, which will affect you and your baby.

Your family or personal health history plays a role in your baby's health as well, and this can be monitored by your doctor. They can keep an eye for any problems due to your age, too. Beside all the concerns about health and safety, your doctor can calculate your due date or the sex of your baby — fun!

Your doctor will schedule frequent check-ups for you and you shouldn't miss any, because they're all important. In addition, they can answer all your questions.

If money is a concern, you can get assisted prenatal care by calling 800-311-2229, which will direct you to your state's family health-care center. Every state in the United States has a center to help you with everything you need to have a healthy baby (Schmitt, 2019).

I will cover prenatal care for yourself, and there will be a few tips for your partner. Let's get into the nitty gritty of it all and help you understand prenatal care.

Chapter 1: Finding the Right Maternity Care Provider and Check-Up Schedule

Choose Your Maternity Care Provider

Whether this is your first time or you're expecting your second or third child, you should gather as much information as you can. You'll want to match your own key principles for a healthy pregnancy to those of your care provider. Perhaps your family's tradition is to use a midwife or have a home birth, but only you know what you want. Your medical history can play a major role in your decision, too. Your family doctor can help you choose the care provider best suited to your individual needs.

However, there's a wide range of care providers for your pregnancy, and this range can differ from expectant mother to expectant mother. This chapter is written to help you learn more about each care provider and how they can help you.

I'll summarize research which identifies overall variances between different types of maternity care providers, such as midwives, family physicians, and obstetrician-gynaecologists (OG-GYNs). I'll focus on research published since 2005 that reports results with three or more studies to strengthen their findings.

These summaries include the best evidence and is a reliable method to learn more about each maternity care provider. In some cases, the results are old, but recent studies suggest that the results remain consistent. Let's take an in-depth look into these studies and their results so you can start deciding what you want in your care provider (Childbirth Connection, 2016).

Please bear with me through this short section, because it contains vital information and statistics.

Physician vs Midwife

Choosing between a physician and a midwife can be a grueling process. Let's take a look at recent revisions of collective studies that show the frequent advantages of midwife care (Childbirth Connection, n.d). These benefits include:

- A lower usage of fetal electronic monitoring;
- Less usage of epidural and spinal analgesia. These can be used during childbirth as a lower-risk anaesthesia;
- Little to no use of pain medication;
- Lower necessity to cut the vagina to widen it during childbirth (episiotomy);
- Increase in vaginal births after caesarean (VBAC);
- Little to no use of forceps and suction during childbirth;

- Lower cost as compared to physicians.

In similar revisions, certain concerns remain constant between midwives and physicians. The following outcome percentages show no variances between the two (Childbirth Connection, n.d):

- No tear or cut between your vagina and anus;
- Fetal distress during labor;
- Excessive bleeding of the mother during or after birth;
- Removal of placenta, as this is done by hand;
- Use of intravenous fluids (IV);
- Baby's condition after birth;
- Baby's convulsions;
- Baby's admission to a neonatal intensive care unit;
- Stillborn baby.

Certain studies suggest that you're less likely to experience the following with a midwife, and other studies say that you're just as likely to experience them with a midwife as you would with a physician (Childbirth Connection, 2016):

- Hospitalization during pregnancy;
- Higher birth weight;
- Speeding up the labor process;
- Breaking the membranes.

I hope this clarifies midwives vs physicians a little more for you. Personally, I know a few women who've had home births with a midwife and none of them have faced negative consequences. But before you make a decision, let's move onto the next comparison.

Obstetrician vs Family Physician

In some cases, you need to choose your care provider according to your medical needs or history. My friend became pregnant a few years back and was immediately referred to a specialist OB-GYN for care. She suffered from type 2 diabetes, polycystic ovary syndrome (PCOS), and a congenital heart defect. Her general practitioner knew her history, and neither he nor a midwife could help her. Her unborn baby wasn't the only one at risk — she was in danger, too. With the right care from her OB-GYN, she had a healthy baby boy six months later.

I want to share a recent review that summarizes various studies. It's old and may seem outdated, but more current individual studies are consistent with the findings.

According to research into maternity care, there's no single example of poor outcomes that can be credited to obstetrician care. Some variances have favored physicians as care providers. Physicians do well to care for women at low risk, and when they can't, they transfer women with special needs to appropriate specialized care. It's better to stick with your family physician, and obstetrician care should be reserved for high-risk expectant mothers. Maternal care by your physician is more cost effective and convenient than having a specialist OB-GYN (Klein, 1993).

To sum up your question: the care provider you choose should be according to your needs — whether you're a low-risk or a high-risk individual, only you and your doctor can make a valid decision here. You can look at your medical history, medical conditions, traditional preferences, and your newfound knowledge combined to make a choice.

Essential Facts to Experience a Satisfying Childbirth

Quality research by Dr. George Hodnett from Bryan, Texas, who specializes in obstetrics and gynecology, has shown that four influences decide a woman's level of satisfaction during childbirth. These four influences are:

1. Having a supportive care provider;
2. Having a good relationship with your care provider;
3. Being involved in decision-making about your care;
4. Your care provider goes above and beyond to create a better-than-expected experience.

Having the right care provider makes it all seem easier and will help you deal with common fears and prevent a bad birthing experience (Hodnett, 2002).

How to Weigh My Options Before Deciding?

Your care provider will be working closely with you and your family through one of the most special and intimate journeys of your life. It's a good idea to make an educated choice. You're welcome to consult with more than one care provider before you decide.

You can also ask a loved one to accompany you to an interview when you first meet a doctor. This enables you to discuss your views with your loved one after the initial meeting. Here's a few pointers on consulting with potential doctors:

- Make sure you're prepared for the interview so you don't waste the doctor's time;
- Create a list of questions to take along;
- Explain that you're keen to be involved in decision-making;
- Make sure you meet stand-ins for your care provider because even though their stand-in will be qualified, they will work differently;
- Tour the birth location. Your care provider will have a certain location where they deliver babies.

Once you have finished your interviews, you can ask yourself the following questions:

- Did they listen to me and respect my wishes?
- Do they share my outlook on pregnancy and birth?
- Do I feel comfortable with them?
- How do I feel about this care provider?

Always follow your gut instinct. It doesn't matter how far along you are; you need to be comfortable with your decision (Childbirth Connection, 2016).

Questions for the Care Provider

It's essential to ask your potential care provider some questions for comparison of your midwife or physician. Here's a list of suitable things to ask (Childbirth Connection, 2016):

How many family members are allowed to attend the birth of my baby? Are siblings allowed? What's the age restriction?

Do you have experience with trained labor support?

How do you feel about induced labor?

When do you recommend I go to hospital once I'm in labor?

How do you feel about intravenous fluids during labor, eating and drinking during labor, and birth positions?

What do you do if labor is progressing slowly?

How often do you have to cut to widen the vagina?

What drug-free pain-relieving options do you provide?

Can I opt for an epidural?

Are alternative pain medications optional, like nitrous oxide?

How many of your deliveries have led to caesareans?

What's your approach to newborn care and what's routine for a healthy baby?

How do you feel about early skin-to-skin contact after vaginal birth and caesarean?

How should I prepare for pain during labor and birth?

What costs are involved? Do you accept my health insurance provider?

I have a certain health issue, how does this affect my care from you?

Additional Questions for the Midwife

What's your level of education? Are you certified in this state? How long have you been practicing?

Where do you attend births? Are they individual or group births? Who attends group births?

How long are prenatal visits? What happens during these visits? If there are complications, would you still be involved in my care?

How do you monitor my baby's health during labor? Do you use a fetoscope or a Doppler to monitor my baby's heart?

Are you limited to your level of care at the chosen birthing location?

What complications would require a physician to step in?

What is your procedure for transfer? Which hospital will my baby be taken to?

Are you certified in neonatal resuscitation and what equipment do you have?

If I don't have insurance coverage, what's your fee and what does it include?

Any possible extra costs I should be aware of?

Do you accept alternative payment arrangements?

Additional Questions for the Physician

What's your educational background and are you board certified?

Where do you attend births and who is present during delivery?

How does your style, values, and hospital standards compare to others?

How frequently do you suggest I attend prenatal visits?

How do I become high-risk and how will that change my care?

How do you monitor my baby's well-being? Do you use electronic fetal monitoring or do you use a fetoscope/Doppler to monitor my baby's heart?

Does the hospital you use to deliver have limits on the care you may provide?

How should I prepare for pain management during labor?

Is the hospital baby friendly and do they offer support for breastfeeding moms?

Does my baby stay in the room with me or go to the nursery?

What if I Doubt My Choice of Care Provider?

It places unnecessary strain on yourself and your loved ones if you have the wrong care provider. Sometimes, you'll need to change because your current care provider is making you feel uncomfortable, preventing you from making decisions, or your appointments are inconvenient to you.

There's no rule that says you can't change your physician, midwife, or obstetrician, but I would suggest that you consider a few things before you do.

First, make sure you have enough time to search for a new care provider. You should also search for a new care provider quietly, because some may have strict policies against this sudden change later in your pregnancy. Last, but not least, make sure your insurance is prepared to make the change, otherwise you'll have to cover the expense and the costs can quickly add up.

Don't beat yourself up for choosing the wrong care provider the first time. You're allowed to change your mind and only you know what makes you and your partner happy. The two of you should make this decision together and be comfortable and confident in your choice.

Check-Up Schedule, Test and Scan/Ultrasound

How many prenatal appointments can I expect?

The number of appointments you have to attend will depend on how far along you are. Some women don't find out they're pregnant until they're three or four months in. This isn't ideal, but it is possible. I knew a woman who never knew she was pregnant until she was nearly in her third trimester. She was used to missing her period, since she had an irregular menstrual cycle to begin with. Fortunately, both she and the baby avoided any complications because she attended all appointments that her doctor set for her.

Anyway, the average woman attends 10 to 15 appointments throughout a full-term pregnancy. If your pregnancy is free of complications, you'll need a monthly appointment from week four to week 28, an appointment every second week between weeks 28 and 36, and finally, weekly visits from week 36 onwards.

Your appointments in the third trimester increase because of a higher risk for complications. You're more likely to suffer preeclampsia — a late-stage pregnancy complication that pushes your blood pressure up, causes severe swelling of your hands and feet, and can cause your organs to stop functioning normally.

You might also have more frequent appointments if you have a history of complications or are a high-risk individual (What to Expect Editors, 2019).

What kinds of tests will I have at my check-ups?

You can expect various prenatal tests, and should just remind yourself that these are necessary. Tests you can expect at each appointment are:

- Blood pressure check;
- Weight check;
- Urine test for sugar, iron, and infections. Sugar is checked for gestational diabetes and iron is checked for preeclampsia;
- Checking your hands, feet, and face for swelling;
- An ultrasound to check on your little one;
- Your doctor will ask you about your overall health.

Some additional tests may be done, depending on your personal risk or health conditions:

- Pelvic exam or pap smear;
- Doppler monitoring;
- Glucose screening;
- Breast exam;
- Biophysical profile;
- A personal stress test.

Depending on your age, ethnicity, or family history, you may be subject to some additional tests, as well. Your care provider could run noninvasive prenatal test (NIPT) or nuchal translucency screening tests to check for abnormalities that can cause Down syndrome between weeks 11 and 13.

Furthermore, a quad screen could be used to check for trisomy 18, tube defects, and Down syndrome. Genetic abnormalities can be found in the first and second trimesters by using chorionic villus sampling test (CVS). Hence, you should discuss all possible risk factors with your doctor if there's a family history or reason for concern (What to Expect Editors, 2019).

What will we talk about?

There's a simple answer to that question: you'll talk about you and your baby. Your doctor's surely not going to want to discuss his golf game last weekend — at least, I hope he doesn't dare. If he does, please find another doctor straight away. This appointment is all about you, your partner, your baby, and your combined well-being.

Your care provider should ask you how you're feeling, both emotionally and physically. They should also offer advice for yourself and your unborn baby. You can ask your care provider all sorts of questions about your pregnancy and they should answer all of them clearly for you. In addition, they should warn you about any changes you should expect as well as changes which could indicate a problem.

It's essential for you to show up with a list of questions and concerns, and another list of any changes you've experienced. I kept a pregnancy diary and would write down my concerns whenever I thought of one so I wouldn't forget it when I saw my doctor.

Now, let's take an in-depth look at your visits (Check-ups, Tests, and Scans Available During Your Pregnancy, 2018).

First visit

If you feel nervous about your first check-up, please relax. Don't feel afraid — enjoy every moment, and look at your journey with an excited heart. After all, you've just found out that you're expecting. You know what this means? It means that you and your partner have taken a blank canvas and started creating a magnificent painting together. The two of you decide each brush stroke and color as it happens. Let's discuss what will happen at your first appointment, besides the tests I've already covered in this chapter.

Your doctor will confirm that you're pregnant and, once it's confirmed, they'll calculate your due date and determine how far you are along. You won't see much other than a little bean on an ultrasound now, but that little bean still invigorates you.

This will be followed by a full blood test to check for anemia, rubella immunity, hepatitis B & C, syphilis, chlamydia, and human immunodeficiency virus (HIV). You'll also have a basic urine test and cervical screening to check for human papillomavirus (HPV), and your doctor will check for vitamin D deficiency if you're at risk.

You'll be required to provide your medical history, current medications, smoking or drinking habits, and decide if you want a flu vaccination. These are all standard and help you pinpoint any issues that may arise or any medical conditions that can harm your baby.

9-20 weeks

This was always a memorable period for me, because something special happens during this time — you hear your baby's heartbeat for the first time. There's nothing that makes you say, "Wow, I have a life inside of me," more than hearing your little one's heart beating. In addition to this, once you see those tiny little hands and feet form, your heart melts and you find yourself yearning to hold them.

You'll have the standard run of tests that you had in the previous section. In addition, you'll have ultrasounds which will show more than a bean this time. Your baby's face and head are forming, and your baby's heart is fully formed at 10 weeks. At 12 weeks, the fetus is fully formed, and at 15 weeks, your baby can start hearing sounds. Yes, you can start talking to them now, or even playing music through prenatal earphones that you use on your navel.

From 19 weeks, your doctor will start measuring your belly and checking on your health. Some parents are fortunate enough to see the gender of their baby between 19 and 20 weeks, if you choose to find out in advance.

22 weeks

Your following check-ups will consist of all the regular blood pressure, urine, weight, and measurements again; however, your baby will start a sleep/wake pattern at 22 weeks which won't necessarily match yours. Your baby could be exploring the land of mummy tummy when you try and sleep at night, and this is when you start feeling noticeable movements. You can discuss your sleep patterns with your doctor if they're of concern. Additionally, you'll undergo a blood glucose tolerance test between week 26 and 27, and your baby's facial features will become more prominent on an ultrasound.

28 weeks

Now, you'll be required to have a few tests at 28 weeks, starting with the usual check-up tests and a whooping cough vaccination. In addition, you'll have blood tests to check for anemia, blood platelet levels, and you may be checked for HIV, hepatitis B & C, and syphilis again. If your blood type is rhesus negative and this is your first pregnancy, you'll receive an anti-D immunoglobulin injection.

Last, but not least, your care provider will discuss your birth plan and go through the basics of taking your baby home at 28 weeks. It's important to have a birth plan established so your doctor knows what you want.

Your baby is perfectly formed now and will just continue to grow. Baby's heartbeat is strong and can be heard clearly through a stethoscope. Your partner may even be able to hear the heartbeat by placing their ear in the right place — if they're lucky enough not to be kicked.

34-36 weeks

Your doctor will do the run-of-the-mill tests again, as they do with every check-up, and you may need a second anti-D immunoglobulin shot. You'll also need a group B streptococcus vaginal swab, and your doctor will assess your baby's position to see which direction your baby's lying in and whether the head is positioning itself near your pelvis.

38-39 weeks

You're nearly there now. Your doctor will check the baby's heartbeat and movement, as well as your urine, blood pressure, and your overall health, as with every check-up. If your baby's head has moved into position in the pelvis, the doctor may say their head is engaged and they're ready for delivery. Your baby's head can engage anytime between now and birth.

40-41 weeks

Your baby's genitals may look swollen on an ultrasound, but this will go back down a little while after birth. The swelling is normal and is caused by your excess pregnancy hormones. However, these should be your final appointments. I don't know about you, but I felt like I had eaten a model scale of a zoo at this stage. I was so excited for it all to be over, and I couldn't wait to meet my baby.

Your care provider will run the standard tests again. And they'll check your baby's heartbeat and amount of amniotic fluid surrounding them if you haven't given birth yet.

Chapter 2: Healthy Options

Healthy Eating Habits When You're Eating for Two

Diet During Pregnancy

A pregnant woman should correct her diet during pregnancy not to lose weight, but to give her body and her baby all the nutrients they need. You'll have to eat from various food groups in order to do this.

Let's take a look at a simple breakdown of your diet.

Fruits and Vegetables: You need 85mg of vitamin C and 0.6 to 0.8mg folic acid daily. You should have two to four fruit servings and four or more vegetable servings each day. Oranges, grapefruit, broccoli, and tomatoes are good sources of vitamin C, while lima beans, legumes, and veal are healthy sources of folic acid. One serving of vegetables is one cup; one serving of fruit is half a cup.

Grains and Breads: You'll require six to 11 ounces of this daily. It's a good source of various vitamin Bs, fibre, healthy carbohydrates, and iron. Some grains also supply you with folic acid. One serving of bread is one slice, and a serving of grains is half a cup.

Protein: Your baby needs a lot of protein. Lean beef, fish, eggs, black beans, split peas, chicken, turkey, veal, lamb, and liver contain protein, vitamin Bs, and iron. It's recommended to consume 75 to 100 grams of protein or three servings of protein daily. One serving of meat protein is approximately three ounces and a serving of legumes is half a cup.

Dairy: Good sources of calcium include milk, yogurt, cream, cream soups, and puddings. You're recommended to consume 1,000mg of calcium daily because your baby needs plenty of calcium and will leach it from your bones if you don't have enough in your diet. You should have four servings of dairy products each day. A serving of yogurt and milk is one cup, a serving of cheese is one and a half ounces, and one egg counts as a serving (American Pregnancy Association, 2019).

Sample Daily Menu

Let's look at a sample menu I've put together for one day.

Breakfast: 1 small cup of oats, an apple, 1 slice whole wheat toast, 2 teaspoons apricot jam, and one glass of fat-free milk.

Snack: 1 cup of yogurt with half a cup of succulent strawberries.

Lunch: a hard-boiled egg with a slice of cheese on whole wheat toast, a small pack of lightly salted popcorn, an orange, and one glass of fat-free milk.

Snack: carrot sticks with a low fat cream cheese and chives dip.

Dinner: four ounces of turkey, one cup wild rice, half a cup of broccoli, half a cup of spinach, and one glass of low-fat milk.

Snack: a small bowl of freshly cut papaya or a low-fat yogurt.

Eating Seafood

While fish is a great source of protein and iron, some seafood should be avoided. The United States Food and Drug Administration (FDA) recommends that pregnant women, or women who plan to conceive, consume fish to acquire essential nutrients such as Omega 3, all ten amino acids from protein, and other vitamins and minerals. These are vitamin B6, B12, D, iron, niacin, selenium, thiamine, and potassium — nutrients which encourage your baby's development.

However, you should avoid seafood that's filled with antibiotics, mercury, and polychlorinated biphenyl (PCB). These include fish like shrimp, tilapia, and farmed salmon. I don't advise you to eat tuna, especially canned tuna. There is a new type of canned tuna which has been approved by the FDA for consumption by pregnant women called Safe Catch Elite. The best seafood you can eat while you're pregnant is wild salmon, rainbow trout, sardines, Atlantic mackerel, and mussels (American Pregnancy Association, 2019).

Personally, I was unable to eat seafood during pregnancy and had to use an omega-3 supplement combined with my multivitamin. Seafood has a strong odor that can make it difficult for a pregnant woman to stomach.

Pregnancy Nutrition

Now, I want to discuss nutrition. Keep in mind that your weight gain shows that your baby is growing and developing in a healthy manner. To target specific nutritional needs, I would suggest that you discuss it with your doctor. Let's take a look at a general nutritional outline.

Some foods can harm your baby during pregnancy. You should always follow these guidelines (American Pregnancy Association, 2019).

- All meat products should be thoroughly cooked through;
- All alcoholic beverages should be eliminated from your diet;
- Remove coffee and sodas that contain caffeine;
- Exercise regularly.

Before you move onto the next section, I want to target some common myths regarding your nutrition.

Myth: You should be eating for two.

Fact: Yes, this is true, but your nutritional needs will only increase by 300 calories from your second trimester onwards.

Myth: If you manage your weight gain during pregnancy, your labor will be easier.

Fact: Underweight mothers place their babies at risk for premature birth, and this can negatively impact your baby's lung and heart development.

Myth: You'll crave the foods you need.

Fact: Yes, you can crave foods you need but this shouldn't be your only nutritional guideline. Besides, I craved things that should definitely not be eaten. The worst was laundry detergent. Yes, I craved laundry detergent with all my pregnancies, but I thankfully never ate any. So, no, your cravings don't always determine what you should eat. However, my detergent craving did help my doctor pinpoint my low level of iron and zinc.

Myth: If you're healthy, you won't experience symptoms.

Fact: Nausea, constipation, and heartburn will still affect you. Following a nutritional diet, exercising, and drinking plenty of water will calm your symptoms, however. It's extremely rare for a woman to experience a pregnancy without symptoms.

Vitamins for You and Your Baby

Types of Prenatal Vitamins

Although the main source of vitamins and nutrients needed during pregnancy should come from your diet (as hard as that may be some days), a daily prenatal vitamin can help fill small gaps — just in case you unintentionally don't get enough key nutrients. Prenatal vitamins should be taken up to three months before conception, if your pregnancy is planned ahead.

Remember that a prenatal vitamin, or any other supplement, can only complement a healthy diet. Consult your doctor about which supplement is best for you.

Over-the-counter (OTC) vitamins are convenient and cheaper to purchase than prescription vitamins. However, they're often made up of low-quality, synthetic mineral salts and vitamins. Let's look at vitamin E as an example. Vitamin E deficiency places your baby at risk of premature birth. OTC products often use synthetic vitamin E instead of its natural counterpart. When you read the label, natural vitamin E will read as d-alpha-tocopherol and the synthetic one will read as dl-alpha-tocopherol. I would advise that you check labels and research before purchasing any of them.

Vegan and organic vitamins usually come from organic or plant-based sources. These vitamins often come in tablet form, because the gelatin used to make capsules comes from animals. Tablets offer limited protection for the ingredients because they have no coating. They're also difficult to swallow, can cause an upset stomach, and do not absorb easily into the gastrointestinal tract. If you're vegan, you'll go for the plant-based vitamin D2, but vitamin D3 — which is derived from animals — absorbs better.

Furthermore, prescription vitamins can be prescribed by your doctor. People automatically believe that prescription medication is better than others, but the ingredients are what matter most. You should look for a multivitamin that contains enough folate, iodine, vitamin D, vitamin B, and calcium for your growing baby (American Pregnancy Association, 2019).

Why Do I Need Vitamin D?

Let's take a closer look at vitamin D. Both vitamin D2 and D3 are essential for your baby's progress, and the recommended dosage for pregnant women is 4,000 international units (IU) per day. Most supplements only have 400 IU, and an additional supplement needs to be taken.

Vitamin D supports your immune system, bone health, healthy cell division, and aids in the absorption of calcium and phosphorus. It helps your baby's bones develop, as well. However, a lack of vitamin D can lead to future problems for yourself, such as cancer, insulin resistance, heart disease, and preeclampsia.

There's a very short list of foods that contain vitamin D, like egg yolk, cod liver oil, and salmon, which is why it's essential to use a daily supplement. Another natural way to absorb vitamin D is by exposing yourself to the sun. Remember to do this in brief sessions, because sunburn will make you feel terrible (American Pregnancy Association, 2019).

Natural Sources of Vitamin B6 and Why I Need Them

Vitamin B6 is another essential vitamin to every part of your body, from brain function to producing blood cells. You can ensure an easier, healthier pregnancy for yourself and your baby by including vitamin B6 in your diet.

Vitamin B6 aids in the development of your baby's brain and nervous system, and improves your baby's birth weight. Furthermore, it helps reduce morning sickness (yay!), maintains healthy glucose levels, and helps your brain release serotonin to keep your stress levels down.

According to the University of Michigan, a pregnant woman should be taking between 10 and 25mg three times daily. However, you should avoid consuming more than 100mg per day, because this can damage your nervous system and cause numbness. With regards to your baby, the National Library of

Medicine reports excessive use of vitamin B6 can cause birth defects.

Vitamin B6 is found in many dietary sources and multivitamins, so you should keep track of how much you're consuming by using a diary. Some natural sources of vitamin B6 are bananas, papayas, lean beef or pork, wild salmon, walnuts, peanuts, hazelnuts, sunflower seeds, whole wheat grains, some cereals, avocados, dried apricots, chicken, turkey, and spinach.

Most of your vitamin B6 will come from your diet, so you shouldn't need a supplement. You can speak to your doctor or nutritionist and share your diary with them. There will be signs if you need more vitamin B6 in your diet, like swollen hands and feet, swollen abdomen, fatigue, anemia, depression, and mood swings (American Pregnancy Association, 2019).

Common Illnesses During Pregnancy Like Headaches, Fever, etc.

How to Avoid Getting Sick

There's nothing worse than getting sick while you're expecting. However, prevention is better than cure, right? I want to share some tips on preventing illness from knocking down your door (American Pregnancy Association, 2019).

- Wash your hands regularly, because everything you touch can have harmful germs waiting to make you sick;
- Exercise to keep your body healthy;
- Follow a nutritious diet to build a stronger immune system;
- Use vitamins, minerals, and natural probiotics found in yogurt to aid in your overall health;
- Ensure you get enough rest.

Initial Steps You Can Take Including Natural Methods

It's a fact that even if you do everything in your power to avoid getting sick, unfortunately, the bug can still bite you and you need to deal with it as fast as you can. I remember my first time being sick during pregnancy. I wasn't sure if I was sick at first, because I couldn't tell the difference between my morning sickness and my flu. But I figured it out when my nose started spraying like a fire hydrant that's been hit by a moving bus.

Now, let's help you understand the first steps you need to take. Sadly, there's no magic trick to remove your flu — you'll need to try the usual natural methods to kick its ass.

First, you need to rest because your immune system works better when you're resting and this can help shorten your suffering. Besides rest, you need to drink plenty of fluids to help flush the bug out, and don't forget to make sure you take your vitamins, because they help your body combat this monstrosity.

Furthermore, you can reduce congestion by placing a humidifier in your room, elevating your pillow, or using nasal strips. You can also suck on ice chips or lozenges and gargle with salt water to relieve a sore throat (American Pregnancy Association, 2019).

Safe Medications

There are some medications which are relatively safe to use during pregnancy, including OTC medications which land in categories A, B, and C. I strongly advise that you always check with your doctor before you take any medication.

However, you can use Tylenol or Ibuprofen for pain and fever, you may use a low dose of Benadryl combined with Flonase spray for allergies, and you may use Vicks sugar-free cough syrup to alleviate your cough. Even though these medications are considered safe, you should wait until you reach your second trimester before using them, and always try natural methods first (Marcin & Westphalen, 2018).

When to See a Doctor

You're pregnant and it's important to listen to your body. If you've shown no improvement for days, you start feeling worse, or your symptoms are making you lose sleep or miss meals, you should see your doctor.

You should also see your doctor immediately if your fever reaches 102 degrees or more, because fever is a warning of infection in your body. If you have chest pain, wheezing, or you're coughing up colored phlegm, you may have a bronchial infection and need an antibiotic. Only your doctor can prescribe an antibiotic that's safe for you during pregnancy.

Chapter 3: Frequently Asked Questions About Safety During Pregnancy

Deli Meat

What are deli meats?

Deli meats are processed meats which have possibly been exposed to the environment and certain harmful bacteria.

Is it safe to eat deli meat?

You're allowed certain deli meats as long as the meat has been stored properly and cooked thoroughly. If you eat any deli meat, you should reheat it at 165 degrees, store it in airtight containers in your fridge for no more than three days, wash your hands after touching it, and make sure it doesn't come into contact with other foods in your fridge.

Which deli meats should I avoid during pregnancy?

Deli meats are mostly raw, however, those that have been cured and contain loads of sodium, salt, and nitrates should be avoided. Some unsafe deli items are pancetta, cured Spanish chorizo, prosciutto, ham off the bone, pepperoni, mortadella, beef pastrami, salami, and sausages. Remember to follow the guidelines on preparing deli meat before giving in to your craving for a piece of pancetta. My kryptonite was salami, because I've always loved salami.

Which deli meats are safe for me?

According to the FDA, it's safe to consume freshly cooked deli meats without preservatives or additives, lean meats that are low in fat, organic deli meats that are free from antibiotics and growth hormones, and low-salt or nitrate-free deli meats. Turkey breast, fresh deli-sliced ham, grilled pork slices, and chicken breast are safer options.

How does deli meat harm me?

Deli meat carries a bacteria called listeria and can make you develop listeriosis. Listeriosis makes you extremely ill and can even land you in the hospital with septicaemia or meningitis. Symptoms alone can be devastating to a pregnant woman, as these include fever, diarrhea, nausea, vomiting, and headaches. Why would you want to be more nauseous? Furthermore, deli meat can raise your blood pressure and cholesterol, which encourage heart problems, and the added nitrates can cause cancer (Pillai, 2019).

Pregnancy and Bed Rest

Many women dread bed rest, but let's take a look at the reasons behind it.

Why would I need bed rest?

Common reasons are preeclampsia, vaginal bleeding caused by a low-lying or prematurely separated placenta, premature labor, a weak or thinning cervix, carrying two or more babies, a history of pregnancy complications, a medical problem that was discovered by a test, or bad development of the fetus.

Am I allowed any activity during bed rest?

This depends on your prescribed bed rest, which you should clarify with your doctor. If your doctor told you to rest *most of the time*, you're allowed non-strenuous activities like bathroom breaks, a quick daily shower, and sitting in a chair or working at your desk for no more than an hour at a time. If your work is stressful, ensure that someone is close by for assistance. You're also allowed brief walks around your home for no longer than 30 minutes each time. However, you should avoid heavy lifting, sexual intercourse or activity, inserting anything into your vagina, or any activity that lasts more than an hour.

What is the best position to lay in?

Your care provider will advise you on different positions that may be comfortable, but most women prefer lying on either side. Personally, I found it most comfortable to lay on my left side or with my head slightly elevated to watch some television.

How will I get to my appointments?

Your doctor will advise you to ask your partner or a family member to drive you to their office. I had a friend who was put on bed rest and was lucky enough to have some consultations at home. It all comes back to choosing the right care provider.

How will I care for my family while I'm on bed rest?

I'm sure your partner understands how important bed rest is, and they should be reading this book with you. You'll likely need to get some outside help with the cooking and strenuous activities if your partner works full time. However, you can still spend time with your family by watching a movie together, reading a story, or playing a game.

Will I become constipated?

Following a healthy diet and drinking plenty of fluids should help. If this doesn't work, speak to your doctor about a safe laxative.

Can bed rest really make me carry to full term?

Unfortunately, there's no scientific evidence to confirm this, but many doctors believe it's the best chance you can give your baby.

Are there any side effects?

You may feel dizzy, isolated, and bored. Your body could ache in some places, too. Speak to your doctor about getting a massage therapist to help you relax your muscles.

What can I do to conquer boredom?

Besides planning your new baby's entrance into the world, you can use your computer or phone, read a book, or start scrapbooking. There are no limits on entertainment (Cleveland Clinic, 2018).

Make-Up Safety: Read the Label

Should I continue wearing make-up?

Yes, but you should be cautious, because your hormones and increased blood flow will make your skin sensitive. You could suffer from skin irritation from products you've used all your life, or notice a heat rash from the sun. Some ingredients can affect the development of fetal and postnatal growth in boys, specifically.

What should I look out for?

Start reading labels and look out for words like phthalates, triclosan, retinoids, bisphenol A (BPA), parabens, and diethyl phthalate (DEP). You should also avoid all fragranced products.

How can I prevent damage from the sun?

Choose a sunscreen with a high sun protection factor (SPF) to protect your skin. Organic and natural sunscreens have fewer harmful ingredients and make good candidates, too.

What make-up products are safe?

Personally, I didn't care much about make-up when I was pregnant, but I know many women keep wearing their favorite products. Here's a list I found online of top-rated cosmetics during pregnancy (Louie, 2018):

- Juice Beauty Stem Cellular CC Cream foundation, an organic foundation that doesn't contain parabens or phthalates;
- RMS Un-Cover Up concealer, which is a perfectly natural product;
- Afterglow Cosmetics Infused Mineral blush is 100% organic;
- Alima Pure Highlighter in Rose Gold is a great vegan product;
- ILIA Limitless Lash mascara uses natural ingredients like beeswax and shea;
- ILIA Tinted Lip conditioner is also organic;
- Superg sunscreen is a natural and mineral sunscreen.

The Effects of Tobacco, Alcohol, and Caffeine

How does smoking harm my baby?

Tobacco contains arsenic, tar products, nicotine, and carbon monoxide, which reach your baby through your placenta. Smoking and secondhand smoke can have disastrous effects, such as premature birth, low birth weight, stillbirth, the chance of sudden infant death syndrome (SIDS) is doubled, and your child could suffer from chronic health issues their entire life. Puffing isn't excluded because the smoke still enters the mucus membranes in your mouth.

How do alcoholic beverages affect my baby?

Drinking during pregnancy can lead to fetal alcohol syndrome (FAS), which causes problems like heart defects, cleft palate, intellectual disability, or physical deformities. Drinking in your first trimester can impact your baby's heart, lungs, and brain development. If you're planning a pregnancy, you should quit drinking before you conceive.

How does caffeine affect my pregnancy?

Although there's no evidence of birth defects in humans, caffeine does cause birth defects in animals. It can be found in chocolate, cola, tea, coffee, and certain pain medications. It's recommended to limit your intake to two or three servings per day to avoid potential complications (UPMC Magee-Womens Hospital, 2016).

Pregnancy and Vices

How can I boost my energy without caffeine?

You can replace your usual caffeine by eating small snacks in between your meals and exercising regularly. Snacks help to regulate your blood sugar and you can incorporate a brief exercise regimen every morning to get your juices flowing.

How do I reduce stress without smoking?

You can speak to your care provider about signing up for prenatal yoga. I joined a prenatal yoga class and it helped me calm down and deal with daily issues. It's a great idea to start a new, relaxing hobby. You could also take a baking class, take up writing, or start making jewelry.

How do I go out with someone without having a drink?

Personally, I didn't enjoy noisy, alcohol-fueled environments while I was pregnant; it increased my stress exponentially. There was one time my husband and I met with one of his high school friends and I didn't want to be the party pooper. They ordered whiskey on the rocks and I sipped a mocktail — a fancy drink that's made to look and taste alcoholic, but isn't. Ordering my mocktail made me feel like I was part of the get-together.

However, my husband was supportive and we would change our date-nights to accommodate me and our unborn baby. Instead of going to a fancy dinner with wine, we would take a walk in the park as the sun sets. I found it easy to remove this vice when I replaced it with equally satisfying adventures (Carepoint Health, 2015).

Good Pregnancy Workouts for Fitness

What exercises can I consider?

You should always check with your doctor before starting your exercise routine, but some good choices are:

Yoga and stretching exercises: This helps you release tension in your muscles and your mind. Please make sure you join a pregnancy class.

Kegels: These exercises help you to strengthen your vagina muscles in preparation for labor. You just clench your vaginal and anal muscles, hold them for a few seconds, and release. This is one exercise I still do today. You'll see more benefits of Kegels in this book.

Walking: Taking a walk in the park is easy and it can lift your mood by providing an unexpected adventure.

Indoor cycling: This is an enjoyable cardio workout that doesn't place too much strain on your body.

Swimming: This is gentle on the joints and relieves swollen ankles and aching muscles.

Water aerobics: Join a low-impact session aerobics class. Aerobics is good for your heart and lungs, and releases endorphins which make you feel good.

What should I consider in my pursuit of fitness?

Don't exercise in high altitudes where oxygen concentration is low, avoid excessive temperatures, slow your pace to accommodate your heart's pressure from your growing belly, move kindly so you don't injure yourself, and avoid strenuous sport. Furthermore, know your limits, stay hydrated, and ensure comfort at all times.

How does my fitness benefit my baby?

Your baby can have a healthier birth weight and a lower heart rate, and exercise eases labor (Johnson, 2018).

Traveling While Pregnant

This was difficult for me personally because I love traveling, but I had complications and wasn't allowed to do so. My husband was fortunate to see all these exotic and strange places, and my inability to travel seriously depressed me. I overcame my depression by reminding myself that once my baby came, I would take them to see the world and all the amazing sights it has to offer.

Is travel safe during pregnancy?

For healthy women and their unborn baby, travel is safe up to 36 weeks. However, most complications happen in the first and last trimesters, which means the safest time to travel is between weeks 14 and 28. Your doctor can tell you whether it's safe for you personally.

When is travel dangerous?

Traveling can be risky if you're carrying twins or triplets, have preeclampsia, a prelabor rupture of the membranes, or other health complications, or you have a history of complications during pregnancy.

Where should I avoid traveling?

You should avoid any area where there is a risk of contracting malaria or zika. Both diseases are carried by mosquitoes and are harmful to pregnant women. Zika can cause birth defects and malaria can affect your health.

How can I prepare for my trip?

You can do the following:

- Schedule a check-up before you leave;
- Know how far along you are;
- Pack all your OTC and prescribed medications, ointments, and vitamins to take along;
- Make sure your vaccines are up to date;
- Choose the fastest method of travel and buy transferable tickets.

How should I travel?

The best way to travel as a pregnant woman depends on where you're going.

If traveling by car, make your driving stints short, wear your seat belt, and stop regularly for walkabouts.

If you decide to fly, you should choose an aisle seat, wear your seatbelt, avoid food and drinks that make you gassy, and take a walkabout every two hours. Walkabouts help to prevent deep vein thrombosis (DVT).

If you book a cruise, make sure the ship stops off at locations with modern medical centers and has a doctor on board, and ask your own doctor for medication to help you overcome seasickness. Seasickness can amplify your pregnancy symptoms and make your trip unbearable.

What is DVT?

DVT can cause a blood clot to form in your veins, which can then shoot to your lungs. Sitting for long periods of time and being pregnant both increase your risk for DVT. You can beat DVT by taking regular walkabouts, staying hydrated, and wearing loose-fitting clothing.

When should I seek medical assistance while traveling?

If you notice any of the following worrisome signs, you should seek emergency medical care (American College of Obstetricians and Gynecologists, 2019):

- Violent vomiting or diarrhea;
- Unexplainable headache;
- A change in vision;
- Excessive swelling in your limbs or face;
- Vaginal bleeding;
- An unexpected water break;
- Severe pelvic or abdominal pain.

I know the thought of travel can be frightening, but many women travel safely while pregnant and enjoy their holidays just as much. Don't allow pregnancy to hold you back. I've always said, "Pregnancy is not a disease, it's merely a temporary condition."

Chapter 4: Pregnancy Fears and Why You Shouldn't Worry

Nausea and Morning Sickness

Morning sickness is a sensitive topic — I know it was for me. If I so much as heard the word nausea or watched a movie where someone threw up, I had to run as fast as my legs could carry me. I'm going to ask that you bear with me through this topic, if you're anything like me. If you're the dad-to-be, you might want to read this section in a supportive way and make sure your wife has a bucket handy while you do.

I want to tell you about the benefits of morning sickness. I know you might be shaking your head in disagreement right now, but there are scientific reasons behind it and benefits thereof.

Cornwell University biologists, Samuel Flaxman and Paul Sherman, confirm that morning sickness happens for a biological purpose. Flaxman and Sherman examined thousands of pregnancies before coming to a conclusion, gathering evidence to prove that morning sickness protects both yourself and your unborn baby.

Professor Sherman, co-author of *Morning Sickness: A Mechanism for Protecting Mother and Embryo*, says that morning sickness occurs at any time of the day. He refuses to call it a sickness and says it should be renamed to wellness insurance. I agree with this statement, because being pregnant is a natural part of life.

Flaxman claims studies suggest that morning sickness is your body's way of protecting itself in your vulnerable state. It causes repulsion of your food to protect you and your developing baby from toxic microorganisms and fetal organ-deforming chemicals. Your body will reject any foods containing these harmful chemicals by making you vomit or become nauseous when smelling certain foods to prevent consumption.

Morning sickness peaks between six and eighteen weeks, when fetal organ development is most susceptible to these harmful chemicals. Two thirds of pregnant women suffer from morning sickness, and the most important thing to remember is that your body knows what's best — listen to it (Flaxman & Sherman, 2000).

Let's take a look at some solutions I found online that align with my own tried-and-true methods (Reutter, 2018).

<u>Stay away from strong smells</u>. If you're cooking, open the windows and let some fresh air into the kitchen to remove pungent odors.

Take your vitamins on a full stomach. An empty stomach combined with iron is a recipe for nausea, and you should always eat before taking your vitamins.

Exercise helps for nausea, too. Yes, this may come as a surprise, but getting on your feet and exercising your nausea away can make you feel a lot better.

Calm your nausea with ginger. You can eat ginger preserve or drink some ginger tea. This helped me on many occasions.

Listen to your body. Avoid greasy, sweet, and spicy foods. You should be eating high carbohydrates, high protein, and bland foods to reduce nausea. Wait until you've finished eating before you drink any fluids, and leave that new Portuguese restaurant for a time when spices don't upset your stomach.

Prepare smaller meals and snacks. Don't eat three large meals daily, aim to eat six small meals, instead. You can also keep tiny snacks at your bedside in case you wake up feeling sick.

Buy yourself scented oils. I used to love scented oil over a burning candle. The smell of orange worked for me, but you can also try lavender, lemon, mint, or whatever scent floats your boat.

If natural methods fail, you can turn to OTC medications. Vitamin B6 reduces nausea, but please beware of an overdose. Furthermore, you can take three 25mg Benadryl a day; it's an antihistamine which is safe and helps for nausea. Please don't take this while driving, however, because it will make you drowsy.

There are worrisome signs that you may experience, and you should visit your doctor if you do.

- Dehydration, dizziness, infrequent urination, and dark or smelly urine;
- Bloody or excessive vomit;
- Abdominal or pelvic pains;
- Sudden weight loss;
- Inability to keep your food down for 12 hours or more.

I know we're all different, but I would like to share my remedy for morning sickness. I'm stubborn as an ox and never used to listen to my body. I refused to give in to my nausea with my first pregnancy and suffered the consequences. Fortunately, with my second, I met a wonderful friend who gave me sound advice — she told me to visit a hypnotherapist. It took a few rigorous sessions, but hypnosis managed to alter my way of thinking and I started listening to my body. My second and third pregnancies went far smoother than the first.

Other Common Pregnancy Problems and Their Solutions

Morning sickness isn't the only pregnancy issue, let's look at a few more. Please keep in mind that every pregnancy and every pregnant woman will experience different symptoms and not every solution will work for you. I will cover as much as I can. If any of the advice in this section isn't working for you, please visit your doctor pronto.

Constipation: Hormonal changes and your baby's growth restricts your digestion and causes constipation in pregnant women. Keep a high fibre diet with lots of whole grains, fruits, and vegetables, and don't forget to drink lots of water.

Bleeding gums: This happens due to swollen mucus membranes. To address this, decrease your sugar intake and increase calcium. Make sure you brush your teeth regularly and ask your dentist for an alcohol-free mouthwash. Don't forget to tell your dentist that you're pregnant if you pay them a visit.

Insomnia: Your body is going through changes and it's no wonder you can't sleep — eight out of ten pregnant women deal with insomnia. You can exercise, read a book, take a warm bath, or have your partner give you a relaxing massage before bed. My partner's massage treatments often did the trick for me. It's essential that you have a calm routine before bed.

Weird dreams: Personally, I found speaking to my husband about my dreams every morning put an end to this.

Indigestion and heartburn: Indigestion is caused by your growing baby placing pressure on your intestines. You should lie on your left side to prevent additional pressure on your esophagus and avoid eating large amounts of food at once. Some low-fat milk will also help soothe your heartburn.

Problems breathing: This is common, because hormonal changes and progesterone directly impact your lungs. Your breathing will become more labored as your baby grows and presses against your diaphragm. The best solution to this is to elevate your body when you're lying down, or to sit with a straight back so your lungs have more space to expand. Remember to take it easy — you have a whole other precious human inside of you.

Fatigue: In your first trimester, your hormones can take their toll on your energy levels. In your second trimester, your body has changed and you're carrying extra weight you aren't used to. Keep your nutrition and exercise in mind to start. Secondly, you're allowed to rest when you need to. Make sure your day isn't overscheduled and that you can either go to bed early at night or take an afternoon nap. I loved sneaking a nap before my older kids came home. Every time I had a new baby,

I would sign my other children into a morning daycare program to allow myself some time to rest when my baby rested.

Edema or swelling: This is one issue that most women will suffer from. Edema is caused by excess fluid trapped in your tissue. Your growing uterus puts pressure on the vena cava and reduces blood flow, causing your legs to swell. You can reduce swelling by drinking lots of water and elevating your feet. I can still remember my husband coming through the door to find me sitting on a recliner in a cartoon-like fashion. Both my head and my feet were elevated, and I looked like a sandwich with a boiled egg between the buns. He would never question my position, though, because he knew how hard pregnancy was for me.

Leaking or itchy nipples: The expansion of your breasts causes the itch and prolactin causes leaking. Prolactin is a hormone that prepares your breasts for milk production. This is an annoying problem because it happens at the most inconvenient times. I used shea butter on my breasts to reduce the itching, and if you're concerned about the leaking, buy some breast pads to wear in your bra.

Backaches: These can be caused by the added weight around your midsection and breasts or by pressure on a specific nerve. I'll mention posture again — keep a good posture and don't sit for too long. Go on a walkabout in between long seatings. Don't lie down, as this can make it worse, and if you bend to pick something up, use your knees and not your back.

Hemorrhoids: These can be a horrible experience — you can have a small or large hemorrhoid on your rectum that may bleed and can be quite painful. Though it's common, you should avoid sitting on hard surfaces for long, do Kegel exercises regularly, and always answer the call of nature — never hold a bowel movement. If you already have hemorrhoids, you can try a cotton pad soaked in witch hazel solution or combine equal parts of glycerine and epsom salts to create a paste. Leave this homemade paste on the area for 20 minutes at a time and wash your anus with warm, clean water. Do this four times a day.

Hypertension: This can be a serious problem for some pregnant women and their babies. You can combat hypertension by speaking to your doctor about healthy weight gain during pregnancy, participating in stress-relieving hobbies and activities, and good nutrition and exercise. Your doctor can prescribe safe treatment as a last resort.

Stretch marks and itching: Your skin is stretching to accommodate your new belly and larger breasts — it's no wonder you're itching. I was lucky to get advice from my mother about this. She told me to control my itch and I'll control my stretch marks. Through all three pregnancies, I used mountains of thick shea butter tubs. It prevented scratching the itch and I developed little to no stretch marks. Scratching encourages stretch marks. Instead of scratching, apply creams and ointments to stop the itch and combat the scars while they're forming. This is an old trick that I'm glad my mom shared with me. If you have stretch marks, you can fade them over time with tea tree oil.

Little to no control of urination: Understand that your growing baby is constantly placing pressure on your bladder. It's common for pregnant women to have an accident. There's nothing you can do to prevent it, so I just accepted it. However, I didn't think it was cute when it happened, and I always wore a thin pad to catch the leak. Don't use a tampon, because this can carry bacteria and infection into your body and it won't stop the leak — trust me. Two ways to reduce incontinence are urinating frequently and practicing those Kegel exercises (Khan, 2018).

Working While Pregnant: Know Your Rights

Being pregnant at work can stress you out. By understanding your rights, you can reduce your stress and decide what's best for you and your baby.

According to the Family and Medical Leave Act of 1993 (FMLA), you're entitled to 12 weeks of unpaid leave if you work for a company of 50 or more employees in America. This act is strictly regulated by the United States Labor Law and hasn't changed, according to a review in 2017. Unfortunately, this discriminates against women who work for smaller companies, and some employers take advantage. The FMLA protects your job security, but doesn't protect it if you receive paid leave. Paid or unpaid leave can only be determined by your employer and maternity leave for men is dependent on your state and company. If you'd like to read more about the current laws on maternity leave, you can visit https://en.wikipedia.org/wiki/Maternity_leave_in_the_United_States#Current_legislation

Furthermore, I would like to give you some practical advice I found online to use while you're pregnant (Murkoff & What to Expect Editors, 2018).

1. You should use the methods you've learned to deal with and possibly prevent nausea and morning sickness at work;
2. Draw up a meal plan and stick to it no matter what;
3. Make sure you're comfortable by dressing comfortably, taking breaks when you need, keep your feet up when you can, adjust your chair, and do some light stretching between work stints. Don't dress up in your two-piece formal suit with the buttons hurting your belly;
4. Stick to your check-up schedule and notify your employer of upcoming appointments in a reasonable

amount of time. You can even give your employer a copy of your schedule;

5. Keep your stress levels down by doing what you can, when you can. Stay well rested, be organized, breathe in some fresh air while on your breaks, and ask for help when you need it.

Whether you're a new parent or a first-time parent, you have to speak to your employer. It's your ethical duty to discuss your pregnancy with them. It doesn't matter if you want to continue working or you want to become a stay-at-home mom, you're obligated to sit down with your employer and do what's right. The link I shared in this section will help you understand the legalities behind your job specific to your state so you may prepare yourself before talking to your boss.

Chapter 5: Late Term Pregnancy Comfort and Preparation

Maternity Jeans and Undergarments

It's inevitable that, as your pregnancy progresses, you'll become uncomfortable. Your baby is growing more and more each day, making you feel like you've swallowed a watermelon. Your breasts are enlarged and your pants can't close anymore. As a matter of fact, your button just shot right off this morning when you sat down. The time has come to make some changes.

I remember waking up one morning with my first pregnancy, feeling as though I'd gained five pounds overnight. I tried to lift myself, but I could feel this immense weight dragging me down like a ton of bricks. Once I was sitting up, I looked down at my belly and my mind created an image of a balloon. Not just a normal balloon filled with lightweight air, though, but a water balloon about to burst. This is when I realized I was no longer comfortable.

The first step you take to find comfort again is choosing the right maternity clothes. I'll go over two types with you, one of which isn't commonly discussed.

Maternity Jeans

Let's start with maternity jeans. The perfect pair of jeans is hard to come by, let alone maternity jeans. If you're a lover of jeans, like myself, you'll want to follow some tips on finding the perfect pair to wear during your pregnancy.

There are three major things to look out for when hunting for a pair of maternity jeans: stretch, waistband, and price. I'll elaborate some more (Shortsleeve, 2019).

Stretch: You need to try on each pair of maternity jeans to find the right one. Stretch is important because your baby's still growing. Don't buy a pair of jeans that have no stretch or sit tight now. In another week, they won't fit anymore, and your partner could gain another black eye from your popping buttons. You should also look out for a firm, yet soft and supportive, stretchy material.

Waistband: Maternity jeans come with a waistband panel that sits either over the bump, under the bump, or to the side. Under the bump waistbands give you support from below, over the bump waistbands give you overall support in your midsection but they sit high, and side panels feel more like a regular jean. Your maternity jean waistband is generally a matter of preference.

Price: Here, I want you to consider two factors. Are you going to wear them after your pregnancy, and how often are you going to wear them during pregnancy? It's unlikely that they'll fit after pregnancy, once you get back to your "perfect figure" again. There's no way you want your pants to look like a circus tent when you're pushing your baby's stroller around. Just like regular jeans, maternity jeans prices can range from affordable to "what the hell did you just say?" You deserve clothes that make you comfortable, but remember that you're going to need money for many important investments other than maternity clothes.

Maternity Undergarments

More important than maternity clothes, however, are maternity underwear. This is crucial for a few reasons. Your current underwear is going to stretch out and lose its shape with your growing tummy and bum. Maternity underwear is designed with comfort and growth in mind, and comes in light colors which make it easy to see any signs of discharge or specks of blood. Blood specks can be an indication of a problem or it can tell you that your baby is on their way.

Maternity underwear comes in low-cut under the bump or high-cut over the bump designs. Over the bump designs offer additional support and feel more comfortable, whereas under the bump designs can feel cooler during the hot summer months. Your choice between the two will depend on the season you're pregnant and the design that makes you feel more comfortable.

There are things to keep in mind if you're struggling to make a decision. Cotton underwear breathes better and is always a good choice — when your underwear breathes better, you're less likely to contract an infection. Most maternity underwear is 100% cotton. Another tip is that maternity underwear comes in a wide range of colors and types to suit your own sense of style. So please, don't allow your 70-year-old grandmother to scare you and tell you that you'll be looking for granny panties. Times have definitely changed (Fritz, 2019).

Maternity wear in general is far more stylish than we're led to believe. What matters most is that you choose the material that is best suited to you.

Furthermore, thick maternity jeans might not be the best idea in the middle of a hot summer, just like a summer-style maternity dress is a crazy idea in winter.

Now, let's look at other steps we can take to find comfort.

Methods to Make Sleep More Comfortable

Clothes are definitely not the only issue making you uncomfortable. Only someone who's had a baby bump can understand how you feel. You're exhausted, uncomfortable, overheating, hungry, and moody, and your bump makes you pee every 15 minutes. Every time I felt overwhelmed by my pregnancy, I would remind myself of our baby and how close we were to meeting them. Soon, I told myself, our baby would come and be a perfect blend of myself and the man I love. My hypnosis sessions continued and my entire outlook changed. When I felt bewildered, I would take a moment to sit back and focus on my baby's movements. Feeling my baby's baseball pitch would put a smile back on my face, even though it hurts.

Okay enough about me again. Here are some tips to help you find enough comfort to rest, because you certainly won't be getting much rest when your baby arrives. Soak it up now, while you feel like a mobile mountain (Miller, 2019).

Place your pillows correctly for maximum comfort. Doctor Christine Greves from the Winnie Palmer Hospital for Women and Babies says, "You should use pillows between your knees to support yourself and you won't roll onto your back and become uncomfortable."

I've used pillows to build a fort around myself when my husband left on a business trip. Having my knees bent and pillows at my front and back prevented me from moving from my ultimate comfort zone. When my husband was home, he would spoon me from the back to help stabilize me.

The weight of your growing belly puts strain on your posture, making you bend over unwillingly. You make a mistake by trying to correct this and lean backwards as you move about, placing unhealthy tension on your back. Your abdominal muscles weaken, which can impact your spine's stability and cause back pain. Additionally, Doctor Medhat Mikheal confirms that using pillows will keep your spine straight while you're resting.

Sleep on your side. According to the American Pregnancy Association (APA), this is the ideal position for restful sleep. Logically, your bump prevents you from stomach surfing, as I prefer when I'm not pregnant. Sleeping on your back can cause breathing issues, low blood pressure, and hemorrhoids. This fact has been confirmed by the American College of Obstetricians and Gynecologists, as well.

Exercise appropriately for your current condition. I know late-term pregnancy can be exhausting, but even short bouts of exercise will help you sleep better. You may check with your doctor and choose a method that's suited to how far along you are. When I was heavily pregnant, I would take short walks that only lasted 15 minutes. I wouldn't walk briskly, but just move along at a slower pace and take in the scenery along the way.

My husband and I also signed up for Lamaze classes. Not only did I learn to breathe better during strenuous activities like childbirth, I also got appropriate exercise. I remember how tired I felt after each class. My husband would try hard to convince me to have a milkshake before I went home, but I only gave in twice because I desperately needed a nap after class.

Stretch those legs at night. Waking up with an intense cramp disrupts your sleep. Unfortunately, even Doctor Greves confirms there's no specific reason behind these cramps in pregnancy. They could occur due to the heavy pressure in your uterus, or you could be dehydrated.

A little trick I used here is to keep a bottle of room-temperature water next to my bed for an emergency. In addition, I have a supportive husband — every night before I went to sleep, he would give my legs a mild stretch and rub to get the blood flowing.

You might have a few stretch exercises from prenatal yoga in mind. Just remember to check with your doctor before doing any stretches at this stage of your pregnancy.

Avoid any heartburn triggers before bed. Even though I've covered heartburn already, I'd like to point out that you should be aware of your triggers in late-term pregnancy. You'll know what causes your heartburn by now, and you should especially avoid eating those triggers as late-night snacks. Instead, change your meals around so you don't suffer excessively at night. If you're anything like me, you should also just forget about late dinners. By week 34, I was unable to eat anything substantial after seven at night.

Pee just before you climb into bed. Besides your baby pressing down on your bladder, your blood count goes up during pregnancy and your kidneys have to filter more fluid. This is why you pee more often.

I used a little trick with my second pregnancy. After eight at night, I would drink low-fat milk instead of water and reserve my water for emergencies only. Milk takes longer to filter through and this trick, combined with peeing right before bed, helped me a ton. There's no guarantee that you won't need to pee through the night, but you'll definitely pee less.

With these tips, you should be getting quality sleep in preparation for your baby.

Preparing for D-Day

I've added this section to help you prepare for D-day. This is one piece of advice that no one gave me, and it's easy to forget something when you're in a rush. I won't go into detail about each item, but I'll tell you how to keep a "ready-to-go" bag during those last few weeks of pregnancy. You can have one in the car and one at home.

Here's a list of D-day items for yourself:

- Your identity card (ID), insurance documents, and hospital paperwork;

- A printed birth plan which you discussed with your doctor;
- Socks and slippers, because your feet can get cold during labor;
- A soft bathrobe that's comfortable and easy to open;
- Flip flops for the hospital shower and a towel;
- Lotion or massage oil so your husband can calmly massage you;
- A spray bottle or hand fan to cool yourself off during labor;
- Lip balm to stop your lips from cracking;
- Extra pillows for assured comfort for yourself and one for your partner;
- An eye mask and earplugs to help you rest during quiet times and after delivery;
- Entertainment to keep you busy in down times and after delivery;
- Soft and comfortable clothes, slippers, and underwear for after delivery — and don't forget a separate bag for dirty clothes;
- Heavy-duty maternity pads;
- Nursing bras;
- Breast pump in case you're unwell and are separated from your baby;
- Toiletries for yourself, including a toothbrush, a hair brush, shampoo, soap, cream, tissues, and hair ties;
- A spare phone charger;

- Money for snacks and drinks after delivery;
- Medications and vitamins;
- This book and any other guide to newborn care;
- A camera for your partner.

A ready-to-go bag for your baby will include:

- Bodysuits that fasten in the front;
- An extra blanket for your skin-to-skin contact and to use on the way home;
- Hats, socks, and booties, because your newborn will get cold even when you're hot;
- Going-home clothes that you choose for the special occasion;
- Baby cream, powder, oil, wet wipes, diapers, and all the baby essentials.

Don't forget that you'll need to install your car seat correctly in your car when you prepare your hospital bags (The Ultimate Maternity Hospital Bag Checklist, 2019).

Now that we've covered prenatal care, it's time to move on to postnatal care.

Part Two: Postnatal Care

Postnatal care is the next fear you may have and it's a common one, shared among many expectant parents. It doesn't matter if you've done this before, you'll worry about all the risks that are involved in the birthing process, the first 24 hours of your baby's life, and how you'll recover physically and emotionally after labor — not to mention the concern surrounding the first year of your baby's life. I'm going to focus on providing as much information as I can to arm you with knowledge and prepare you for what lies ahead.

Postnatal refers to the moment your gorgeous baby enters the world and consists of many processes and learning curves while you get to know your baby. Your health and the health of your baby is at stake, and the best precautions you can take to ensure optimal results is to follow postnatal guidance from this book, your doctor, and the support group around you.

Chapter 6: Taking Care of Yourself

Recovering From Labor and Childbirth

This can be a scary and beautiful moment, all in one. You and your partner get to meet the new addition to your family, but you're still recovering from a traumatic event. Doctors will be poking and prodding you when all you want to do is rest and be with your family. It's the most invasive moment you'll ever experience. Yet, amidst the chaos, you'll be guided to restoring yourself to your former glory in no time.

Recovering From a C-Section

Many women believe that a C-section comes with a gruelling recovery process. Yes, I confirm that it is challenging, but it's not impossible whatsoever — and with the right care, you'll be well on your way to looking after your baby and enjoying every moment thereof.

How Will I Feel After Surgery?

Surely you're going to be groggy from anaesthesia or itchy from spinal or epidural narcotics. You'll also possibly experience nausea, mood swings, inflamed breasts, and vaginal discharge. This is normal after extensive surgery. However, you'll be holding your bundle of joy and I can promise you one thing, even though you feel detached from reality right now, you'll know it was worth it when you look down to see your baby snuggled in your arms.

How will I be relieved of pain?

You've just had major surgery, and you'll need medication to recover and cope with the pain. There's no shame in asking for more, if you think your care provider has underestimated your agony.

If you were given an epidural or general anaesthesia, you were probably given morphine, too. Morphine will reduce your pain for up to 24 hours and leave you feeling less groggy. Furthermore, you'll receive narcotic pain medication intravenously.

Once you're in the recovery room, you'll be given prescription pain medication. This can be used for up to a week and then you'll gradually transition to OTC medication. Be sure to drink lots of fluids to avoid constipation, because it can worsen your pain. Finally, you can use a hot water bottle or a gel ice pack in addition to medication.

Another note: Let your doctor know if you're itchy, constipated, or nauseous and they'll give you medication to reduce these issues.

When does breastfeeding start after surgery?

Breastfeeding can commence a half-hour after surgery, whether you're in the recovery room yet or not. I will cover breastfeeding extensively in chapter eight.

What are the first few days like in recovery?

You can most definitely expect a busy day. A nurse will stop in every few hours to check your vital signs, the amount of vaginal bleeding, and feel your stomach to check whether your uterus is firming. Your body will be discharging lochia, which is a vaginal discharge every new mother experiences. This bright red discharge consists of bacteria and tissue from your uterus lining — some people call this afterbirth.

Your nurse will remove your catheter and IV line within 12 hours. She'll also instruct you on how to cough and help you with deep breathing exercises to avoid fluid build-up on your lungs and prevent pneumonia. In addition, your doctor will check on your wound daily and your nurse will help you get up and walk around. Walking is essential because you need to keep your circulation flowing to avoid blood clots. You can also roll your ankles, wiggle your toes, or have your partner do a circulation massage.

Something nurses often forget to tell you is that you need to walk straight. My friend had two C-sections and with her first, she was uneducated and suffered the consequences. She forgot to mention her allergies and they covered her drainage hole with a plaster that contained an ingredient that she was allergic to, leading to septic complications. That was her own fault. However, neither her nurse or doctor corrected her posture as she bent over when she walked. Her wound took longer to heal because of the infection, and she wasn't walking upright. You're not supposed to stretch excessively, but you do have to walk straight after a C-section. Her road to recovery was long and treacherous with her first child.

Anyway, walking will help your digestive system as well, because your intestines are listless after surgery which can cause gas and bloating. In addition, you should empty your bladder often so your uterus stays contracted and doesn't add pressure to your wound. Take short walks after you've taken your pain meds.

Your doctor will also prescribe some stool softeners, some form of simethicone for gas, any vaccines you've missed, and they'll discuss birth control options with you.

What's recovery like when I leave the hospital?

You're recovering from surgery while taking care of a newborn — admit it, you need help. Make sure your partner, family, friends or even hired help are around for you during your recovery time. Don't lift anything heavier than your baby, and give your incision time to heal. Medications will help, and your incision may start feeling better after a few days. However, it can remain tender for a few months.

Your doctor will give you instructions on wound care, but you can use antibacterial soap and warm water to clean it daily. Do this in the shower but don't submerge yourself in water for the first six weeks, as this could lead to an infection. Your wound should be dried properly after cleaning. You'll most likely have dissolvable stitches, otherwise your doctor will remove the metal staples a week later.

Your vaginal discharge should gradually turn from dark red to pink and finally to yellow/white. If your bleeding returns or you have menstrual cramps, you should see your doctor. Whatever you do, don't use tampons until your six-week check-up. Even then, you can only use them with the consent of your doctor.

How active should I be during recovery?

You should continue walking, but only return to moderate exercise and sexual intercourse after six to eight weeks. In addition, don't do any strenuous housework or lifting for eight weeks. Even sweeping the floor is more strenuous than you may think. You can drive after two weeks if you aren't taking sedative pain medication and as long as you feel no discomfort from checking your blind spots, depressing the pedals, or turning the wheel. Finally, you can return to work in six to eight weeks, if your work isn't physically strenuous.

What will my C-section scar be like?

Your scar will look darker than your skin and bulge out at first, however, the bulge will grow smaller within six weeks. It will be a low-lying scar which will sit just below your pubic hair line and eventually, you'll hardly notice it — don't concern yourself with the tales you've heard of massive scars on your lower abdomen.

If your incision becomes warm and red, swells, or oozes, you need medical attention. Other common signs of infection are feeling feverish, sudden or worsening pain, smelly discharge, and burning urine.

What should I expect emotionally?

A C-section isn't to be taken lightly. There are various reasons you may have one — you could have been in labor for many hours before you were rushed to surgery, leaving you either disappointed or feeling cheated, or you might even feel relieved. It depends on your outlook and reason.

However, it's easy for frustration to take hold, because your recovery undoubtedly feels endless at first. You can only listen to your doctor's advice and follow a healthy diet.

Furthermore, it's common to have the blues after a C-section. These sneaky feelings of sadness come on about three days after your surgery and last for days. However, you should seek help if you think they're getting worse or have persisted for too long. Postnatal depression is serious and needs urgent treatment (Boyd-Barrett & Alrahmani, 2019).

Recovering From a Vaginal Birth

Why do I keep urinating so much?

Your body stored a lot of excess fluid while you were pregnant, and now it has to go somewhere. You'll urinate more frequently and have stronger, lengthier streams. It will take a few days for the excess fluid to exit your body, and you may notice swelling in your hands and feet that is worse than when you were pregnant. It's important that you stay hydrated, because your kidneys need a constant flow of fresh water to flush any toxins out.

Is it normal to leak when I cough or laugh?

Your pelvic muscles are weak from labor — this is called stress incontinence. You may not feel much in your pelvic area for about a week. Don't be embarrassed, and remember to wear your maternity pads to absorb the unexpected splash. I used many packs of maternity pads to avoid embarrassment. I'll advise you to continue your Kegel exercises to strengthen your pelvic muscles again, but if your incontinence persists longer than two weeks, consult your doctor.

Why am I getting stomach cramps after delivery?

The pains you're feeling are contractions from your uterus. Remember, your uterus stretched up to 20 times its normal size during pregnancy, and now it has to shrink back down again. Your doctor will feel your uterus at each check-up and should no longer be able to feel it at six weeks postpartum. However, if the pressure from your doctor's hand hurts you, it could indicate an infection.

Why is my belly still big?

Your stomach doesn't magically flatten after delivery because your muscles are stretched, tired, and weak. You need to follow a healthy diet and start a more vigorous exercise regimen. Remember to listen to your body and only push it as far as it can go, because you're still healing. You can also discuss exercises that target your stomach with a fitness specialist. Personally, I conveniently joined a postnatal exercise group at the same place we attended our Lamaze classes.

Why does it hurt to sit?

Many women experience a small tear between their vagina and anus during delivery. Occasionally, your doctor or midwife will cut you if you aren't wide enough for your baby to exit through. Some women need stitches, and a few lucky women don't. Clean your wound regularly with warm antibacterial soap water and keep it dry. Furthermore, you may use ibuprofen to ease the pain.

Why are my emotions all over the place?

Whether you're a new mother or a first-time mother, your body and hormones have gone through changes — you're sleep deprived, worried about bonding with your baby, nervous about your parenting skills, or you had a difficult and long birth. You're allowed to have the baby blues. However, if you find it difficult to cope and can't take care of your baby, speak to your partner or doctor to find help straight away.

How can I cope when I'm feeling exhausted?

Whether you've done this before or not, you know you can ask for help. Nine months of physical changes during pregnancy, your body trying to correct itself in a few weeks, and dealing with the stresses of a newborn baby can affect anyone. Reaching out for help isn't a crime (Recovery After Vaginal Birth, 2017).

Adapting to Your New Lifestyle

According to Dr. William Dement, a sleep specialist, parents lose an average of two hours of sleep per night for the first five months — with this in mind, let's look at practical advice for you to gain more sleep.

- Have a network of friends, family, and your partner on speed dial for times you need help.
- Alter your baby's environment to get them to sleep so that you can sleep. You can switch the television off, dim the lights, and close your curtains. As your baby's biological clock matures, they'll fall asleep easier.
- A trick I used with two of my children was to put them in their car seat and drive around the block a few times. The car's vibrations lulled them to sleep — and still does.
- If you can afford one, hire a domestic worker to take care of any strenuous activity that exhausts you.
- You can catch up on your own sleep by sleeping when your baby does. Make sure your environment is dimly lit, a well-controlled temperature, and avoid stimulants like caffeine and coffee. Don't forget to switch your phone off, because your baby will wake you up like an alarm when needed. This is how I often got extra sleep in.

What do I do when I can't sleep?

Without sufficient rest, you won't cope — and that's a fact. I didn't just use hypnosis throughout my pregnancy; I listened to many relaxing self-hypnosis videos on YouTube to help me calm myself into drowsiness. If you don't want to follow a guided meditation, you can just sit back and picture yourself on a beach while you focus on your breathing. If all else fails, go to another room and read a book for a few minutes before trying to sleep again (Ding, 2019).

Getting Comfortable With Chaos

I want to share some practical advice about coping with your newfound chaos because, let's face it — your life will be chaotic now (Avery, 2018).

- Realize that this chaos is only temporary. Your house *will* be clean again, and you should only worry about your baby and enjoy every moment that you share. Your standards for a clean house can be readjusted again later.
- Speak to other parents to gather advice, whether you're new to parenting or just want some fresh opinions. Trust your instincts and filter the advice you get to best suit you.
- Communication between parents is essential to get through this chaotic stage. Tell your partner about your day, even the little things.
- As a stay-at-home mom, I cooked dinner in the morning because if the day became chaotic, I'd feel better knowing I already planned ahead.
- Don't be humble; acknowledge your hard work. Your partner can take you for a nice dinner to show appreciation for your effort.

- Lastly, get out of the house. You can't clear your mind if you're cooped up in chaos. Take your baby and have a lovely stroll in a quiet park where you can both relax and breathe in the fresh air.

Adjusting to Your Role and Handling New Baby Stress

Now it's time to accept that you're a parent for the first time or once more by reading some advice about handling new baby stress from experienced people (11 Ways to Handle New Baby Stress, 2018).

- You've already taken the first step in preparation by reading this book. The more you prepare, the less you'll be overwhelmed.
- Work as a team. Both parents should plan postnatal schedules together. Divide and conquer all plans, tasks, and decisions.
- Don't fret about your baby each time they cry. It will take you some time to grow accustomed to their cries and the meaning behind each one, and you'll learn to know every sound by heart. Besides, your baby's more resilient than you think — and so are you.
- When you bring your newborn home, you can never have enough essentials. Stockpile any diapers, medications, and toiletries you need as they go on sale.

- Allow yourself some 'you' time. One parent can watch the baby or a nanny can come over. Get out and have some fun together, because you both need and deserve it.
- Keep your camera handy because you don't know when something happens that's going to go viral.
- Don't criticize or compare yourself, your partner, your parenting skills, or your baby to another — everyone is unique and comes with their own strengths and weaknesses.
- Become a huggy-bear. Hug your partner, your mother, your brother, your friend, and, most importantly, your baby. There's a special kind of comfort that comes from hugging another person.

Chapter 7: Baby's First Days

Let's take a moment to learn about the first days you'll spend with your new baby. This chapter focuses on in-depth information about the basics, and even second-time parents can read through to find out something new by learning about the reason behind a certain test or procedure. For first-time parents, I know you're nervous, but you'll be fine. The more you learn, the better equipped you'll be. The first 24 hours is a trying time for everyone.

Baby's Appearance

Your baby will be born looking like an adorable little alien, no matter how silly that seems. Their skin will be blue and mottled, and they'll be covered in a cheesy white substance called vernix, amniotic fluid, and blood. The amniotic fluid and vernix is crucial for your baby to taste and smell when they first come out, as this helps make them feel safer in the outside world. Their skin will change to a pinkish color when they start breathing, but their hands and feet will retain a bluish hue for a few hours.

Your baby will also appear to have birthmarks on their face. Many babies are born with white, pimple-like blotches on their face that disappear over time. Some birthmarks are temporary while others are permanent. My eight-year-old has a brown birthmark on his back which looks like the Australian continent. When he was born, though, it was a colorless blotch.

If your baby was born vaginally, they could have an elongated head at first because they spent a long time squeezing through the birth canal. No one really prepares you for this and if you're a first-time parent, you'll be taken by surprise. Your baby will have soft spots at the front and back, which helped them squeeze through the birth canal. The rear soft spot takes four months to close, but the front can stay soft for nine to eighteen months. In addition, their face will be puffy, but this will change over the next few days as the accumulation of fluid and trauma of birth subside. However, your baby's genitals will be swollen, too, as you might've seen on your last ultrasound.

Some babies are born bald and some have a bush of hair. All three of my children were born with thick, dark hair. Just as their eye color changes, their hair color can change, too (What a Newborn Looks Like, 2017).

Bonding: Skin-to-Skin Contact

If you had a vaginal birth, the nurse will place your baby on your chest immediately. Skin-to-skin contact isn't only about bonding. It allows your baby to feel safe when introduced to a new world, reduces crying, regulates their body temperature, and helps to start the breastfeeding process.

If you had a C-section, you can ask your nurse for skin-to-skin contact as early as possible. This can happen in recovery with either you or your partner (Baby's First 24 Hours, 2018).

Personally, this moment was the most precious to me. I managed to forget all the pain and hard work the last nine months had been and I'd never felt closer to another person in my life. This was the very moment I felt a strong family connection to my husband and baby.

Weighing and Measuring

After your initial bonding and feeding, the nurse will take your baby to weigh them and measure the circumference of their head. Funny enough, you'll never forget these numbers for the rest of your life. Furthermore, you don't need to wash your baby for the first 24 hours.

Vitamin K

Why is it important for my baby?

Vitamin K is what helps your baby's blood clot and without it, they can suffer from vitamin K deficiency bleeding (VKDC). Although VKDC is rare, it can cause complications, such as bleeding in the brain. Babies don't get enough vitamin K during pregnancy or breastfeeding and will need to be supplemented after birth.

How is it administered?

Vitamin K can be given orally but if your baby throws up within an hour, they'll need another dose. It's absorbed better through an injection, and most hospitals will opt for a shot. One injection can protect your baby for months. If you choose oral doses, your baby will need one at birth, another at five days old, and a third at four weeks if you breastfeed. A third dose isn't needed for babies on formula because formula contains vitamin K.

Can all babies have Vitamin K?

Oral doses of vitamin K aren't suitable for all babies. Premature babies need smaller doses and it's difficult to measure this orally. Another factor is a sick baby. If your baby is ill when they need their second dose, they'll have to switch to the injection. In addition, if you were personally treated for epilepsy, tuberculosis, or blood clots during pregnancy, your baby won't be able to absorb vitamin K orally and will need the horrid jab.

Does my baby need to have it?

This is a personal preference. Medical authorities in Australia encourage all parents to give their babies vitamin K, whether they're premature or having surgery like circumcision.

Are there any side effects?

According to the Australian National Health and Medical Research Council, one study showed that vitamin K injections are associated with cancer; however, six studies done recently denied any link. The council confirms that there's no link to childhood cancer. Vitamin K injections have been administered for 30 years and there's no evidence to prove any harmful side effects.

What should I look out for?

You should watch for any unexplained bruising or discoloration of your baby's skin. If they haven't had vitamin K or need more, their blood will be thin and gather under their skin, and you should contact your doctor right away. Babies with jaundice are more susceptible to VKDB, as well.

How do I get Vitamin K for my baby?

Your care provider should ask you during pregnancy if you want oral or injected vitamin K when your baby is born. It's part of your birth plan and it will be administered after birth. Be sure to check with them and ensure that it's recorded on your baby's hospital file, even if you didn't allow a vitamin K dosage (Vitamin K at Birth, 2018).

Cord Blood Collection and RH Negative

Rhesus (RH) is an inherited protein on the surface of your red blood cells. If you're RH negative, you're missing this protein, which can complicate your second pregnancy. Your blood will be tested to see if you're RH negative. If you are RH negative and your baby is RH positive, a tiny amount of your baby's blood can contaminate yours during pregnancy or birth. Your body will build antibodies toward RH positive cells, and this can affect your second pregnancy with an RH positive baby.

Your body will release these antibodies during pregnancy and breach the placenta, dissipating your baby's blood cells and causing Rhesus disease (RHD) that can lead to brain damage, jaundice, and anemia in your second baby. Fortunately, there's an injection you'll be offered during pregnancy to prevent this and Rhesus disease is rare nowadays.

However, if your body already has these antibodies, the injection won't help. Your pregnancy and, subsequently, your baby will need to be watched closely and a cord blood collection will be taken from your baby to test if you're RH compatible (Rhesus D Negative in Pregnancy, 2018).

Feeding and Sleeping

Your baby should latch onto your breast within the first hour after birth and keep feeding for about an hour. If they don't, you can try and coax them with some breast milk on a spoon. If this fails, speak to your doctor or a specialist nurse.

You'll keep your baby with you and, once they've been fed, they'll fall asleep. Your baby will sleep for about six hours the first time and probably half of their first day in the world.

Apgar Scores

The Apgar score is named after Dr. Virginia Apgar and is used to determine your baby's overall health one minute and five minutes after your baby's birth. This is how your care provider decides whether your baby needs emergency or medical care.

Skin color, heart rate, muscle tone, breathing rate, reflexes, and responsiveness are each measured individually. Each measurement is rated between zero and two, with two being the highest. These five measurements make up your baby's Apgar score out of ten.

An Apgar score of six or less is normal with the one-minute check-up and a score of seven or more is normal at the five-minute check-up. It's considered low if your baby's score is less than seven in the five-minute check. If your baby's score hasn't improved in the five-minute check, your doctor will watch your baby closely and treat them appropriately.

However, a low Apgar score doesn't mean your baby will have lifelong problems, it just means your baby possibly has a breathing problem that needs urgent attention by your care provider (Apgar Score, 2017).

Your Baby's First Brush With Their Senses

The first thing your baby will recognize is your voice, because they've heard it for the past nine months, and they'll respond by looking at you. They may even recognize your partner's voice, if your partner has been talking to them. Something that still amazes me is that your baby will also continue to hear your heartbeat, as they did in your womb.

However, your baby's vision is blurry when they're born, and they use their sense of sound and a 30-centimetre visual distance to recognize you. This is the perfect distance between your breasts and your face and is often called the cuddle distance.

Furthermore, your baby will taste and smell your milk and amniotic fluid, which is familiar to them (Baby's First 24 Hours, 2018).

Urine and Meconium

Your baby will pass urine and newborn poop, or meconium, at least once. Your baby's poo will change color and consistency over the next few days, but meconium is commonly seen as a black, sticky poo.

Newborn Issues

Jaundice

Jaundice is a yellowing of the skin and eyes and is rather common in babies. Your baby's jaundice may go away on its own, or they could need hospitalization. You need to keep an eye on your baby and if they're not eating well, looking more yellow, or urinating less, they might need medical treatment.

Eating problems

Your baby will lose some weight after they're born, but should gain it back within 10 to 14 days. In the first two weeks of their life, they should have two bowel movements and soak six diapers a day. This will be a good indication that they're eating well and staying hydrated.

However, your baby's spit is important, too, and you should keep an eye on it. It's normal for your baby to bring up some food spit when they burp, but you need to look out for vomit. Vomit is more violent and more substantial than spit up. If your baby keeps vomiting frequently and the vomit is darkish green in color, you should take them to the hospital.

Infection

If your baby suddenly starts crying more often and becomes restless, you should measure their temperature. An oral temperature above 100 degrees in a newborn is worrisome. A fever is the first indicator that your baby is fighting an infection. Watch carefully for fevers, especially in the first month (SickKids Staff, 2019).

Newborn Screening Test

What is newborn screening?

Newborn screening is done at the hospital. Various tests are undertaken to check for disorders that could affect your baby's development. The disorders checked for in newborn screening can seriously harm your baby's intellectual and physical well-being. These tests also look for life-threatening conditions that could arise in infancy and childhood. Early treatment is always best.

How is newborn screening done?

Newborn screening is standard and you don't need to request it. It will begin with a blood test within the first 48 hours, and a second test could be required when your baby is a week or two old. Your care doctor or midwife will prick your baby's heel to collect a few drops of blood and place it on a special type of paper which goes to the laboratory. Your baby hardly feels this and the results will come back in two to three weeks.

In addition, your baby's hearing will be tested and a pulse oximetry, which uses a sensor on their skin, will be used to see how much oxygen is in their blood. A low level of oxygen can indicate a heart issue. Both of these tests are painless to your baby.

What disorders are included in newborn screening?

Screened disorders differ from state to state. However, most states test for the following: cystic fibrosis, sickle cell disease, critical congenital heart disease, hearing problems, and phenylketonuria. Early detection and treatment can prevent life-threatening complications.

Who pays for newborn screening?

Newborn screening isn't optional. Your insurance provider will cover the costs or, if you don't have insurance, you're looking at $15 to $150 for initial screening. Additional screening will cost more. Price is dependent on your state, but some hospitals don't charge at all.

What happens if a newborn screening test comes back negative?

A negative result means your baby has no disorders checked for by the screening process. In rare cases, there could be a false negative. This only happens if the laboratory mixes the tests tubes or the screening is done too early. Don't fret, though, as this is extremely rare. A negative result means no additional testing is required, and you can take your baby back to your doctor if you notice problems down the line. Keep in mind that your care provider might not call you with a negative result.

What happens if a newborn screening test comes back positive?

A positive result means that one or more of the tests came back abnormal. A positive result doesn't guarantee that your baby has a disease — further diagnostic tests will be done. If they do have a disease, your baby will start treatment right away. It's possible to receive a false positive result as well, and the diagnostic tests will come back normal. Furthermore, your baby's results could be borderline and your doctor will need to repeat the tests.

What is newborn genomic sequencing?

Genomic sequencing is technology that determines the order of deoxyribonucleic acid (DNA) building blocks in your baby's genetic code. This technology is used to test for genetic disorders (What is Newborn Screening, 2019).

Newborn Check-Up Expectations

Check-ups are just as important to your little one as they were to you. Let's take a look at what you can expect from each visit.

At birth

Your doctor will start by recording your baby's height, head circumference, and weight on a growth chart, so your newborn can be compared to others of their age to identify any potential problems.

Your baby will have a physical examination of their ears, eyes, lungs, heart, hips, mouth, skin, abdomen, legs, and genitals to look for any abnormalities. The soft spots on your baby's head and the shape of their head will be checked, too, to see if their head is shaping well after birth.

Your doctor will test otoacoustic emission (OAE) by placing a headphone and microphone in your baby's ear to measure how sound reflects off their ear canal. They will also test auditory brainstem response (ABR) by placing electrodes on your baby's head to check the response of their hearing nerve to sound. Both tests will indicate a problem with hearing. Furthermore, a hemoglobin screening involves a blood sample taken from their heel to check for sickle cell disease, hyperthyroidism, and other inherited diseases. Lastly, your baby will receive a hepatitis B injection on their first day.

Five days after birth

Your baby will undergo another full examination on day five, which will involve a few more tests. Your baby will be measured again to keep track of their growth and feeding, have a second physical examination to look for any changes, and have a hemoglobin screening if they haven't had one yet.

Chapter 8: Baby Essentials: Feeding

Let's start with this classic face-off to decide what's best between bottle and breastfeeding. This chapter will help you understand the differences between the two and the benefits of each.

Breastfeeding Basics

The American Academy of Pediatrics (AAP) recommends exclusive breastfeeding for the first six months of your baby's life and using it to complement their diet up to two years of age (Breastfeeding Overview, 2019).

Breastfeeding provides the perfect combination of proteins, fat, and vitamins to make your baby healthy, and breast milk digests easier. It's filled with antibodies that kill bacteria, and breastfed babies typically have fewer problems like asthma, diarrhea, ear infections, allergies, respiratory illnesses and hospitalization. Furthermore, the contact allows you to bond with your baby and make them feel safe. Who wouldn't want that? The AAP confirms that breastfeeding can lower your baby's risk of specific cancers, obesity, diabetes, and possibly sudden infant death syndrome.

In addition, breastfeeding lowers your risk of osteoporosis, cancer, encourages weight loss, speedily returns your uterus to normal size, and reduces uterine bleeding. Besides, it saves you the cost of expensive formula and bottles. I'm sure you're familiar with those costs by now.

If you're concerned about your ability to produce milk, you needn't be. No matter how short your baby's feeds are, you need to keep feeding for your breasts to continue producing milk. A hormone called oxytocin sends signals to your brain to produce more milk when your breasts run low. Your first milk, called colostrum, can look a little odd. My colostrum looked like watered-down milk, at first but that's just how it looks when it starts. The color and consistency of your breast milk will change over the next few days. It's best to stick to a breastfeeding routine and your milk production will be fine.

Additionally, there are easy-to-learn positions for breastfeeding. The most important position is the one that makes both of you comfortable. Here are some helpful positions:

- *Cradle position:* Allow your baby's entire body to face you and rest the side of their head in your elbow's crevice. Keep your baby's tummy against your body to ensure that they feel secure, and support your baby's lower back by placing your free arm through their legs.
- *Side position:* This is a great option if you're recovering from surgery or feeding at night. Lie on your side with your head elevated by pillows and use your free hand to

move your breast into position. As soon as your baby latches on, you can support their head with your free hand.

- *Football position:* This is an ideal position for after a C-section, because you don't place strain on your wound. However, this is best with newborn or small babies. Lay your baby along the length of your arm, supporting their head with your palm. Your baby is supposed to look like a football.

I had trouble with my second baby. My baby's body would often hurt when held for a long time. I made use of the cradle position to prevent this and bought a baby breastfeeding sling to help. My baby soon latched on like a hungry little monster after I introduced the sling cushion.

If your baby isn't keen on feeding, try repositioning your baby and they'll latch on once they're comfortable. Then, use your free hand to cup your breast and caress their lips with your nipple. Their natural instinct is to open their mouth and latch on. Your nipple and areola should disappear into their mouth and their lips should resemble an outward sucking position. If your baby isn't latched on correctly, use your pinky finger to gently break their latch from your nipple and try again. Keep your nails short and smooth so you don't hurt their gums.

You should always follow the ABC's of breastfeeding to ensure smooth sailing.

- *A is for Awareness:* Keep supply and demand in mind here. Watch for signals that your baby's hungry or that they've had enough. Your baby will feed eight to twelve times daily for the first few weeks. Don't wait for your baby to cry, because this means they're too hungry. They'll make sucking noises, move toward your breasts, or suck their hands to indicate that they're ready to feed.
- *B is to Be patient:* Your infant will feed between 10 and 20 minutes on each breast. Don't rush them — they know how much they need. I used to divide my baby's feedings evenly between my two breasts to avoid discomfort.
- *C stands for Comfort:* Breastfeeding must be comfortable for you, too, not just your baby. Make sure you're sitting or lying comfortably when you're feeding your baby.

Medical Concerns with Breastfeeding

Sometimes, breastfeeding isn't possible and you have to use formula. Breastfeeding isn't an option if:

- You have active and untreated tuberculosis;
- You're undergoing chemotherapy for any form of cancer;
- You suffer from human immunodeficiency virus (HIV);

- You smoke cigarettes or marijuana, use cocaine, or drink alcohol;
- You're on prescription medication for Parkinson's disease, arthritis, or taking certain pain and cold medications.

It's good to know that your baby can't contract your influenza or even the common cold through breastfeeding. However, consult with your doctor about any conditions or medications that can prevent you from breastfeeding.

Reasons Some Women Are Against Breastfeeding

You know the reasons why some women can't breastfeed, but breastfeeding is still optional even though it's recommended. There are a few reasons for women refusing to breastfeed:

- They fear that their breasts will become ugly, deformed, or sag, even though age, genetics, and smoking do more harm;
- Breastfeeding in public can be difficult and non-parents, strangers, and work colleagues can often make a woman feel uncomfortable for no reason. Not everyone understands that breastfeeding is natural;
- They feel the pressure of having to take all the responsibility of feeding and won't seek help from their partner, friends, family, or a nanny;

- Formula digests slower, which means less frequent feedings.

However, the truth is that breast pumps solve most of these issues. Unless a woman is educated about breastfeeding, she may never learn to overcome these problems and give her baby the recommended start in life.

Common Challenges

When you start breastfeeding, you'll likely experience some difficulties along the way, especially the first time around. As a matter of fact, you may find ways of improving your method second time around, too. Let's take a look at common challenges and how to overcome them.

Sore nipples

There are a few easy ways to prevent sore nipples:

1. Make sure your baby's latched on correctly and don't tug them away. Your nipple is sensitive and tugging will hurt.
2. Feed or pump more often, because full milk ducts are painful.
3. Keep your nipples dry and allow some fresh air between feedings.

4. Start with your least tender nipple, because the baby will feed more rigorously until they're past their initial hunger stage.
5. My personal favorite is to use a warm cloth and lay back for five minutes.

However, if breastfeeding has already taken its toll on you or you're suffering common nipple issues, there are a few ways to make them feel better.

Dry or cracked nipples: If you're using bra pads, change them often to keep your nipples dry and use an unscented nipple cream daily to stop them from drying further.

Inverted nipples: I had this problem at times and would stimulate my nipples by gently rubbing my fingers over them. If you struggle with inverted nipples and can't correct them, use a breast pump or call a lactation specialist.

Engorged breasts or blocked ducts: Full breasts can cause your blood vessels to clog up. I prevented this by gently massaging my breasts once a day to stimulate circulation, no matter how weird it looked every time my husband stepped in. Another tip is to use alternating ice packs and hot showers to soothe your breasts once a day to help reduce the swelling.

Mastitis or breast infection: A breast infection is accompanied by fever and warmth. You should visit your doctor to get antibiotics that are safe to use while you continue breastfeeding. Use a warm cloth compression four to five times a day on your breasts to relieve any pain.

Stress breasts: Stress hormones interfere with your oxytocin hormone, which signals milk production. You need to be relaxed when you're feeding. I used a meditative soundtrack whenever I felt stressed during feeds. As a matter of fact, both baby and myself nodded off like this a few times.

Premature troubles: Premature babies can't breastfeed yet and you'll have to pump breast milk and feed them with a bottle or feeding tube.

However, there are some danger signs. You should contact your doctor if you see the following:

- Strange nipple discharge or bleeding;
- Your baby isn't gaining weight or filling their diapers;
- Your breasts are abnormally enlarged, painful, red, or hard.

Breastfeeding looks easy, but it isn't — and you should ask for help when you need it. Besides consulting with your doctor, you can talk with other mothers or a family member for help and advice. It's a good idea to ask a trained professional to physically show you the best ways to hold your baby and treat any problems.

Pumping Your Breasts

Using a breast pump helps a woman who can't breastfeed for various reasons. Before you start pumping, learn about the basics by visiting www.ameda.com/milk-101-article/when-and-how-long-to-pump/. Furthermore, you can read the instruction manual that came with your breast pump to make sure you're using it correctly.

Once you have an understanding of how a breast pump works, you can move on to the next stage.

Breast-milk storage

It's important to learn about storing your breast milk the right way. You can use an airtight and leak-proof glass bottle, a thick Bisphenol A (BPA)-free plastic bottle, or special breast milk freezer bags to store your milk correctly. In the first two weeks, your baby will drink 60 to 90ml per feeding, and between two weeks and six months, your baby will need 90 to 150ml each time. It's better to store individual quantities to ensure freshness and not reheat it too many times. If you're freezing the milk, leave a gap as milk expands when it freezes.

Your breast milk can survive up to eight days at the back of the fridge, where it's coldest. Label your containers and keep them away from contaminants like shellfish. Freshly pumped milk can also be kept in a cooler bag with ice packs for 24 hours and in the freezer for 12 months. However, don't refreeze milk once it's thawed. It's best thawed in your fridge and used within 24 hours (Breast Milk Storage Guidelines: How to Store Milk Safely, n.d).

Going back to work

Start pumping three to four weeks before you return to work so you can practice and build a reserve. Remember to breastfeed your baby frequently before you return to work so your body keeps producing milk. Practicing breast pumping will make sure your baby will drink from a bottle. Besides, you should stick to your routine with your baby before you go to work and as soon as you return home.

Federal law requires that workplaces have a private office or lactation room. If this weren't the case, pumping your breasts at work could be a whole lot more complicated. Your company should follow regulations, and there should be a wash basin in the designated pumping room. You'll need to wash your hands and your pump kit after each use. If you can't do this, take a few kits with you daily. You'll need 20 to 30 minutes per pumping session (Breastfeeding at Work, n.d).

Breastfeeding Health

You need to care for your own health in order to provide your baby with the best health while you're breastfeeding.

Surprisingly, you're allowed to eat anything you want, as long as you follow a balanced diet filled with nutrients. You can safely add 500 calories to your diet and eat a variety of vegetables, fruits, protein, whole grains, and healthy fats. It's also essential that you stay well hydrated and continue your prenatal vitamins.

Furthermore, don't neglect yourself or deny yourself well-deserved rest. You're most welcome to become physically active and pursue weight loss, but keep in mind, your body has gone through changes and your energy levels will be low. Remember to look after your hygiene and mental health, as well (Nagin & Shur, 2019).

Weaning

Your baby will be ready to start the weaning process at six months. They'll continue to breastfeed but will begin to eat other foods now, too. However, you should wean them gradually over weeks or months.

You can start by replacing one meal a day, moving on to two when they're doing well with the first. Keep an eye out for signals from your baby and they'll let you know when they're ready for more. Never force your baby to wean off breast milk faster than they can. Additionally, choose a new place for mealtime and avoid sitting in the same place where you breastfeed your baby to show them that there's a change happening (Weaning Your Child from Breastfeeding, 2019).

I held my baby on my lap to bond with them further and to reassure their feelings of safety after changing from lying in my arms to sitting and eating. There were a few struggles at first, when my baby would pinch my enclosed breasts, but persistence paid off well.

Bottle Feeding

Should you choose to bottle feed, this option comes with its own list of advantages and disadvantages. Let's listen to bottle feeding's argument next.

Pros and Cons

Just as anything in life has pros and cons, there are pros and cons to bottle feeding (Arora, 2019).

Advantages

- Anyone can feed your baby, giving you more freedom to finish chores.
- You can feed your baby in public without wandering eyes staring at you.
- It's easy to keep track of your baby's intake, as most bottles have measurements on the side and you can record your scoops.

- You don't have to follow a balanced diet (even though you should).
- Bottle feeding comes in handy for lactose intolerant babies.
- Formula has vitamin D already built into it.
- It's easier to go back to work.

Disadvantages

- Bottle feeding is way more expensive.
- It may impact your baby's immune system and they won't get the same nutritional value they do with breast milk.
- It becomes inconvenient when you have to prepare the bottle in the middle of the night in the dead of winter, or if you forget your formula at home when you go out.
- You miss out on the healthy benefits as a mother.
- Bottle feeding can put your baby at risk for certain health issues, like sudden infant death syndrome.

Okay, I know the disadvantages of formula are frightening and I agree that whenever possible, mothers should bottle feed. However, the method of feeding you choose can't be justified by anyone else.

Bottle Feeding Basics

Bottle feeding is fairly straightforward, if you know the basics. Let's learn more about formula in this section.

There's no evidence to show that expensive branded formulas are superior to cheaper generic brands. Both have to abide by FDA regulations. However, the major difference is that brand names change up their flavors and ingredients, and try to match breastmilk as much as they can (Bloch, n.d).

Let's look at some facts regarding bottle feeding in general. Some of this information is learned through experience, and I've also searched for answers through research to help you better understand bottle feeding (Alli, 2019).

1. All plastic bottles sold in the U.S. are BPA free, which means it's simply a matter of preference. Plastic is lighter and can't shatter, but glass lasts longer.
2. You should try various shapes, sizes, and flow rates to learn what your baby likes. All nipples are made of silicone or latex and should be examined frequently and replaced when necessary.
3. You can wash baby bottles by hand or in the dishwasher with hot water and an anti-bacterial detergent. However, plastic bottles should be hand-washed because extreme temperatures can cause chemicals to be released from the plastic. I'll discuss

safe methods of cleaning your bottles and nipples in a later chapter.

4. Mix your formula exactly as the instructions direct. Watered-down formula deprives your baby of nutrition, can cause salt deficiency seizures, and can be tough on their kidneys and tummy.

5. You can start with a formula derived from cow's milk, soy-based, or a hypoallergenic type of formula that is iron-rich. Check the label to see whether your formula is iron-fortified. Formulas come in either ready-to-use, concentrated, or powder forms. Fair warning, my children hated soy formula.

6. Room temperature formula is perfectly fine, but if you want to heat your formula, hold it under an open hot water tap for a minute or two. You can test the temperature on the top of your hand to feel if it's warm but not too hot. Don't heat formula in a microwave, because this creates hotspots which will burn your baby's sensitive mouth.

7. Don't change formulas without speaking to your doctor. They'll be able to check for allergies from your current formula by using a simple method. Similar to the way a doctor tests adults for allergies, your doctor will place samples of each worrisome ingredient on your baby's skin and wait to see if there's a reaction.

8. Powdered formula that's been mixed can be stored in the fridge for 24 hours, opened packets of liquid

formula can stay in the fridge for 48 hours, and if your formula is left out for more than two hours, chuck it.

Furthermore, here are some useful feeding tips (Alli, 2019).

1. Cradle your baby with their head higher than their body and burp them mid-feed, if they'll allow. This prevents a buildup of excess winds.
2. Don't feed your baby by allowing a pillow to support their bottle even though it seems like the easier method when you're busy. Your baby's more likely to suffer from early tooth decay, ear infections, and possible choking if unsupervised.
3. Don't force your baby to keep drinking formula if they're finished. If they pull their face sideways, push the nipple out, or stop sucking, they've had enough.
4. Place a cloth over your shoulder before you rest your baby against it and gently rub or pat their back to release their winds. There's no need for hard knocks. Some babies don't need to be burped after feeding, so don't be surprised if your baby doesn't bring up any winds.
5. If your baby spits up a lot when you burp them, you should place them in a supportive seated position for 45 minutes. Don't lay them flat or play with them.

I'm confident that these tips have provided you with simple, yet practical advice to feed your little munchkin. Now for the next step: introducing solid foods.

Introducing Solid Food

Your baby is ready to eat solid foods from six months and will begin to show an interest in food. You can start when your baby is able to sit with support, shows good head and neck self-support, and they stop pushing spoons out with their tongue.

The order of introduction doesn't matter, but you should keep feeding them formula or breast milk anyway. You can start by giving your baby iron-rich foods like minced meat, infant cereal, mashed beans, or mashed egg yolk with a spoon. Try mixing their food with water, formula, or breast milk, and gradually thicken it over a few days. Next, start adding vitamin C, which helps them absorb iron, such as oranges, tomatoes, and spinach. Introduce a variety of soft textures including mashed, finely minced, pureed, and tender foods.

However, you should avoid mixing textures, and watch out for choking hazards like chunky vegetables, popcorn, hard candy, marshmallows or sausages. Peanut butter should also be thinly spread to prevent the baby's mouth from sticking together. Never leave your baby unattended when they're eating or drinking, and don't add any sugar or salt to their diet.

Experts advise against avoiding foods that may cause allergies like peanuts, yogurt, and seafood. Instead, you should observe your baby and immediately report any reactions to your doctor. If you introduce solid food one type at a time, you'll identify problematic foods (Introducing Solid Foods to Your Baby, 2019).

Furthermore, it's important to avoid cow's milk, as it can cause iron deficiency. Create manageable meals by sitting your baby in a comfortable, supportive position, and allow them to explore their food. Give your baby their own spoon to hold while you feed them with another spoon and let them drink from a cup. Dish up single servings and don't allow them to eat from a container, because their saliva can spoil the remainder of their food.

Don't force your baby to finish their food when they start crying or push it away, especially when their growth is on target. Overfeeding your baby doesn't make them sleepy, so forget about that old wives' tale. As a matter of fact, an overfed baby suffers from stomach cramps and can become restless (Mayo Clinic Staff, 2019).

Chapter 9: Baby Essentials: Clothing, Diapers, Bathing, & Skincare

Now, let's get started on the second part of your baby's basic care. I've filled this chapter with my own personal experience, practical advice from other mothers, and some basic information that you may be too shy to ask about.

Baby Clothing

When to Start Shopping

Personally, I'm not superstitious and have always started shopping from the time I found out I was pregnant, because baby shopping is one thing all parents look forward to. I know there's a higher risk of miscarriage in the first trimester, but buying clothes certainly won't improve or decrease your chance of this happening. If you see something on sale, grab it. Once you realize how expensive a baby can be, you'll want to take advantage of all opportunities. If you've had a child before, you know this well.

However, you're also allowed to wait until you pass the first 12 weeks or find out the gender of your baby. It's up to you and your partner. Here are some key factors to know about shopping for baby clothes (Nishapro, 2018).

- They don't need to cost an arm and a leg.
- Your baby is growing fast, and you shouldn't stock up on items for the same age range. You'll learn to determine your baby's growth rate and buy sale items appropriately.
- Keep comfort in mind and avoid wool, lace, and frills, because your baby's skin is ultra-sensitive and these fabrics may cause irritation. Keep it simple with onesies and rompers made from cotton, fleece, and blended materials. I first dressed my babies inside out to protect their skin from irritation from tags and stitching.
- You should set up a changing station with all your essentials at hand, because in the beginning, changing your baby won't be easy. Even if you've done it before, you'll know that it takes getting used to.
- Your baby's body isn't able to regulate temperature yet, and you can layer clothes as the temperature changes. You can also use a swaddle blanket to prevent your baby from startling themselves with their own movements by wrapping them burrito-style but not too tight.

Washing Your Baby's Clothes

Next up is washing their clothes. This information is crucial because your baby's immune system is still developing and it's easy to overlook the bacteria in your baby's clothes. Rule number one is you should always wash new clothes to avoid the harmful chemicals found in new garments. You can prepare to wash their clothes by taking the following steps:

- Read the label for instructions specific to the fabric;
- Use a chemical-free baby detergent;
- Pre-soak in warm water and soak after your wash to kill any chemicals from your detergent;
- Use sunlight to dry their clothes and avoid chemical-based dryer sheets and electric dryers;
- Avoid fabric softeners and fragranced detergents, even if you want your baby to smell like a field of cherry blossoms;
- Wash reusable diapers separate from your baby's clothes.

If you hand-wash your baby's clothes, start by washing your hands with antibacterial soap, and use infant detergent. Make sure the temperature of the water is warm and not boiling hot, and remember your soaking and drying methods. However, if you use a washing machine, you should wash your baby's clothes before yours. You must pre-soak them with soap and use the rinse cycle twice.

Furthermore, you should disinfect your baby's clothes before you pre-soak them. Use a disinfectant baby detergent from the pharmacy to spot-treat any stains, because protein stains and bodily fluids attract bacteria. You can also add a small cap of white vinegar to your water — white vinegar also kills bacteria.

If your baby has any skin allergies, speak to your doctor about products that are safe to use (Khan, 2018).

Diapers

The next step in basic baby care is to learn about diapers. Yes, even diapers aren't as straightforward as they seem. I'm going to cover the most common concerns.

Disposable vs. Cloth

Cloth diapers are cheaper, reusable, eco-friendly, gentler on your baby's sensitive skin, and adjustable. However, they're also less absorbent, use loads of electricity and water to keep them clean, and require rigorous effort when you're cleaning them. Disposable diapers, on the other hand, are convenient, more absorbent, and come in many sizes. Unfortunately, they also cost more, aren't environmentally-friendly, are surprisingly a choking hazard, and can cause skin irritation because of gels and dyes.

Getting Equipped

There's no escaping diaper duty, but you can make it easier by preparing your essentials. Let's look at what you'll need (Murkoff & The What to Expect Editors, 2019):

You'll want to find a sturdy changing station with plenty of drawers, and make sure it's a good height so you don't hurt your back when you bend over. You can add a safety strap to secure your baby — some changing stations come with a strap installed. Next, you'll stock your changing station with diapers, creams/ointments, onesies, hand sanitizer, nail clippers, a first aid kit, pacifiers, an odor sealing diaper pail, wet wipes, and an extra change-station cover pad.

I often made my own wet wipes, inspired by a friend, and would love to share the recipe with you. The ingredients you need are:

- Two tablespoons of witch hazel extract
- Two teaspoons of liquid castile soap
- Two tablespoons of pure aloe vera
- Two rolls of heavy-duty paper towels
- An empty one-gallon ice cream bucket
- One and three-quarter cups of warm, distilled water

- Ten drops of your choice of essential oils such as tea tree or rosemary — I loved using lavender oil for this
- Optional extras include three capsules of vitamin E and two teaspoons of baby oil

Cut your paper towel rolls in half and fold them into your ice cream bucket. Mix your ingredients in a separate bowl and pour the mixture over the paper towels. Leave it to absorb for ten minutes, and shake the bucket around to make sure all the towels are soaked. Keep in mind that you should avoid using essential oils if your baby has sensitive skin.

Changing Diapers

Let's get the low-down of changing diapers and what's normal.

Urine

Baby urine is very much like yours. However, it will have a pinkish tint for the first few days — this is just a chemical reaction of your baby's first concentrated urine and the diaper. There's no need for concern when you see this.

Should your baby be urinating less or have cloudy, foul-smelling urine accompanied by a fever, you should call your doctor. Your baby should soak six diapers a day after the first week, and could be dehydrated. Fever could indicate a urinary tract infection that needs treatment.

Stools

Your baby's meconium will change to a seedy, runny, yellow poop if they're breastfeeding or soft, tan-colored poop if they're on formula. They'll likely poop up to four times a day, but this will decrease after six weeks.

However, you should watch out for red poop, which indicates gastrointestinal bleeding; black poop that can be a sign of lactose intolerance; pale or chalky poop that indicates liver problems; hard or pebble-type poop, which can indicate constipation; or any mucus in their poop. As for diarrhea, you should be aware of constant, unchanging diarrhea that's more frequent and watery than usual. If it persists and is accompanied by fever or restlessness, you should call your doctor.

Gas

Gas is normal and your baby needs to be burped regularly. This is caused by indigestion, poorly-shaped bottles, and even your own diet, if you're breastfeeding. Avoid eating gassy foods and drinking gassy sodas while you're breastfeeding.

Should your baby's stomach be bloated and harder than normal, and burping them doesn't calm them down, you should call your doctor (Bell, 2009).

Diaper Rash

Diaper rash is a common problem with babies and can appear red, tender, speckled, and raw when it's bad. Mild diaper rash will go away with simple changes.

Diaper rash can be caused by irritation from poop, urine, or even just the diaper rubbing against your baby's skin for too long, or it can be caused by allergies to skin products, ingredients in the diaper, or soaps and detergents. Furthermore, the rash could be a bacterial or fungal infection.

You can prevent diaper rash by changing your baby often and dabbing their skin with warm water. Avoid rubbing their skin, which causes further irritation. Next, you can allow them to air dry before generously adding a petroleum-based cream and, finally, replacing their diaper loosely to prevent chafing. I used to leave my baby in their crib with waterproof sheets for a few hours daily to ensure their skin stayed dry.

Should your baby's rash get worse, look raw, form pus-filled sores, or if your baby has a fever, you should contact your doctor (Tellado, 2019).

Bathing and Skin Care

Next up is bathtime basics, which is definitely another important section for new and first-time parents.

Bathing Basics

A newborn baby doesn't need to bathe daily — two to three times a week will be sufficient. Bathtime makes your baby sleepy, so you should implement a bedtime bathing routine. Start with a sponge bath before you try using a baby bath tub. Sponge baths are recommended until the umbilical cord dries up and a newborn baby boy's circumcised penis has healed.

Your baby gets cold fast, so you should find a flat surface in a warm room to bathe them. You'll need a bowl with warm water, a soft blanket for them to lay on, a soft sponge, and your essential bathing supplies. You can use the soapy, soft sponge to dab their little body clean.

Once you move onto a baby bath tub, fill it enough just to cover the bottom of your baby's bottom, and ensure your room is between 70 and 80 degrees to prevent your baby from getting cold. You can test the water with your elbow and make sure it's just comfortably warm. Place your baby in the water feet first and support their head and neck with your arm. You can slide your hand under the arm furthest away from you. Your baby will be slippery at first, but you'll learn to handle this. Don't forget that you should always support your baby with one hand while using the other to bathe them.

Use cotton swabs dipped in warm water to gently wipe your baby's eyes, from their nose to the outside of the eye. Then you can wet your soft cloth and wash their face, chin, and inside and behind their ears. Now, you can soak your cloth again and move to their neck and torso, and then down to their arms and fingers. Next, you can move down to the legs and toes.

Now you can move to their genitals. Wipe from front to back for girls, and move the foreskin back for uncircumcised boys. Use a fresh cloth with soapy warm water for this and be gentle when you wipe their genitals and backside.

If your baby has hair, you should wash it with a tear-free baby shampoo. Remember to be gentle around your baby's soft spots. If they don't have hair, you can just wipe their head with the cloth before you rinse your baby. You can hold your baby football-style again and use clean, warm water to rinse.

Now you can pat your baby dry by using a soft towel. Don't miss any folds of skin. If your baby hated his bath, you can return to sponge baths for a few days before you try again. Remember to allow your baby's skin to dry before applying the cream to their bottom (Murkoff & the What to Expect Editors, 2019).

A personal tip I'd like to share here is to use an extra towel when bathing your baby. My second child was born in the beginning of winter and there was a problem with our thermostat. When I absolutely had to bathe my baby, I wrapped them in a spare towel before submerging them in the baby bathtub and then removed the towel slowly to help them get used to the water.

Furthermore, there are some critical hygiene tips you'll need to know, which I'll cover in the next three sections.

Umbilical Cord Care

Your baby receives vital nutrients through an umbilical cord while you're pregnant, but this cord is no longer needed after birth. The doctor cuts and clamps it, leaving behind a stump which will dry up and fall off. Expose the stump to fresh air by folding your baby's diaper down in the front so it can dry out faster and allow the stump to fall off on its own.

It's normal for your baby's stump to bleed a little and crust close to the skin, especially just before it falls off. If it becomes red or swollen, oozes, creates a moist pink bump, or hasn't separated after three weeks, you should contact your doctor. This could be a sign of infection and must be treated promptly (Mayo Clinic Staff, 2018).

Circumcision Care

Circumcision is an optional route chosen by some parents. It's a simple procedure where the foreskin is removed two or three days after birth and heals in seven to ten days.

Keep the area clean by gently using unscented soap and warm water with every diaper change and allow it to air dry. Then you can smear some petroleum jelly on the tip of his penis and either wrap it with a piece of gauze or leave it bare. Gauze prevents friction caused by rubbing against his diaper, and you can even put two diapers on for extra cushioning from the discomfort and tenderness.

Your baby's penis will be a little red, there could be a drop of blood in his diaper, or you can see some yellow liquid ooze from the tip — this is all normal. However, if foul-smelling drainage, fever, swelling, fluid-filled sores, persistent bleeding, redness after more than five days, trouble urinating, or if the yellow ooze is still there after a week, you should contact your doctor (Murkoff & the What to Expect Editors, 2018).

Nail Care

Your baby's nails are sharp even though they're softer than yours. It's easy for your baby to scratch themselves when they're waving their little arms around. You should trim their fingernails three times a week and their toenails less because they grow slower. You should use an emery board for the first few weeks.

Some babies are rather fussy when it comes to nail trimming — I know mine were. You can try clipping their nails after their bath or while they're sleeping. Use baby clippers to do this and push their finger tip back so you don't clip their skin. You should cut fingernails with a curve and toenails straight, after which you should smooth out rough edges with an emery board. Ask your partner to hold or distract your baby if they wake up or become restless. I used to sing a nursery rhyme if my baby was awake and made it seem like playtime.

If you should snip their fingertips, don't panic. It happens more often than you think. Run their little finger under a stream of cold water and use a cotton swab to apply pressure for a few minutes to stop the bleeding. Don't wrap their finger in a plaster because they can choke on the plaster if they chew their finger (Montgomery, 2019).

Common Skin Conditions

There are a few common skin problems that come with babies, and you may experience one or two of them. Let's have a look at some common issues to give you an idea of what to expect (Newborn Rashes and Skin Conditions, 2018).

Pimple-like rash: Baby acne is common and will clear up on its own. It can show up on your baby's cheeks, forehead, or nose.

Blotchy skin: Some babies are born with tiny, red bumps which sometimes contain pus. This is called erythema toxicum and isn't harmful. It can appear on their entire body and should disappear within a week. In addition, African-American babies can get pustular melanosis. This rash forms blister-like pimples that break open and leave dark spots. The rash disappears a few days after birth, but the dark spots take a few weeks or months to diminish. Furthermore, your baby can have mottled skin from the cold, and you can just warm your baby up to make the 'rash' disappear.

Heat or moisture rash: A heat rash is caused by weather and overdressing your baby. You can cool your baby down by dabbing them with a wet cloth and removing a few layers of clothing. A heat rash appears as small red specks under their clothes. A moisture rash, however, is caused by their bodily fluids. Whether it's spit or sweat, it will look similar to a heat rash but can be prevented by keeping your baby's skin dry and clean.

Newborn red specks: Your newborn could be covered in tiny red specks. These are bits of blood that have surfaced due to birth trauma and will disappear after a few days.

Cradle cap: Many babies suffer from scaly and crusty skin around their head. It's an accumulation of dead cells, scales, and skin oils. It should disappear after 12 months and must be treated at home with shampoos and mineral oil from your drug store.

However, you should contact your doctor if your baby has the following worrisome signs:

- Excessive pus from any rash
- Red streaks running the area in question
- Swelling in their neck, armpit, or groin lymph nodes
- Pain or warmth in the area

On a lighter note, some common birthmarks — or angel kisses, as some people call them — are common and present themselves as a discoloration of the skin around the upper lip, between the eyebrows, upper eyebrows, and the back of the neck. Some examples are:

1. A mole is a smallish brown mark that can be hairy.
2. Mongolian spots are flat, smooth, and have a grey-blue color to them — they look like a bruise. These are common and most fade by six years old. These are likely with darker skinned babies.
3. Port-wine stains appear pinkish at birth and darken to a red-purple color over time. These are caused by underdeveloped blood vessels and can appear anywhere on your baby's body.
4. Finally, you can spot a capillary hemangiomas on your baby's skin. This can be a pink, reddish purple raised mark, or it can be flat and smooth. These are common on your baby's upper body and can grow rapidly for no

reason. However, once this form of birthmark's growth halts, it starts to shrink and eventually disappears.

There are more birthmarks, but these are some of the more common ones you are likely to notice and wonder about.

Chapter 10: Care Provider and Childcare

How to Choose Your Baby's Care Provider

Getting Started

Whether or not your pregnancy is planned, you've made the first decision regarding your baby's future when you choose their doctor. All decisions are up to you, as parents, and choosing your baby's doctor is essential. You should begin your search about three months before you deliver. You can even ask your prenatal doctor or midwife for advice on choosing a postnatal doctor, or you can get recommendations from family, friends, colleagues, and parents you meet in Lamaze classes. I entered this journey with two other moms-to-be with my second and third babies which helped me a lot. Once you have a pediatrician in mind, or a few options, you can check with your insurance provider to see if they cover that specific doctor.

On the American Academy of Pediatrics (AAP) website, you'll find a section where pediatricians are listed. This is especially helpful if you're new to an area or don't have anyone you can ask. You can look at the positive and negative reviews left by previous patients for each doctor before you make your decision. Let's have a look at some other factors you'll need to consider.

Pediatricians vs. Family Physicians

Family physicians and pediatricians have the same amount of experience, but pediatricians specialize in the health, growth, behavior, and development of children up to the age of 21, whereas family physicians treat people of all ages, from children to adults and seniors (Sheahan, 2019).

Factors to Consider

Training: Is your pediatrician trained as a doctor of medicine (MD) or a doctor of osteopathy (DO)? An MD is trained in traditional medicine and a DO is trained in medicine holistically. Both are trained to diagnose and treat ailments and prevent future health issues where possible. MDs and DOs have to complete residency programs, which means they have to spend a certain amount of time doing practical work under the supervision of qualified doctors.

Choosing your doctor based on their training is your own personal preference. Every MD and DO will have to pass a difficult exam after their residency to become qualified and board certified.

Personal approach: Doctors' offices approach new parents differently — some may want a private interview and others invite expectant parents to come to their office in groups to learn more about their practice. You should aim for a private interview.

Cost: You should call each doctor's office to make an appointment and they'll inform you of any costs involved in the interview consultation. Many insurance providers pay for interview consultations.

Location: Keep in mind that your chosen doctor needs to be within close range to you. I'll tell you from experience that you shouldn't choose a doctor who's 15 miles away because if your baby chokes on something, you need to get your little one in as fast as possible. Location is vitally important.

Accessibility: On the one hand, you want a doctor who's great at their profession and on the other hand, you want one that's available for all your baby's check-ups. In my opinion, you should aim for both. My friend missed vital vaccinations for her baby because her doctor was away. His personal assistant wasn't a qualified nurse, so she couldn't help. Use a doctor who works in a partnered office or has a qualified nurse available — you can't risk your baby missing essential care.

Hours: You'll want a care provider who makes themselves available during weekends and after hours. My pediatrician was amazing, especially with my first baby. He didn't mind being disturbed after ten at night. As soon as I chose my doctor, I was given a cell number for emergencies. Little did I know, I would need it.

I will never forget my first baby scare, when I checked on my seven-month old in his crib late one Saturday night. I still tear up when I recall the dreadful feeling that came over me when I saw him. He was laying on his side with his eyes wide open when I noticed that his head and shoulders were curling backward. I felt like I was in a Stephen King novel when I saw my baby; I'd never been more afraid in my life. I shrieked for my husband to get the car keys and my phone as I grabbed my baby and scrambled for the front door.

My baby's entire body was folding over backwards as my husband jumped in the driver's seat. I called my pediatrician immediately and he urged me to rush my baby to the hospital and promised to meet us there. After we arrived, our baby was taken away from us and we were forced to sit in the waiting room. My pediatrician arrived minutes later and reassured us that he will personally handle our baby.

We sat in the waiting area for two hours, grinding our teeth and thinking the worst, before our pediatrician came to speak to us. I remember frantically asking him where my baby was as he calmly sat me down. He had a smile on his face. He explained that our little guy was in agony from biting his tongue, which was why he was doing backflips. Besides the pain, our baby was perfectly fine.

The reason I'm sharing my story with you is because that night could have been worse — our baby could have suffered a seizure or brain aneurysm. However, thanks to our choice of pediatrician and his association with the closest hospital, our nightmare turned out to be nothing.

Interviewing Pediatricians: Good Questions to Ask

There are some questions you can ask your pediatrician when you're interviewing them to help you decide if they're the right choice for you. Take the time during your interview to notice the cleanliness and friendliness of the staff at the practice and speak to other parents who are there to see the doctor while you wait. Here's a list of the questions you need to ask in your interview (Sheahan, 2019).

Is your practice a group effort? Who will help my baby when you're unavailable?

Do you provide weekend and after-hours care?

Are you affiliated with a hospital that specializes in child care?

Can someone answer all my questions if I call your office and you're busy?

Do you always call back when I leave a message?

Do you offer video consultations if I'm away?

Do you use electronic medical records to store my baby's information?

Is there a website where I can find test results or keep an eye on my baby's developmental progress?

Will you personally handle emergencies or refer me to an emergency room?

How much are your services if my insurance provider doesn't cover costs — and even if they do, do you require me to pay cash and claim it back from my insurance?

If my baby needs specialist care, do you refer them to a specialist?

Is your vaccination policy standard with the immunization schedule of the Center for Disease Control and Prevention?

Will you be present at the initial examination of my newborn baby?

Evaluating Your Options

Now that you've interviewed potential pediatricians, you can evaluate your options. The doctor you choose will treat your baby for many years to come, and choosing a doctor that you can work well with makes you more confident and puts you and your partner in the driver's seat.

How does the doctor feel about circumcision, breastfeeding, bottle feeding, alternative medicine/treatment, and medications? Does the doctor make you feel comfortable and confident? Will they listen to your queries and explain things in language you can understand?

There's nothing wrong with having multiple interviews and comparing notes on each doctor before you decide. Your doctor needs to match your own ideals.

Choosing Your Child Care Provider

Another key aspect of your new baby's life is choosing a care provider. Planning is how you will ensure a successful life for yourself, your partner, and your baby. It's never too early to start planning for your baby's care. You may choose to be a stay at home parent. However, placing your child in someone's care allows you to go back to work, spend time alone with your partner, and may increase your baby's learning and socialization skills. Let's take a look at the advantages and disadvantages of each type of care, as well as the average costs involved to help you prepare (Dorning, 2019).

Stay-at-home parent

The advantages of raising your child at home are:

- You decide the quality of your childcare;

- You get to raise your child with the values and traditions you believe in;
- You're there for every milestone in your baby's development;
- You get to bond with your baby every day;
- You avoid the struggle of juggling work and raising a child.

The disadvantages are:

- You don't have much support and have to do everything yourself;
- Your baby misses out on socializing and play dates have to be arranged to have them build social skills;
- You'll suffer a loss of income, medical benefits, and retirement annuities from your job if you were previously employed;
- You can become lonely if you're used to being out and about with colleagues and friends;
- You'll impact your future work possibilities — you'll have to explain why there's a gap in your resume when you do return to work.

The good news is that becoming a stay-at-home parent doesn't cost you any extra; however, the bad news is that you'll lose the income you had before.

Family care

The advantages of family care are:

- Your family member is likely to share your values and traditions;
- They have a personal interest in your baby and will provide them with familial love and attention;
- This is often a cheaper option, because your relative might refuse payment or require less compensation.

The disadvantages are:

- The way you raise a child may differ, especially if an older family member offers to assist. Their methodology could be outdated;
- Your baby doesn't socialize in this situation, either;
- You could damage your relationship with your relative because working for family can cause conflict;
- Old relatives may find it difficult to handle the responsibilities that come with a baby.

Family care can be cost effective, as most relatives won't want payment. Instead, you can pay your mother's gas bill every month to thank her for looking after your baby.

Nanny

Your baby will enjoy the following advantages:

- They'll be in a familiar environment at home;
- Your nanny is trained and experienced in modern childcare;
- There's more flexibility with a nanny and you aren't restricted to certain hours;
- It's convenient because everything your nanny needs is at home;
- Your baby will receive individual attention.

The disadvantages are:

- Unless you have a nanny-cam, you can't see what's going on;
- Play dates must be arranged again;
- Your nanny can become sick or have a family emergency and ditch you;
- There's loads of paperwork and complex taxes involved with a nanny;
- Your privacy suffers with live-in help;
- A nanny is the most expensive form of childcare.

A nanny can cost between $500 and $700 weekly, or $2,100 and $3,000 monthly. However, a live-in nanny will cost less.

Home daycare or day mother

Let's look at the advantages that come with this form of childcare:

- Smaller and more individualized care than you'll find at a daycare;
- Costs less than most childcare options;
- Your baby can socialize with other babies;
- They're normally flexible with pick-up and drop-off when you have an emergency;
- Your baby's in a home-like environment.

The disadvantages are:

- Day mothers aren't always qualified in early childhood development;
- They follow less strict licensing policies than daycares;
- They're often closed over holidays;
- Your baby's more prone to getting sick in a group environment;
- There's no direct supervision around the clock;
- Your day mother can become ill and temporarily leave you without childcare.

The cost of home daycare can vary from $300 to $1000 per month.

Daycare center

Here are some advantages of full-time daycare:

- They're reliable and won't let you down;
- Your baby is well supervised;

- Social skills flourish in daycares;
- The staff are well trained in early childhood development;
- Daycare is cheaper than a full-time nanny;
- A daycare is regulated by strict guidelines and policies.

The disadvantages can be:

- Some daycares have minimum age requirements and finding one that has space for your baby can be tedious;
- Many daycares don't facilitate sick children and a nanny will have to step in;
- Strict operating times are non-flexible;
- Closed on most holidays;
- The care is impersonal because the carer has to look after up to three babies at once.

Full-time daycare can cost between $380 and $1564 monthly.

Preschool

Preschool isn't something you need to worry about in the first year of your baby's life, but I'll cover it nonetheless. While Preschools are similar to daycares, they follow different regulations and are education-based. Your child can attend preschool between the ages of two and five.

The advantages of preschool are:

- Preschools are reliable;

- The teachers are well trained;
- Your child will improve their social skills;
- Preschools are well regulated;
- It's a structured environment with regular outings;
- Their educational curriculum is focused on your child's precise level of development.

The disadvantages are:

- Your child gets sick often in a group environment and you're not allowed to send them to school when they're sick;
- Preschools close for holidays;
- Strict hours in which you need to drop off and pick up your child;
- Each teacher attends to an average of eight children at a time.

The cost of full-time preschool currently ranges between $372 and $1,100 a month. However, by the time your little one goes to preschool, these amounts may change.

Chapter 11: Check-Up Schedule and Vaccinations

Check-Up Schedule

It's important to understand your baby's necessary check-ups to ensure their growth and development. The AAP recommends the following check-ups, which I've placed in a simple-to-understand set of guidelines for new or curious parents (Yang, 2019).

One Month

Your baby will be measured, assessed behaviorally, physically examined over their entire little body, and undergo a developmental surveillance similar to the tests done at birth. These tests will help your pediatrician determine if your baby is developing normally in comparison to other babies of their age. Your doctor will ask about your baby's sleeping, eating, bowel movements, responses to sound, movements, and their development in flexing their arms and legs.

Next, your doctor will review the screening done at the hospital and rerun any tests if necessary. If your baby's hearing wasn't tested or their screening wasn't done, they'll do it this time. Your doctor will then give your baby a second HepB shot with either this check-up or the next.

Finally, your doctor may test your baby for tuberculosis (TB). TB causes heavy breathing, night sweating, swollen glands, a persistent cough, fever, slow growth, and weight loss. Your doctor will inject an inactive strain of TB into your baby's arm and you'll wait 48 to 72 hours to see the result. If the result is positive, your baby's arm will turn red around the injection site and swell up. You'll need to inform your doctor if this happens.

Two Months

Your baby's two-month check-up isn't for the faint-hearted. Your pediatrician will examine your baby physically and check all the basics again. Weighing your baby will help the doctor determine their growth and whether your baby's eating well. But this is when the terrifying needles come out, so brace yourself.

Your baby will receive their second HepB shot if they haven't received it yet. This will be followed by a rotavirus vaccine (RV), which could be the first of up to three doses by the time your baby is six months old. The number of times your baby receives the RV vaccination depends on the brand your doctor uses. Next, your baby will receive Haemophilus influenza type b conjugate vaccine (Hib), pneumococcal vaccine (PCV), diphtheria and tetanus toxoids and acellular pertussis vaccine (DTaP), and finally, inactivated poliovirus vaccine (IPV).

I cried with my first child because I couldn't stand my baby's crying. Yes, the doctor does combine some of these shots, but it still shattered my heart into a million pieces when I watched my baby screaming.

Four Months

Even though you and your baby may be traumatized after your last check-up, the four-month check-up can't be missed. Your baby will get the regular weighing, measurements, behavioral assessment, and physical exam for their record. The doctor will continue comparing your baby's development with other babies' charts to look for any worrisome inconsistencies.

In addition, your baby will have a hemoglobin screening to check for anemia and will have second doses of Hib, PCV, IPV, RV, and DTaP. I'm sure you'll be stronger for these this time round.

By the way, my husband and I decided to attend all check-ups together after the trauma of the first. That way, we were able to support each other when we heard our baby crying, because those cries resonate through a parent.

Six Months

Your baby will go through the regular checks of weight, physical examination, and developmental surveillance for their comparison chart.

Furthermore, your pediatrician may do a lead screening to ensure that your baby hasn't been exposed to worrisome levels of lead — high levels can impact your baby's development. In addition, your baby will likely have their first tooth, and an oral check is in order. If your baby hasn't been tested for TB, they'll be tested now.

As far as vaccines go, your baby will receive an influenza shot on your request if it's winter, and they'll receive their third doses of PCV, DTaP, and perhaps Hib. Additionally, your baby may need another RV vaccination, a third IPV vaccination between now and 18 months, and a final HepB shot before 18 months.

I would strongly recommend the influenza shot if it's midwinter, because you can save your baby and yourself from a nasty flu.

Nine Months

Your baby will undergo the regular weight, measurements, behavioral, and physical examination for their chart. Your doctor will also check their oral health again, and they may receive a HepB or RV shot if they didn't get one last time.

However, your pediatrician will perform a development screening at this time, which is more formal than previous assessments. The test will include a bunch of questions about your baby's behavior and growth. Your doctor may request that you play with your baby while he questions you, because this will help your doctor visualize your baby's behavior and movements to see if they're learning fundamental skills appropriate to their age.

This screening will help your doctor decide if your baby needs further developmental screenings. If your baby is a high-risk infant, these screenings will happen frequently. Low birth weight, premature birth, and having a sibling diagnosed with autism spectrum disorder (ASD) automatically places your baby at a higher risk.

Finally, your doctor will take a small amount of blood to check for iron deficiency and lead levels again.

Twelve Months

It's rather common for your baby to celebrate their first birthday with a check-up. Your doctor will check measurements, weight, do a physical exam, and assess your baby's development.

Your baby might receive another lead screening or TB test, a hemoglobin screening, and their cute milk teeth will be examined once more. Next, your baby will be poked and prodded.

Your baby will get their final dose of HepB and their third shot of IPV if they haven't received it yet. This will be followed by a third or fourth dose of Hib and a fourth dose of PCV between now and 15 months. Next, they'll receive their first dose of measles, mumps, and rubella (MMR) shot and a varicella vaccine now or at their following check-up. The prodding will end with the first dose of HepA vaccine, which must be administered again after six months.

Fifteen Months

I must admit, you start growing accustomed to these check-ups by 15 months. Of course, it still hurts like hell when your baby cries, but you know it's for their own benefit.

At 15 months, your baby will get all the regular weight checks, measurements, and a physical exam again. They'll also receive the HepB, Hib, PCV, varicella, HepA, MMR, and IPV shots if they didn't receive them last time. Your doctor will further administer the fourth dose of DTaP between now and 18 months.

Eighteen Months

Your 18-month check-up will comprise of the usual physical exams, weighing, and developmental assessment for record. In addition, your doctor might do a TB test, oral examination, lead screening, and hemoglobin screening. Your baby will also receive any outstanding HepB, DTaP, HepA, and IPV shots.

Furthermore, the 18-month check-up is crucial for the first autism screening. Your doctor will run tests to check for ASD warning signs. ASD can halt your baby's communication, social, and behavioral skills. This is a common screening between a year and two years in a child's life and should your doctor find a problem, they'll refer you to a specialist or program that can help your baby.

Twenty-Four Months

Wow, your baby is two years old now. Irrespective, your baby will undergo the usual physical exam, weight check, behavioral assessment, autism screening, and developmental surveillance. Additionally, your child may have a TB test, oral examination, hemoglobin screening, or a lead screening.

Furthermore, your child should receive two quadrivalent meningococcal conjugate vaccines (MCV4) eight weeks apart. This should happen between the ages of two and ten. Your doctor may also do a blood test to check for lipid disorder, which can lead to heart problems.

Otherwise, you're out of the heavy check-up battlefield and you no longer need to hear your little one scream blue murder.

Questions and Concerns About Check-Ups

You may wonder why vaccines are necessary, and I'll answer this question for you in the following section. I haven't sugarcoated the information, because it's vital for you to understand why your baby needs vaccinations. Shall we proceed?

How Do Vaccinations Work?

A vaccine teaches your baby's immune system to identify and kill bacterial or viral pathogens. When certain antigens are injected into their bodies, their body triggers an immune system reaction. Antigens are tiny molecules of bad pathogens, and your baby's body is able to react appropriately to these minimal forms of pathogens. When the pathogen reappears naturally, your baby's immune system creates antibodies and kills them.

Your baby can also be vaccinated using inactive pathogens. Even though the pathogens are dead, your baby's immune system will still identify and destroy them. A conjugate vaccine contains pathogens which have been immobilized and they can't make your baby sick, allowing your baby's immune system to safely do its thing (How Vaccines Work, 2019).

Why Should Our Baby Be Vaccinated?

The best way for me to answer this question is to provide you with a list of the many ways vaccination helps your baby (10 Reasons to Get Vaccinated, n.d).

- It will keep your baby healthy;
- Your baby's immune system is built with vaccinations and nutrition because they're born with an undeveloped immune system;
- Vaccines are one of the safest medical products in the world;
- They don't make your baby sick with the disease they're meant to prevent;
- The diseases that are prevented by vaccines haven't disappeared and you need to prevent them from happening to your baby;
- It can impact whether your baby lives or dies;
- Vaccine-preventable diseases can cost an arm and a leg;
- When your baby gets sick, they risk the health of everyone around them.

Are Vaccine Additives Safe?

Once a vaccine is issued in the United States, the FDA and CDC place these vaccinations under a microscope to ensure their safety. Many vaccines contain adjuvant, which is a specific ingredient that helps the vaccine work better by creating a stronger immune response (Vaccine Safety, 2018).

Can Vaccination Affect an Autistic Child?

A study published in the Journal of Pediatrics, 2013, proved that vaccinations in the first two years of a child's life didn't contribute to the development of ASD (DeStefano; Price; & Weintraub, 2013).

Vaccination Schedule

Now, I need you to grit your teeth as I go into some tough-to-read information.

Childhood Vaccinations

Let's have a look at common childhood diseases, their symptoms, their complications, and the vaccines that prevent them from making your little one dangerously sick (Centers for Disease Control and Prevention, 2019).

Hepatitis A is restricted with a HepA shot. It's contracted through contaminated food or water and direct contact. Symptoms can include loss of appetite, fatigue, vomiting, jaundice, fever, and dark urine, but your baby may not even show symptoms. Your child can suffer from kidney or pancreatic issues, blood disorders, liver failure, and joint pain if they contract hepatitis A.

Hepatitis B is contained with a Hep B vaccine and can be contracted through contact with contaminated blood or bodily fluids. There can be no symptoms or your baby can suffer from a headache, fever, weakness, vomiting, joint pain, or jaundice. Complications include cancer, failure, or chronic infections of the liver when they get older.

Your child is protected from *diphtheria* with a DTaP vaccine. This is contracted through direct contact and can be airborne. Symptoms include a mild fever, weakness, sore throat, and swollen neck glands. Complications include heart failure, death, paralysis, coma, and swelling of the heart muscles.

The RV vaccine protects your little one from *rotavirus*. This is contracted through the mouth and diarrhea, vomiting, and fever are common symptoms. Complications are severe diarrhea and dehydration.

The PCV vaccine protects your child from *pneumococcal* disease. This disease is transmitted through direct contact and is airborne. Symptoms may include an infection of the lungs (pneumonia), but it can have no symptoms at all. However, complications include an infection of the blood, infection of the spinal cord and brain (meningitis), and death.

The MMR vaccine prevents *measles*. This is contracted through direct contact and is airborne. Symptoms include a cough, runny nose, pink eye, fever, and, most noticeably, a rash. Complications can include swelling of the brain (encephalitis), pneumonia, and death.

The varicella vaccine prevents *chickenpox* which is airborne or contracted through direct contact. Symptoms are headache, fever, fatigue, and rash. Complications are bleeding disorders, encephalitis, infected blisters, and pneumonia.

The MMR vaccine also protects against *rubella,* or German measles, which is airborne or contracted through direct contact. Symptoms can include swollen lymph nodes, fever, and a rash. Complications cause birth defects, miscarriage, premature labor, and stillbirth in pregnant woman.

The Hib vaccine fights against *haemophilus influenzae type b* diseases that are airborne or contracted through direct contact. This disease can present no symptoms until bacteria enters the bloodstream. However, complications include intellectual disability, meningitis, a life-threatening infection that causes breathing issues (epiglottitis), pneumonia, and death.

The MMR vaccine fights *mumps* which is also airborne or contracted through direct contact. Symptoms include a fever, headache, fatigue, muscle pain, and heavily swollen salivary glands. Complications include hearing loss, swollen testicles or ovaries, encephalitis, and meningitis.

The IPV vaccine protects your child against *polio*. Polio is contracted through the mouth, direct contact, and is airborne. There may be no symptoms, but if there are, they include a fever, headache, sore throat, or nausea. Complications are paralysis and death.

The DTaP vaccine prevents *tetanus,* which is contracted through a cut, bite, or lesion. Symptoms include muscle spasms, fever, neck and abdominal stiffness, as well as difficulty swallowing. Complications are labored breathing, broken bones, and death.

The DTaP vaccine also protects against whooping cough, or *pertussis*. Pertussis is contracted through direct contact and is airborne. Symptoms include a runny nose, severe cough, and a pause between breaths (apnea). Complications include pneumonia and death.

The flu vaccine protects your child from *influenza,* which is airborne and contracted through direct contact. Symptoms include muscle pain, cough, fatigue, sore throat, and fever. Complications can lead to pneumonia.

If you're traveling, please speak to your doctor about any additional vaccines your baby may need.

Side Effects of Vaccines and How to Manage Them

Common side effects include fever, a small lump at the injection site, tenderness, swelling, and redness around the site, a restless baby, or an oddly drowsy baby.

Here's some advice on how to treat these side effects:

- You may use a cold, wet towel for compression twice a day to help a site lump go down faster. However, it should go down on its own.
- Change your baby's clothes when they're hot so you don't encourage a fever.
- Allow your baby some extra fluids to rehydrate.
- You can speak to your doctor about liquid form paracetamol for your baby to ease the pain and bring their fever down. Just remember that your baby needs natural probiotics whenever they're taking any form of medication. A smooth, plain spoonful of yogurt before each intake of medication helps your baby's tummy deal with medications.

There are some rare side effects of vaccinations, too. One of the rare side effects is anaphylaxis, which should be treated by your doctor or emergency staff. It's a severe allergic reaction to the vaccination, and is completely treatable if handled swiftly. Another rare side effect is a blockage of their bowels. This is highly unlikely to happen if you keep your baby hydrated. Finally, a one or two-minute febrile seizure can take place, which scares the hair off your head. Febrile seizures happen when a child's temperature rises too fast (Immunisation – Side Effects, 2018). However, your doctor will bring your baby's fever down quickly.

Weighing the Risks and Benefits

Refusing your baby's vaccinations can place your baby, your family, and everyone around you at risk for serious complications and diseases. Vaccinations are medication that help you prevent serious illness or even death for your baby. Any side effects are easily manageable, and serious side effects are rare. The benefits outweigh the risks. If you have followed the guidelines in this book and have your doctor close by, you have nothing to worry about (Immunisation – Side Effects, 2018).

I apologise for the brutal information in this section, but you need to learn the hard facts about vaccinations. Now you can take a deep breath and relax as we move onto the next chapter.

Chapter 12: Baby's Safety and Medical Emergency Concerns

A crucial part of raising a healthy baby is to ensure their safety, and to know when to call for help. In this chapter, we'll look at important safety measures, emergency situations, and travel tips.

Home and Outdoor Safety

The Nursery

There are a few ways to make your nursery safer for your explorative little one. Let's delve into the details (St Clair DiLaura, n.d).

Anchor your furniture: Your baby is a strong and curious soul who loves to explore. Make sure that all nursery furniture is anchored against the wall or floor, secured with studs or drywall screws. You want your baby to be able to pull themselves up against furniture when they start learning to lift themselves — secure furniture isn't only safe, but it gives your baby the freedom of learning to stand.

Toy storage: Yes, your baby is going to have a mountain of toys. You should ensure that your toy chest has no sharp edges and that any lid can be easily removed. You don't want your baby trapped in the toy chest or injured by a falling lid. I had a special toy chest made for my kids. It was made of thick, durable plastic that had rounded edges, and instead of inserting the toys at the top, it was open in the front. Sure, it was larger than other "toy chests," and messier — but it was safer, too.

Declutter the nursery: You should remove all small items from your baby's reach. Pack everything in drawers and make sure the drawers are locked. This includes any choking hazards, disposable diapers, creams, ointments, toiletries, coins, anything small enough to fit in their mouth, and anything long enough to string around their neck or hands. You'll be surprised what your baby will want to shove in their mouth or bite; it's the way they learn.

Electricity: Your baby is curious as heck and wants to touch everything and place everything in their ear, nose, and mouth. I had a shelf that was high up on the wall and placed everything there after each use. And don't forget the outlets. You can purchase fake covers for each outlet in your house. It looks like a flat plug that you insert so that your baby can't stick their wet little fingers into an outlet.

Secure your windows: If you have blinds in your nursery, remove any decorative strings attached to them, and when you open or close them, make sure to secure the strings up high again. Additionally, your baby is going to climb out of curiosity. Remove any furniture that can help your baby get near the window.

Crib: Issue number one with cribs is safety standards. Yes, I know, cribs are pricey, but you should avoid your ancestral crib. Safety standards for cribs have changed and improvements have been made. The old drop-side models were painted with lead paint and their slats are too far apart.

Furthermore, the AAP advises against the use of crib bumpers and too many loose, soft items around your baby. Remove any extra blankets, duvets, pillows, and teddy bears from your baby's crib. You should also place your crib away from the wall and avoid hanging a mobile overhead. As your baby gets stronger and uses their surroundings to lift themselves, they'll pull anything down. You can hang pictures against the wall if you use earthquake-safe screws and your crib is away from the wall. Mobiles look cute, but they're a dangling hazard.

Feeding Safety

Food safety is another important aspect. I've compiled some advice on food safety that hasn't been mentioned yet, but if your baby was premature, had a low birth weight, or your baby's unhealthy, you need to speak to your pediatrician about this topic (NSW Food Authority, 2015).

When it comes to breastfeeding, make sure you follow the guidelines I provided earlier to store your milk properly, and keep your hands sanitized at all times. Formula should be prepared with sterilized hands, too. Wash your hands with warm water and antibacterial soap, and you should do the same with any countertops you use for preparation.

You should avoid using homemade formula, because this isn't restricted or regulated by FDA guidelines. Homemade formula often uses raw milk or raw milk products and contains several disease-causing organisms.

As far as solid foods go, you must avoid raw or partially-cooked eggs because they could contain salmonella. Eggs need to be hard-boiled and then mashed for your baby's consumption. Honey can't be fed to babies younger than 12 months, as this can cause botulism. Finally, salt can harm your baby's kidneys, because their kidneys are still developing and cannot expel the excess salt. Besides, your baby's taste buds are still developing, too, and they don't need to grow accustomed to salt and spices.

Every single utensil, cup, bottle, and nipple your baby eats with needs to be rinsed in cold water, washed in warm, antibacterial soapy water with a bottle brush, and then rinsed again before you sterilize them using steam or hot water. Fortunately, there are modern-day steamers for baby bottles which come with easy-to-follow instructions. Otherwise, you can boil all these eating utensils in a pot of water for two minutes and add a sterilizing agent purchased from your local drug store. Remember not to use excessive heat.

The Bathroom

Next, I'll focus on some bathroom safety tips (The Editors of Parents Magazine, n.d).

You can start securing your bathroom by removing any hazardous items. These can include razors, hair clips, toothbrushes, make-up, and soap. Fasten a shelf against the wall, out of reach of your baby, and place all these hazardous items on the shelf. Make sure they can't fall off the shelf by labeling some containers and placing all loose items inside. Remember that your baby will eat your soap. You can also secure your laundry basket against the wall so they don't crawl into it or topple it over on themselves, and do the same with the garbage bin. Finally, you should throw out any cat litter box, because your child will eat it. Your kitty will have to use their litter box outside.

Watch out for any water hazards. Get into the habit of running your water out after each bath, no matter how little water was used. You should secure all water outlets with padded child-proof knobs to prevent your baby from burning against the hot surface and opening the faucet. You should also check that your water heater isn't set above 120 degrees.

Next, you need to check all electrical outlets again and cover them once more. Hair dryers and electric shavers should be stored out of reach after every use. Hide all cords and wires that can wrap around any part of your baby or that your baby can chew on.

Your medicine cabinet needs a change, too. Yes, it's convenient to keep your medication in the bathroom, but you need to either place a lock on the cabinet or move it away from the basin and fasten it securely to a wall that has no climbing assistance underneath. The same goes for any cleaning chemicals or toiletries. These should all be placed in a child-proof, locked cabinet.

Finally, throw out your old bathroom rugs and replace them with rubberized non-slip rugs to secure your baby's first wobbly steps. You can use a rubber mat in the bathtub as well for when they start bathing in the tub.

The Front Garden and Backyard

The garden is another place many people forget to secure properly, but your baby will spend time there and it should be as safe as possible (How to Make Every Yard Safe, n.d).

Your garden can be a treacherous arena for your baby, and it's important to look at your groundcover and hazards. Start by removing all plant fertilizers and tools by placing them in a locked shed. Then you can look around your garden and remove any garden terrifying gnomes, sharp garden bed surroundings, and rocks. If they're fixed in the ground, dig them up and toss them.

Next, if you have a pool, make sure it's securely fenced in and there's no way for your baby to access it. You can also fence your wood pile, barbecue, and anything that doesn't go into your garden shed. Do away with any glass-top tables and metal outdoor chairs.

Finally, if you have a playground, make sure your swing or slide is surrounded by soft, shock-absorbing ground cover like grass or rubber mats. Avoid rope swings and use chain swings, instead. Additionally, make sure your slide ends where there's no hazards around and keep a sand pit covered from pets and bugs that will contaminate it.

General Safety Tips

Here are a few more safety tips to consider when your baby is around the house (Safety Inside and Outside the House, 2019).

You can prevent burns by keeping hot things out of reach, turning pot handles away from the edge of the counter, never allowing electrical cords like a kettle cord to hang within reach, using a fire guard around your fireplace and radiator, and removing tablecloths. In addition, keep lighters, matches, and Christmas tree lights away from your baby.

To prevent falls, you can round furniture corners or add pads to them, avoid allowing your baby to sleep on a bed instead of their crib, use the seatbelt in your highchair, and teach your baby to stop climbing up onto high things. Furthermore, you shouldn't leave your baby unattended on a high surface and install baby barriers or keep doors locked to keep them away from dangerous areas.

Sadly, as little as a few teaspoons of water can harm your baby, which is why you need to remove any pools of water that gather after some rain, never leave your baby unattended in water, and drain the baby splash pool when you're done.

Furthermore, you should avoid buying toys that aren't age appropriate. Your baby's toys should be checked regularly for splinters, sharp edges, and loose bits. You should buy soft or large toys with no small breakable parts. Keep safe toys low so your baby doesn't need to climb to reach it, and avoid walkers altogether. I know that sounds crazy but walkers have all those little buttons on the front that tend to break off and become a choking hazard.

Remember that your baby knows nothing and they need to be taught. Your baby will fall and bump their little noggin here and there; it's all part of learning. There's no need to panic — just remain vigilant and supervise your baby at all times. If you've taken all the necessary precautions, you can take a breath of relief because you've minimized the chances of accidents.

Unwell Baby: When to Seek Help

Let's face it, your baby will have a fever or vomit from time to time. I'll cover common reasons for seeking medical attention from your pediatrician in this section, because whether you're a new parent or a first-time parent, it remains challenging to identify an unwell baby. Here are some signs that your baby needs medical attention that haven't been covered yet in this book (Mayo Clinic Staff, 2019):

Fever: Your baby has a concerning fever if they are younger than three months; your three- to six-month-old baby's temperature is 102 degrees or higher and accompanied by other symptoms; your six-month-old baby's fever is above 102 with other symptoms; or there are no other symptoms and their fever persists for more than a day.

Tender navel or penis: Contact your pediatrician if your baby's navel or penis turns red and starts to bleed.

Dehydration: Additional signs of severe dehydration include a sunken soft spot on their head, dry mouth, and no tears when they cry.

Changes in appetite: Your baby's eating too little or has refused food for the last few feedings.

Changes in behavior: Your baby may cry more than usual, be more floppy, sleep more than they normally do, or they don't allow you to comfort their cries.

The common cold: It becomes worrisome when your baby's nasal mucus lasts longer than 10 to 14 days, they have trouble breathing, or they suffer from a cough or ear pain for more than a week.

Eye discharge: Watch out for red eyes that leak any form of mucus.

When to Seek Emergency Care

Before an incident happens, you can ask your doctor for advice on how to treat certain symptoms on your way to the hospital. After my own scare that Saturday night, I took a first aid course that specializes in babies. I paid $88 for it at the time, and I don't regret it one bit. It helped me cope with a few emergencies over the years while I was en route to the hospital. However, you should seek emergency care for any of the following signs or symptoms, because I'm not a licensed healthcare provider (Mayo Clinic Staff, 2019).

- Your baby's choking.

- They got burned with boiling water or against a hot surface.
- Your baby's having a seizure. They'll become less responsive and they may foam from their mouth.
- You can't stop their bleeding.
- They suffered an electrical shock from a power outlet or cord.
- Your baby's skin and face turned blue, purple, or grey.
- An animal or person bit them.
- They had a near-drowning incident in any amount of water.
- They suffered an injury to their head or face after a fall.
- If their skin or eye came into contact with any poisonous substance.
- If they inhaled a poisonous substance.
- If they accidentally consumed a poisonous substance.
- If their breathing is labored or they've stopped breathing. Your baby will need cardiopulmonary resuscitation (CPR). This is one of the first things they teach you with first aid, and I suggest you take a class.

However, it's important to know why your baby's in the condition they're in. The medical staff can help your baby faster if you know what happened. These are questions they may ask you upon arrival at the emergency room.

1. What symptoms does your baby have?

2. What's your baby's medical history? (Having their history at hand is a great idea. Make sure it's always ready in the car.)
3. Has your baby had any changes in their feeding, bowel movements, or temperature?
4. Have you tried any home remedies we need to be aware of?
5. What possible toxins, environmental factors, foods, or dangerous elements has your baby been exposed to?

Keep in mind that when your baby needs urgent care, the best thing you can do is keep a clear head and do what needs to be done. Standing in a corner and freaking out won't help your baby. Allow your autopilot to take over and steer yourself to a solution.

Traveling With an Infant

Finally, I'd like to cover travel tips for you and your baby. Having a baby doesn't mean you don't have to travel, you should just be better prepared before you do (Wears, 2013).

If you're planning to fly, there are a few things to consider. Call the airline and check whether the flight is fully booked. If it isn't, ask them to block off the middle seat and book the aisle and window seat. You'll want some space for supplies and your partner can have the aisle seat opposite you. You'll also need your car seat, and you should make sure it's up to standard with flying regulations — not all of them are. Don't forget to let the airline know that you'll be traveling with your baby.

Pack well for a flight, because airlines charge for extra luggage — and your stroller and car seat are considered extra luggage. Take into consideration your hand luggage, too, because you'll need baby essentials more than your make-up bag. Another item I packed was extra cotton wool. Flights can make babies' ears hurt and you can use cotton wool soaked in warm water to insert into their ears to help. Besides the essentials, you'll need entertainment for your baby to distract them from boredom and crying, so pack a toy or two in your hand luggage that you can use to play with your baby.

If you're traveling abroad, pack your formula, breast pump, and baby foods into your luggage. Just remember to include these food items on your declaration checklist. Chances are, they won't have the formula or food your baby loves and you'll have trouble feeding them. Next, you can pack the stroller that suits your trip. If you're stopping multiple times on your journey, pack a light, easily foldable stroller. However, if you're doing a lot of sightseeing when you get there, you may need a stronger stroller in which your baby can nap. Furthermore, a car seat is required by law in most countries, so don't forget your car seat even if your cruising over on a ship.

Call your hotel before you confirm your booking and tell them about your baby. You can request a room that's away from others so your baby won't cry people awake, and you can ask them if their rooms are baby-friendly with cribs.

Finally, make sure you plan ahead for your baby's vaccinations. They may need additional shots, depending on your destination. Do your homework and ensure a memorable holiday for all of you.

Conclusion

Congratulations, you've made it — and don't you simply feel relieved now? Before you started this book, you were in a state of confusion and doubt. You struggled to believe in yourself and your ability to bring a beautiful, healthy baby into this world and raise them for the first 12 months. You were overwhelmed by worries about pregnancy and all it entails. Even if this is your second baby, you weren't sure about your previous knowledge and methodology. You never expected to feel those underlying concerns a second or third time around, yet, they were present. If you're new to being a parent, you saw parenthood as an insurmountable task ahead of you. You didn't believe that you had it in you to overcome that terrifyingly big obstacle.

You found yourself staring up at a giant, barely able to catch your breath. You could feel your feet slipping over the edge of pre- and postnatal sanity. You weren't sure how you would carry another human being inside of you. You questioned how your body could handle two people at once. You found yourself worrying about your health during pregnancy, and the health of your baby before and after pregnancy. Suddenly, your mind was flooded with ideas about what to do after your baby was born. You felt weak and uneducated, whether you'd been a parent before or not, whether you're an expectant mother or father.

However, after finishing this book, you feel a strong sense of freedom from these horrid concerns, and you know you're ready for whatever pregnancy and the first year of your baby's life can throw your way. Among many topics, we've covered essential know-how in this book, including:

- Choosing the right doctor or midwife for your pregnancy;
- An in-depth look at your prenatal check-ups;
- All the medication, supplements, and the best diet for your pregnancy journey;
- The impact of your possible smoking, caffeine, and alcoholic habits;
- Finding rest and preparing for the big day;
- Realistic expectations of the first 24 hours and the 12 months that follow;
- Postnatal care and essential check-ups;
- What to do and what not to do;
- Immunizations and how they impact your baby;
- Recovering from the birth of your baby;
- The need-to-know basics of your baby's skincare, health, hygiene, and nutrition;
- Concerns about baby illnesses and red flag alerts;
- Securing your baby's environment to keep them safe.

I know how challenging motherhood or fatherhood can be, and that's why this book covers all the topics I know concerned me. There are typical questions all parents-to-be will want answered, and I've provided straightforward knowledge and experience to correctly portray solutions. You might find yourself doubting something your mother told you. Here, I've used information from reliable and modern sources to back my own experience and knowledge. There are things I learned while writing this book that helped me understand the reason why my baby had those vaccinations. The average Joe doesn't know the scientific reasons behind them and will think it's okay to skip one.

I've come across information on pregnancy that I didn't know and other data that I did. I can guarantee you that the knowledge shared in this book helped you heal your C-section wound, reminded you of every item you needed on the first day, prevented harm from befalling your baby, taught you how to hold your baby correctly when breastfeeding, and explained useful methods to bond with your baby. Additionally, it helped you overcome concerns about what you'll do when your baby falls ill after hours, what foods to avoid while pregnant, what foods to avoid giving your baby, and how to distinguish one skin condition from another.

Furthermore, you've learned about what's normal in your baby's urine, birthmarks, common ailments, and when to call your pediatrician. We've covered questions and answers that needed to be asked, which helped you choose your doctor. You found comfort in knowing that you can hold your baby a certain way, you can use certain methods to help them sleep, and you've even prepared for childcare if you do go back to work or just need a night off. Your brain has soaked up enough information to give you the best chance of providing the greatest future to your baby.

Here comes the most difficult part. This book is filled with information that can only allow you to take a step forward. However, if there's one thing I want you to take away from this book, it's that you need to ask for help when you're unsure about anything. There's absolutely no shame in seeking assistance from a friend, a family member, your partner, or even a support group you may be part of. I could never imagine having completed my pregnancy journey, or the first year, if my loving partner hadn't been by my side.

If you choose to delve deeper into any concerns you may have, make sure you confirm your findings. Google is a wonderful tool, but anything you find online should be checked with your supportive partner, evidence-based facts, or other people you confide in. So go out there and gather up your support group, keep this book close by for reference, and take the bull by its horns.

References Section 2

10 Reasons to Get Vaccinated (n.d) Retrieved from www.nfid.org/immunization/10-reasons-to-get-vaccinated/

11 Ways to Handle New Baby Stress. (January 11, 2018) Retrieved from https://blog.pregakem.com/handle-new-baby-stress.html

Alli, R.A. (February 25, 2019) Get the Facts About Bottle Feeding. Retrieved from www.webmd.com/parenting/baby/ss/slideshow-baby-bottles

American College of Obstetricians and Gynecologists (June 2019) Travel During Pregnancy. Retrieved from www.acog.org/Patients/FAQs/Travel-During-Pregnancy?IsMobileSet=falseWorking

American Pregnancy Association (2019) Diet During Pregnancy. Retrieved from https://americanpregnancy.org/pregnancy-health/diet-during-pregnancy/

American Pregnancy Association (2019) Eating Seafood During Pregnancy. Retrieved from https://americanpregnancy.org/pregnancy-health/eating-seafood-during-pregnancy/

American Pregnancy Association (2019) Getting Sick While Pregnant. Retrieved from https://americanpregnancy.org/pregnancy-complications/sick-while-pregnant/

American Pregnancy Association (2019) Natural Sources of Vitamin B6 During Pregnancy. Retrieved from https://americanpregnancy.org/pregnancy-health/natural-sources-of-vitamin-b6-during-pregnancy/

American Pregnancy Association (2019) Pregnancy Nutrition. Retrieved from https://americanpregnancy.org/pregnancy-health/pregnancy-nutrition/

American Pregnancy Association (2019) Types of Prenatal Vitamins. Retrieved from https://americanpregnancy.org/pregnancy-health/types-prenatal-vitamins/

American Pregnancy Association (2019) Vitamin D and Pregnancy. Retrieved from https://americanpregnancy.org/pregnancy-health/vitamin-d-and-pregnancy/

Apgar Score (October, 2017) Retrieved from www.pregnancybirthbaby.org.au/apgar-score

Arora, M. (August 16, 2019) Bottle Feeding Advantages and Disadvantages. Retrieved from https://parenting.firstcry.com/articles/bottle-feeding-advantages-and-disadvantages/

Avery, N. (2018) 10 Tips for Coping with a New Baby. Retrieved from https://planningwithkids.com/2009/05/12/10-tips-for-coping-with-a-new-baby/

Baby's First 24 Hours (June, 2018) Retrieved from www.pregnancybirthbaby.org.au/babys-first-24-hours

Bell, K. (2009) Diaper Duty Essentials: What's Normal? Retrieved from www.parents.com/baby/diapers/dirty/diaper-duty-essentials-whats-normal/

Bloch, E. (n.d) Are Generic Formulas as Good as Brand Names? Retrieved from www.parents.com/baby/feeding/are-generic-formulas-as-good-as-name-brands/

Boyd-Barret, C. & Alrahmani, L. (October 28, 2019) C-section healing and recovery time. Retrieved from www.babycenter.com/0_recovering-from-a-c-section_221.bc

Breastfeeding at Work (n.d) Retrieved from www.ameda.com/milk-101-article/breastfeeding-at-work/

Breastfeeding Overview (2019) P. 1–5. Retrieved from www.webmd.com/parenting/baby/nursing-basics#1-2

Breast Pumping Guide: When and How Long to Pump (n.d) Retrieved from www.ameda.com/milk-101-article/when-and-how-long-to-pump/

Breastmilk Storage Guidelines: How to Store Milk Safely (n.d) Retrieved from www.ameda.com/milk-101-article/how-to-store-breast-milk-safely/

Carepoint Health (February 17, 2015) Surviving pregnancy without your favorite vices. Retrieved from https://carepointhealth.org/surviving-pregnancy-without-favorite-vices/

Centers for Disease Control and Prevention (February 5, 2019) 2019 Recommended Vaccinations for Infants and Children (birth through 6 years) Parent-Friendly Format. Retrieved from www.cdc.gov/vaccines/schedules/easy-to-read/child-easyread.html#table-child

Check-ups, tests and scans available during your pregnancy (2018) Retrieved from www.pregnancybirthbaby.org.au/checkups-and-scans-during-your-pregnancy

Childbirth Connection (2016) What to Ask a Midwife Who Might Provide Your Maternity Care. Retrieved from www.nationalpartnership.org/research-library/maternal-health/what-to-ask-midwife.pdf

Childbirth Connection (2016) What to Ask a Physician Who May Provide Your Maternity Care. Retrieved from www.nationalpartnership.org/research-library/maternal-health/what-to-ask-physician.pdf

Childbirth Connection (n.d) Retrieved from www.childbirthconnection.org/healthy-pregnancy/choosing-a-care-provider/collecting-information/

Cleveland Clinic (September 24, 2018) Pregnancy Bed Rest. Retrieved from https://my.clevelandclinic.org/health/articles/9757-pregnancy-bed-rest

DeStefano, F.; Price, C.S.; & Weintraub, E.S. (2013) The Journal of Pediatrics. P. 561. Increasing Exposure to Antibody-Stimulating Proteins and Polysaccharides in Vaccines is Not Associated with Risk of Autism. Retrieved from www.jpeds.com/article/S0022-3476(13)00144-3/pdf?ext=.pdf

Ding, K. (2019) Sleep Deprivation and New Parents. Retrieved from https://consumer.healthday.com/encyclopedia/parenting-31/parenting-health-news-525/sleep-deprivation-and-new-parents-643886.html

Dorning, A. (March 20, 2019) Childcare Options: Pros, Cons, and Costs. Retrieved from www.babycenter.com/childcare-options

Flaxman, S.M. & Sherman, P.W. (June, 2000) The Quarterly Review of Biology. Vol. 75, No. 2, P. 113-148

Fritz, A. (October 14, 2019) The Best Maternity Underwear to Keep You Comfortable Throughout Your Pregnancy. Retrieved from www.whattoexpect.com/baby-products/pregnancy/maternity-underwear/

Hodnett, E.D. (2002) Pain and women's satisfaction with the experience of childbirth: a systematic review. Retrieved from www.ncbi.nih.gov/m/pubmed/12011880/#

How to Make Every Yard Safe (n.d) Retrieved from www.safetyed.org/howtomakeeveryyardsafe.html#.XeYP70BuLIV?

How Vaccines Work (2019) Retrieved from www.publichealth.org/public-awareness/understanding-vaccines/vaccines-work/

Introducing Solid Foods to Your Baby (June 11, 2019) Retrieved from www.healthlinkbc.ca/health-topics/te4473

Immunisation Side Effects (April, 2018) Retrieved from www.betterhealth.vic.gov.au/health/healthyliving/immunisation-side-effects

Johnson, T.C. (May 16, 2018) Pregnancy Fitness: Your Best Moves Before Baby Arrives. Retrieved from www.webmd.com/baby/ss/slideshow-pregnancy-fitness-moves

Khan, A. (June 20, 2018) Washing Your Baby's Clothes – How to do it Rightly. Retrieved from https://parenting.firstcry.com/articles/washing-your-babys-clothes-how-to-do-it-rightly/

Khan, A. (May 22, 2018) 21 Common Pregnancy Problems and Their Solutions. Retrieved from https://parenting.firstcry.com/articles/21-common-pregnancy-problems-and-their-solutions/

Klein, M. (1993) The effectiveness of family practice maternity care. Primary Care, Iss 20 (3), P. 523–536.

Louie, K. (August 20, 2018) Best Pregnancy-Safe Makeup and Beauty Products. Retrieved from www.whattoexpect.com/maternity-products/beauty/best-pregnancy-safe-makeup/

Marcin, A. & Westphalen, D. (September 14, 2018) What Medicines Can I Take While Pregnant? Retrieved from www.healthline.com/health/pregnancy/what-medicines-are-safe-during-pregnancy

Maternity Leave in the United States (November 26, 2019) Retrieved from https://en.wikipedia.org/wiki/Maternity_leave_in_the_United_States#Current_legislation

Mayo Clinic Staff (August 13, 2019) Sick Baby? When to Seek Medical Attention. Retrieved from www.mayoclinic.org/healthy-lifestyle/infant-and-toddler-health/in-depth/healthy-baby/art-20047793

Mayo Clinic Staff (February 17, 2018) Umbilical Cord Care: Do's and Don'ts for Parents. Retrieved from www.mayoclinic.org/healthy-lifestyle/infant-and-toddler-health/in-depth/umbilical-cord/art-20048250

Mayo Clinic Staff (June 6, 2019) Solid foods: How to get your baby started. Retrieved from www.mayoclinic.org/healthy-lifestyle/infant-and-toddler-health/in-depth/healthy-baby/art-20046200

Miller, K. (January 31, 2019) 7 Ways to Make Sleep More Comfortable When You're Pregnant. Retrieved from www.self.com/story/pregnancy-sleep-comfort

Montgomery, N. (January 9, 2019) How to Trim Your Baby's Nails. Retrieved from www.babycenter.com/0_how-to-trim-your-babys-nails_10027.bc

Murkoff, H. & The What to Expect Editors (December 19, 2018) Newborn Circumcision Care. Retrieved from www.whattoexpect.com/first-year/circumcision-care

Murkoff, H. & The What to Expect Editors (January 9, 2019) Essentials for Diaper Changing Stations. Retrieved from www.whattoexpect.com/baby-products/diapering-potty/essentials-for-diaper-changing-stations/

Murkoff, H. & The What to Expect Editors (March 30, 2019) Baby's First Bath. Retrieved from www.whattoexpect.com/first-year/first-bath/

Murkoff, H. & The What to Expect Editors (November 27, 2018) 5 Strategies for Working While Pregnant. Retrieved from www.whattoexpect.com/pregnancy/working-while-pregnant

Nagin, M.K. & Shur, M. (November 13, 2019) Self-Care for the Breastfeeding Mother. Retrieved from www.verywellfamily.com/taking-care-of-the-breastfeeding-mother-431683

Newborn Rashes and Skin Conditions (December 12, 2018) Retrieved from www.uofmhealth.org/health-library/zx1747

Nishapro (May 4, 2018) Shopping Tips for Newborn Baby's Clothes. Retrieved from https://community.today.com/parentingteam/post/shopping-tips-for-newborn-babys-clothes

NSW Food Authority (March, 2015) Retrieved from www.sahealth.sa.gov.au/wps/wcm/connect/5514158047d940a7ac79adfc651ee2b2/Feeding+babies+and+food+safety+Fact+Sheet.pdf?MOD=AJPERES

Pillai, S. (November 8, 2019) 5 Reasons Why it is Unsafe to Have Deli Meats in Pregnancy. Retrieved from www.momjunction.com/articles/is-it-safe-to-eat-deli-meats-during-pregnancy_00118527/#gref

Recovery After Vaginal Birth (August, 2017) Retrieved from www.babycentre.co.uk/a553491/recovery-after-vaginal-birth

Reutter, K. (November 16, 2018) 8 Ways to Treat Morning Sickness Naturally. Retrieved from www.onemedical.com/blog/get-well/natural-morning-sickness-remedies

Rhesus D Negative in Pregnancy (May, 2018) Retrieved from www.pregnancybirthbaby.org.au/rhesus-d-negative-in-pregnancy

Safety Inside and Outside the House (September 24, 2019) Retrieved from www.facs.nsw.gov.au/families/parenting/keeping-children-safe/around-the-house/chapters/at-home

Schmitt, J.W. (April 1, 2019) Prenatal Care. Retrieved from www.womenshealth.gov/a-z-topics/prenatal-care

Sheahan, K.P. (September, 2019) Choosing a Pediatrician for Your New Baby. Retrieved from https://kidshealth.org/en/parents/find-ped.html

Shortsleeve, C. (June 10, 2019) The Best Maternity Jeans for Every Body Type. Retrieved from www.whattoexpect.com/baby-products/maternity/best-maternity-jeans/

SickKids Staff (January 7, 2019) Health Issues in Your Newborn Baby. Retrieved from www.aboutkidshealth.ca/Article?contentid=453&language=English

St Clair DiLaura, A. (n.d) Creating a Safe Nursery: 10 Mistakes to Avoid. Retrieved from www.babycenter.com/101_creating-a-safe-nursery-10-mistakes-to-avoid_10414382.bc

Tellado, M.P. (September, 2019) Diaper Rash. Retrieved from https://kidshealth.org/en/parents/diaper-rash.html

The Editors of Parents Magazine (n.d) 5 Things You Can Do to Get a Safer Bathroom. Retrieved from www.parents.com/baby/safety/bathroom/bathroom-safety-basics/

The Ultimate Maternity Hospital Bag Checklist (May 1, 2019) Retrieved from www.pampers.com/en-us/pregnancy/giving-birth/article/what-to-pack-in-your-hospital-bag-go-bag-checklist

UPMC Magee-Women's Hospital (March 23, 2016) How Smoking, Alcohol, and Drugs Can Harm Your Baby. Retrieved from https://share.upmc.com/2016/03/how-smoking-alcohol-drugs-harm-your-baby/

Vaccine Safety (October 22, 2018) Retrieved from www.cdc.gov/vaccinesafety/concerns/adjuvants.html

Vitamin K at Birth (June, 2018) www.pregnancybirthbaby.org.au/vitamin-k-at-birth

Weaning Your Child from Breastfeeding (June, 2019) Retrieved from www.caringforkids.cps.ca/handouts/weaning_breastfeeding

Wears, C. (September 2, 2013) Traveling with an Infant: 8 Things You Must Know Before You Go. Retrieved from www.flightnetwork.com/blog/traveling-with-an-infant-things-to-know-before-you-go/

What a Newborn Looks Like (August, 2017) Retrieved from www.babycentre.co.uk/a178/what-a-newborn-looks-like

What is Newborn Screening? (November 26, 2019) Retrieved from https://ghr.nlm.nih.gov/primer/newbornscreening/nbs

What to Expect Editors (May 21, 2019) Prenatal Appointments.
www.whattoexpect.com/pregnancy/pregnancy-health/prenatal-appointments/

Yang, S. (2019) Baby's Check-Up Schedule. Retrieved from www.thebump.com/a/new-baby-doctor-visit-checklist

Section 3: Smooth Transition to Parenthood for First Time Mothers and Fathers

How to Adapt and Embrace your New Life as a Parent without Stress and Worries

Regular exercise has numerous health benefits, all of which apply equally to new mothers as at any other stage of life. Some of the benefits are weight loss, increased aerobic fitness, social interaction, and psychological wellbeing. Exercises after giving birth can also speed up recovery and assist with muscle strength and toning.

Always consult with your doctor before starting any postnatal exercise program. Whether or not you are ready to exercise depends on individual factors. For instance, you may be advised to wait until your six-week postnatal check-up. In other cases, especially if you were exercising regularly throughout your pregnancy, you may be able to return to exercise sooner than that, perhaps within the first week or two.

Here are some of the benefits of postnatal workout to your health and your fast recovery.

- It can improve your physical and mental wellbeing.
- Help restore muscle strength and firm up your body
- Make you less tired because it raises your energy level and improves your sense of wellbeing
- Promote weight loss
- Improve your cardiovascular fitness and restore muscle strength
- Condition your abdominal muscles
- Improve your mood, relieve stress and help prevent postpartum depression.

So, get your **"36 Minute Postnatal No Equipment Workout"** in MP4 (video) format for free by clicking the entering the link or scanning the QR Code below:

https://harleycarrparenting.com/a-smooth-transition-to-parenthood-book

or

- Download the video
- Watch it and follow the workout steps
- This Postnatal workout is only 36 minutes and you can do it in the comfort of your home without using any equipment
- Do it everyday

Let´s get started …

Enjoy and Best Wishes to your Parenting Journey!
Harley Carr

Introduction

Welcoming a baby and entering parenthood is the beginning of a new chapter in your life. It is a significant change, and your life will change in ways you may not have imagined. As daunting as parenthood may sound, it is all good and there is nothing to worry about. However, learning to deal with this new change is an essential aspect of becoming a new parent. A common problem a lot of expectant parents as well as new parents face is the lack of confidence and knowledge on what to expect. This, in turn, can make it difficult to cope with all the changes that parenthood brings about.

Where is the instruction manual? Will I be a good parent? How will my life change? Will I ever lose this pregnancy weight? To breastfeed or not to breastfeed? Am I a bad parent because....? These are just some of the questions every first-time parent has. If you have them, don't worry, you aren't alone. Forget about all unrealistic advice you might have come across, this book has everything you need to cope with the days and months ahead as you enter parenthood.

In this book, you will learn about all the possible changes that can crop up when you are a parent. Learning about what you can expect makes it easier to cope with these changes. You will learn about dealing with the different aspects of your life, physical, emotional, and mental, that change once you are a parent. Being armed with all the information will make you feel in control of your life. Instead of being caught unawares, you will be better prepared to deal with any possible challenges that crop up.

How do I know all this? Well, as a mother of 3 children, I have had plenty of experience dealing with the post-pregnancy phase. Hello! My name is Harley Carr, and as a mother of three kids aged 8, 5, and 3, I know a thing or two about parenthood. Raising a child, let alone three, is quite a challenging role. You will be responsible for your young one's well-being, and that's an added responsibility. I faced plenty of challenges and difficulties after my first pregnancy. There were different life-altering questions I had to answer.

The toughest choice of all was to decide whether to resume work or become a stay at home mom. I couldn't bear the thought of spending even a minute away from my newborn. So, I chose to stay at home and become a full-time mom, and the rest is history. It was perhaps the best decision I ever made. I love spending time with my children, and they keep me fully occupied. From changing diapers to late-night feeding sessions while managing a house and concentrating on my personal relationships, I have dealt with it all. I wouldn't have been able to do all this if I didn't have the support of my partner and our family.

In this book, I will share insights, tips, and tactics you can use to deal with and manage all the challenges during your baby's first year. Apart from this, you will also learn about coping with different struggles and challenges of parenthood and how you should embrace it with open arms. Becoming a mother is one of the most rewarding feelings ever. When you welcome your little bundle of joy into your life, it will change you. No, this is not a scary change, and I will guide you through every step of the way. You can rest easy knowing that you aren't alone.

In this book, you will find all the information you require to address all your needs during the first year of your baby's life. It will prepare you for parenthood. Once you are armed with all of this knowledge, it becomes easier to deal with the challenges that come your way. It will make you feel more confident to face and adapt to the changes in your life as a new parent.

You will experience a rather potent mix of overwhelming emotions as you step into parenthood. This book will help you deal with it all. Apart from this, you will learn about simple tips you can use to strengthen and nurture a relationship with your partner. Learning to cope with and balance all the different aspects of your life is essential, and even more so after you become a mom.

Do you want to learn to deal with all the mixed emotions you might be feeling right now? Do you want to learn to secrets to rekindling the romance in your life after pregnancy? Do you want to learn about the right way to get back to shape after pregnancy? Do you want to learn to manage your expectations about yourself and your partner? If yes, then look no further, because this is the perfect book for you!

So, if you are eager and excited to learn more, let us get started without further ado!

Part 1: Adjusting to Parenthood

Becoming a parent is a major transition in your life. In fact, it might be one of the most challenging transitions ever. I know it can take some time to get used to the new reality - emotionally, mentally, and physically. All of a sudden, you are now responsible not just for your well-being, but for your baby's too. The best way to get adjusted to all these changes is to understand what you can expect along the way.

Adjusting to parenthood is a gradual process. Even if you feel a little lost initially, you will slowly find your footing. Being a parent is an ongoing process and it never truly ends. You will always be a parent to your child. You will keep learning and discovering new things about yourself, your partner, and your child. This process never ends and unless you make your peace with it, it will be a little tricky. The good news is that parenthood brings with it an immense sense of satisfaction and happiness.

In the first section of this book, you will learn about certain tips and strategies you can use to get accustomed to parenthood.

Chapter 1: Becoming a Parent! What to Expect?

For Moms

Changes in life

Giving birth will change you; it will change your priorities and your life in general. Various issues will become a priority during different phases of your life. Life without a baby is quite different from life with a newborn, and life with a toddler is different from living with a teenager. Before you entered parenthood, professional growth might have been one of your priorities. However, once you become a parent, you might have to start considering how you can balance your professional life with your personal life and the newfound responsibility of parenthood. If you were working, then you will have to reconsider all your priorities and decide whether you want to take a break from work or keep working.

The person you were before becoming a mom will be quite different from the person you are right now. When I look back, I realize how much I have changed. I'm not complaining about the life I have now, but I know it is quite different from what I was used to. I love being a full-time mom, and I have no regrets about it. Once again, it is a personal decision, and you're the only one who can determine how your life will change. There are various changes you will have to deal with.

Not just emotional ones, but physical and mental ones as well. Even science agrees that there are certain physiological changes associated with pregnancy and birth. You don't have to be afraid of all these changes, as changes are a natural part of life. Change is also a sign of growth.

Priorities change

Every mother will agree that pregnancy and the birth of a child has changed her in one way or the other. During the course of pregnancy, you have plenty of time to think and worry about maybe losing your sense of identity. However, once you hold your child in your arms, you will not have much time to think about all these things. Why? Because life is happening right this instant. As a mother, I know that my life is happier and richer because of my children. They added an additional dimension of love to my life that I never knew I needed. Now, I cannot imagine my life without them.

There were times when I used to miss my private time and old life. Life with a child is certainly quite busy and hectic. Well, everyone needs a little "me" time, and this is true for moms as well. A lot of my single friends used to ask me if I would want to change anything about my life. I am telling you exactly what I used to tell them: "I love my life, and I wouldn't have it any other way." I would trade a hundred years the other way instead of giving up spending time with my children. They make me a better person, and I am more "me" than I ever was.

My children certainly changed me. They made me emotionally vulnerable and empathetic towards others. I wasn't an extremely emotional person, but now that I have my kids, I have become emotionally attached. Emotional detachment is a thing of the past, and I am glad I am more in touch with my emotions than I ever was. I remember times when I used to watch any news on TV about children in distress, or any suffering. I was quite passive towards it, and it did not bother me. I did feel a little sad, but that's about it. I couldn't exactly understand what those news stories portrayed, and there was always a sense of disconnection.

Now that I am a mother, I feel deeply about these issues. These days, I try to do my bit for the needy. Before having kids, I used to worry about not having sufficient money to buy fancy clothes, go on exotic holidays, and so on. I was worried my life was boring and that I wasn't cool enough. These days, I worry about whether I will be able to provide my kids with everything they will ever need. Even if you're not especially fond of kids, it will all change once you are a mother. The first time you hold your little baby in your arms, you will experience this overwhelming and powerful urge to protect the little one. The kind of love that you cannot express in words and which is quite hard to understand. I know how much I have changed because of the love I have for my children. I didn't even know I was capable of experiencing such a powerful feeling of love. Yes, I love my partner, parents, and even myself. But the love I have for my children is something new. That was the moment when the phrase "mother's love" finally made sense to me.

At my core, I am the same person I always was. My beliefs are the same, but my outlook on life has changed. Life seems more real, beautiful, peaceful, and better. So, be prepared for a drastic change in your priorities, but also be prepared to welcome and embrace the joys of motherhood.

Good or bad change?

Pregnancy isn't a hurdle; it merely changes the course of your life. This change is always for the better. You don't have to worry about compromising on any aspect of your life. You must come up with new ways to do whatever you love. It all depends on your perspective. If you keep a positive mindset, this change will seem positive, and a negative mindset will fester more negativity. For instance, before parenthood, I was not used to waking up early in the morning. These days, I wake up early in the morning and exercise too. After all, I need to set a good example for my kids. I know I am a better person today than I ever was, and it is mostly because of the ways motherhood has changed me. So, I think you don't have to be scared of this change and, instead, should come up with ways in which you can deal with it.

Emotions

You will experience a variety of emotions when you become a

mother. You might feel happy, anxious, worried, nostalgic, and so on the minute you see your baby's face. I know I did. It is your first meeting with your baby who will, from that moment on, become the center of your universe. You might not know how to react, and it will certainly be a lot to process. Most of these emotional changes are directly associated with the fluctuations in the endocrine system. It, in turn, is often the cause for postpartum depression or baby blues.

The oxytocin levels in your body tend to increase right after giving birth. This chemical released by your brain is a love-inducing hormone. The love that you feel for your child and the protective instinct that comes over you whenever you look at your little one are all because of this chemical. After pregnancy, you not only have to deal with plenty of physical changes, but even emotional ones. On a psychological level, welcoming a baby into your family is a significant life event, and it can leave you feeling a little blue. No two people are alike, and the way we all process life-changing events is quite different.

Remember that you are not obligated to feel happy and excited all the time. You are entitled to feel whatever you want to feel. If you're feeling unfulfilled after the pregnancy period, it is known as postpartum depression. If you're feeling a little low, all that it means is that you need a while longer to feel better. So, give yourself the time to feel like yourself once again. You probably need a while to get used to the new situation, but don't allow this to make you feel guilty. You are entitled to your emotions, and you don't have to suppress them because you are worried about what others might say. You don't owe anyone any apologies for feeling under the weather. This is often the phase wherein new mothers resign themselves to their feelings of being a "bad mother." Before you start feeling guilty for something you haven't voluntarily done, try to consciously understand why you are feeling the way you are feeling. During this period, you will need plenty of support from your partner, family members, friends, and other loved ones. They will be your support system, and they will help you get used to the new changes in your life.

Let's try to understand how the postpartum mind works, and you will be better equipped to deal with it. Expectant mothers, especially first time mothers usually have lofty and unrealistic expectations about motherhood. After all, for the last nine months, they have been repeatedly told about how joyous, exciting, and amazing motherhood will be. So, you eagerly await the moment you can be the happiest person on Earth. Then comes along the baby, and you hold your little one in your arms, and you don't experience the euphoria you are expecting. The lack of this feeling can make you feel sad, strange, confused, and even guilty. Weren't you supposed to feel extremely happy?

Well, becoming a mother is one of the most amazing moments you will ever experience, but everyone is different. Different women require varying timeframes to get used to their new roles and situations. My reaction after giving birth was always different. I experienced different emotions and feelings with each pregnancy. Therefore, I suggest that you cut yourself some slack and don't worry too much about what you are supposed to feel. Try to keep a positive attitude, surround yourself with your loved ones, and you will feel better.

For Dads or Partners

Pregnancy is undoubtedly a significant change for a woman, but this doesn't mean it is any less overwhelming for their partners as well. A lot of first-time dads also experience a variety of emotions and feelings. The way you might have felt shocked, anxious, excited, and even scared, your partner has felt it too. After all, even your partner's life is about to change. Even he needs to prepare for the pregnancy. So, it is time to concentrate on your partner. He might be experiencing a variety of emotions like guilt for feeling unprepared and anxious too. Sit down with your partner and discuss what the future will be like. You need to be his support system, the way he will be yours. He needs to be comfortable with this process, or he might end up panicking. A little preparation, and plenty of open discussions about what lies ahead will be quite helpful. Here are a couple of questions he might be thinking about.

When I first found out that I was pregnant, my husband and I were quite thrilled. However, after a couple of days, I noticed that he was always anxious. When I asked him, he looked at me with a frightened expression and asked, "Am I capable of taking care of our baby?" His question caught me off-guard, but I realized his worries are justified. Most expectant mothers are so caught up in their own emotions that they forget about their partner.

Babies don't come with manuals. An expectant parent doesn't always have to know everything about pregnancy, childbirth, and parenting. There are classes you can attend, but parenthood is a continuous process. It doesn't end after a specific exam, and it is a full-time job. A lot of first-time dads tend to experience nervousness and anxiety because they don't know what to expect. You both can join a class to prepare yourselves for different stages of pregnancy, from handling labor to changing diapers. Once your partner knows that he can do all this, he will feel more confident. Encourage him to reach out to you, his family, and loved ones for some support. It is an emotionally challenging time for him, as well.

Another question a lot of first-time dads wonder is whether they will be good dads or not. The way you keep wondering about it, your partner does as well. Fatherhood is like any other new role he might have to take on in life. It takes effort, practice, and plenty of experience. I know my partner, and I have come a long way since our first pregnancy. We do face a little self-doubt now and then, but now we know that there is no instruction manual about raising kids. You can read all that you want, but ultimately, it all depends on you, your partner, and your child. So, if you notice that your partner is experiencing self-doubt, you have to reassure him.

Your partner might be worried about the finances, as well. After all, thinking about all the expenses you both will need to accumulate as the child grows up can be a little scary and overwhelming. However, there are a couple of things you can do together to reduce the financial burden and stress. Start planning ahead. Create a college fund for your child, along with an emergency fund. Start planning your finances to reduce unnecessary stress. If you want, you can consult a financial planner as well and come up with a plan to tackle all the financial issues that lay ahead. Once you are prepared and have a rough idea about the kind of expenses you will incur, you will be better equipped to deal with it.

The way you might be worrying that parenthood is the end of your independence, your partner will also be worrying about the same thing. You don't need to feel guilty about thinking this. After all, your life is about to change, and it will be a significant change. Therefore, start talking about these things. You don't necessarily have to compromise on your lifestyle or your independence, merely because you are both parents. However, your list of priorities is bound to change. True, during the initial phases, you both will need to give up on a little sleep and deal with tiredness as well. As your baby grows, it will all become easier. Start working together and communicating about all the shared responsibilities and duties you will each need to take up when the child comes along. It is the best way to ensure that neither of you is overburdened. It would be a good idea to meet other expectant parents as well as. When you talk to others who are in the same situation that you are in, you will feel better. You will realize that you aren't alone.

Pregnant women tend to experience drastic emotional changes. As the pregnancy progresses, you and your partner might both feel emotionally overwhelmed. Keep in mind that he not only has to deal with his emotions, but even your mood swings as well. Therefore, be a little empathetic towards him. After all, he is also going through the same changes that you are. Even if he doesn't understand what you're going through physically, emotionally you both are on the same page. Be kind to each other and love each other. After all, you are supporting each other.

Spend some time together, and think about ways in which you can support each other. Ensure that neither of you is being judgmental and narrow-minded while the other is talking. Even if you don't agree with everything your partner says listen to him. He will feel better after expressing himself. He must not be scared to share his thoughts and opinions about the pregnancy and what the future holds. After all, if not you, whom will he go to? Ensure that the channels of communication between you and your partner are always open and free. Don't be scared of how he will react. He must not be afraid of how you will respond. Start spending as much time together as you possibly can. This is the best way to prepare yourself for the pregnancy.

Make a conscious effort to keep your relationship stable even when the baby comes along. Until now, it was just you and your partner, and that meant you both had all the time in the world for each other. Once you have a baby, this is about to change. Your priorities will change, and so will your partner's. Even if your partner's preferences have not drastically changed, he will need to deal with your changing priorities. It is important to concentrate on the baby, but it is also essential to concentrate on each other. If your partner feels left out or unwanted, he will start withdrawing. Be kind to him and talk to him about things. You never know, he might be more scared than you are. Encourage him to share his feelings with you. And when he does, don't be harsh towards him.

Tell him about how he can help you. Talk to him about your needs as well. Encourage him to do the same.

Chapter 2: Adjusting to Changes

Things will be different after pregnancy. Not just physically, but emotionally too. Apart from this, there will be changes in your usual lifestyle as well as relationships. Becoming aware of these changes and understanding them is the best way to adjust.

Physical Changes

Your baby is finally here; after nine long months of waiting and labor, you are now a mom. Congratulations! You must be quite excited, happy, and elated. However, you might also be exhausted, uncomfortable, and on an emotional rollercoaster without any breaks. You might also be wondering if you'll ever be able to fit into your favorite pair of skinny jeans ever again. Childbirth classes might have helped you get through the pregnancy, but you might not be prepared for all the physical changes that follow pregnancy. In this section, let us look at the different physical changes your body goes through after childbirth.

Sore breasts

Swollen and engorged breasts are quite common. When your breasts are full of milk, they might feel quite tender. Even your nipples might be painfully sore for a couple of days. Once you start breastfeeding your baby, this soreness will reduce. You must be wondering whether to breastfeed your baby or not. I suggest breastfeeding. I breastfed all my children, and as they are growing up, I see the difference it makes. It not only strengthens their immunity and gives them the nutrition they need as babies, but also helps enhance the bond with your infant. Breastfeeding is also believed to reduce the chances of breast cancer. So there are no downsides to breastfeeding, and I suggest you get on board!

Body aches

All the contractions and pushing you underwent during labor will make you feel fatigued and achy all over. You might experience abdominal aches and cramps while the uterus contracts itself back to its normal size. These pains might become quite pronounced while breastfeeding. This discomfort should not last more than a couple of days, and it can be easily counteracted using over-the-counter painkillers. However, if it lasts longer, it is time to consult your doctor.

Vaginal discharge

The vaginal discharge you notice after delivery is known as lochia. It can be speckled with blood, and you don't have to worry about this. Lochia is the remaining tissue, blood, and mucus present in your uterus after childbirth. It doesn't sound pretty, but it is natural and you don't have to worry about it. The vaginal discharge you notice will not be heavier than your usual menstrual discharge. Instead of tampons, opt for sanitary napkins since tampons can be quite uncomfortable. You might need to change your pad quite frequently immediately after the delivery.

Back pain

During pregnancy, your abdominal muscles are stretched. To compensate for this, your body shifts all the extra pressure to your back. Apart from this, new mothers also suffer from back pain after delivery because of poor posture during pregnancy. If these problems don't go away within six weeks of delivery, it is time to visit a chiropractor.

Swollen feet

To support the growing fetus during pregnancy, your body tends to produce at least 50% more blood than usual. This, combined with other hormonal fluctuations in your body, tends to cause swelling of feet, hands, ankles, and other extremities. It is quite normal. You might notice that your shoe size has also increased! It can take a couple of weeks for all this extra fluid to exit the system. Consuming a diet that's rich in potassium helps get rid of all this water weight.

Vaginal pain

The area between the vaginal and the anal openings is known as the perineum. Women who opt for vaginal delivery often experience tearing in this region. It takes at least six weeks to heal fully, and it can cause vaginal pain. The best way to prevent this is by massaging this area during the final weeks of pregnancy. To speed up healing, I suggest that you get postpartum massage daily.

Urinary incontinence

Your bladder control primarily depends on the strength of your pelvic floor muscles. During the final weeks of pregnancy, the entire weight of your body tends to increase the strain on these pelvic floor muscles. This, in turn, reduces your bladder control. I remember, during the final couple of weeks of my pregnancy, I had to pee quite frequently. I used to be wary about drinking even a glass of water because I knew I would have to pee again. It's an unavoidable part of pregnancy, and this can continue even after your delivery. Once your pelvic floor muscles are stronger, your bladder control will automatically improve. The best way to strengthen these muscles is by performing Kegel exercises. They don't take much of an effort and are quite easy to do.

Soreness in limbs

Expectant mothers usually avoid exercising during pregnancy. It causes the accumulation of flab and induces extreme weakness in the muscles. Apart from this, your body produces a hormone known as Relaxin in huge quantities. It tends to have a weakening effect on all your joints. Therefore, sore wrists, aching shoulders, or even tired arms are all part of the postpartum body experience. To manage and relieve the strain in the muscles of your upper body, opt for toning and strengthening exercises of the muscles in your arms, shoulders, and back. There are certain exercises you can start performing even six weeks after your delivery. You will learn more about all these exercises in the subsequent chapters.

Heat flashes

Your body takes a couple of days to readjust its hormones after undergoing labor. During this period, you can experience heat flashes or night sweats. All the extra fluids that your body is still retaining after childbirth is the main reason for these heat flashes. The best way for your body to get rid of all these excess fluids is through sweating. Avoid wearing warm clothes or sleeping under too many blankets. Also, place a towel or an extra sheet on your side of the bed to ensure that the sheets stay dry.

Hair loss

Your mane may no longer be as lustrous or thick as it was before pregnancy. The high levels of hormonal changes in your body during pregnancy can cause hair loss. Hair loss should stop anywhere within six months after childbirth, and your hair will resume its original look within a year. Ensure that the diet you consume is rich in fruits and vegetables. Different nutrients present in these ingredients help your hair grow. Apart from this, follow a gentle hair care regime and avoid using any heat.

Hemorrhoids

Any swollen and painful veins present in and around the anus are known as hemorrhoids. Hemorrhoids can also cause bleeding and extreme discomfort. These are quite common during and after pregnancy. Soaking yourself in warm water, consuming a high-fiber diet, and drinking plenty of water can help treat this condition. Apart from this, you can consult your healthcare provider for any topical ointment for pain relief.

Constipation

An irregular bowel movement, the inability to have a bowel movement or any difficulty while having a bowel movement are all signs of constipation. Constipation is quite common, especially during the days immediately after childbirth. A high-fiber diet, coupled with plenty of fluids can alleviate constipation. Your healthcare provider might also recommend any medicines for the same.

Weight gain

You might lose up to ten pounds immediately after delivery and a couple of more pounds during the first week. Regardless of all the excess pounds you have piled on during pregnancy, you can attain your ideal weight once again. Exercise and a healthy diet are the keys to losing weight and maintaining weight loss. You will learn more about all this in the subsequent chapters.

I know that most of the changes discussed in this section are certainly not pretty. However, keep in mind that your body has just been through a lot. Childbirth is not easy. Not only did you carry your baby for nine months, but you gave birth to your little miracle too. Therefore, it is but obvious that your body will bash certain scars. The good news is, with conscious effort, patience, and self-love, you can get your pre-pregnancy body back. Keep in mind that nothing is impossible.

Note: If you notice that any of these changes become persistent, contact your healthcare provider immediately.

Emotional Changes

There is plenty of advice about what you can expect during pregnancy. But, no one warns you about the emotional roller coaster you will go through after pregnancy. After every pregnancy, I felt like my emotions were all over the place. I would be lying if I said it wasn't overwhelming. However, I was better equipped to deal with the emotional changes after my first pregnancy. In this section, let us look at the emotional changes you will experience as a new mom.

Sadness

Experiencing over-sensitivity is a regular aspect of becoming a new mom. Feelings of weepiness and intermittent sadness are quite common, and they are known as baby blues. Don't think that it means you aren't happy to be a mom. It merely means you need a while to get used to it. I remember I was bawling like a baby when I couldn't figure out how to change the diaper. If you experience any overwhelming urge to cry, cry it out. You will feel better. Don't allow your emotions to make you feel like you aren't doing your job well. Remember that this is a phase and it too shall pass. It is a temporary state of mind, and it isn't permanent. Anxiety disorder and the postpartum mood are not the same as baby blues. When in doubt, reach out to your support system!

Happiness

You've probably heard it a thousand times by now that you will be delighted when you become a mother. However, you cannot even begin to comprehend the overwhelming joy you will experience when you hold your little one in your arms for the first time. As with sadness, even the happiness you experience will be over-exaggerated. You tend to feel every emotion quite deeply, and it will take a while to get used to this. This overwhelming sense of joy you experience can make you feel incredibly high at times. It is unbelievable that someone so small and tiny can bring about this kind of happiness. Even the simplest of faces your baby makes will be a source of your happiness. From getting teary-eyed to giggling uncontrollably, they are all parts of becoming a mother. I remember after my third child, my husband and I were watching a movie, and I started giggling uncontrollably. Eventually, we had to stop the movie because he feared that I would end up hemorrhaging or hurting myself.

Fear

Fear is a potent emotion, and motherhood brings along with it a set of emotions you might not have even been aware of yourself. Also, if you are not usually a worrier, you might have already started to notice changes in your usual attitude. Regardless of whether the fear is a complex or a minor one, it can be somewhat overwhelming, especially during the initial stages of motherhood. Experiencing fear is quite common, and you're not the only one. You might be worried about how you will deal with your new baby. After delivering my first child, I was thinking, "How will I know when to feed the baby? How do I know when to stop? What will I do if the baby cries?" If you find yourself thinking all these questions and getting scared, then rest easy knowing that you are not alone. Every mother tends to think of all these things. It is quite normal and common. Most of these fears stem from not knowing what the future holds. You might have been anxious and scared when you started school, college, or even a new job. Now, when you look back, you will realize your fears were misplaced. Likewise, this too shall pass. If you have any fears or worries, I suggest that you talk to your partner about them.

Anger

No one would want to admit it, but anger is also a very common emotion women experience after delivery. Anger often stems from the frustration of not knowing what to do. You might be angry with yourself for not knowing how to soothe or breastfeed your baby. Usually, it is also triggered because of any unrealistic expectations about motherhood. If you try to be a perfectionist, you'll experience plenty of anger.

Anger and irritability for prolonged periods can also be a sign of postpartum disorder. Therefore, if you notice that your anger isn't going away, or that you are always frustrated with the world around you, it might be time to seek a little extra help.

Doubt

There will be moments of extreme self-doubt as well. You might be left wondering whether you'll be a good enough mother or whether it was the right time to have a child. This often stems from the misconception that maternal instinct is a natural one. This is not necessarily true. You might not have planned on having a baby, but once you have a baby, your maternal instincts will kick in—if not immediately, then eventually. After my first pregnancy, I was not sure how to breastfeed my baby. This made me doubt whether I was fit for motherhood or not. Well, before you start going down the spiral of self-doubt, I suggest you take a break from it all. Calm yourself down and take a deep breath. It will all be fine, don't doubt yourself. If you need help, ask for it. Keep in mind that the weeks following the delivery are meant for discovery. You will learn, and you will get the hang of things. Don't be too harsh on yourself.

Jitters

Experiencing jitters is also common after delivery. You might feel like you are on edge, anxious, and tense for no apparent reason. Even when your logical brain says everything is alright, your emotions seem to be telling you otherwise. If you aren't used to feeling all this, then it can be a little overwhelming. Cut yourself some slack because all of this is normal. It is perfectly alright to feel anxious. The lack of sleep, combined with the fact that you just had a baby, can make you feel uneasy. These feelings will disappear once you get used to motherhood.

Everything and anything might be a trigger. You will feel extremely overwhelmed by the world around you. During this phase, you will feel deeply emotional. Once again, it is normal. Oversensitivity is common, and so are extreme mood swings. Experiencing all these emotions is normal. Don't let anyone tell you otherwise. You don't have to suppress them but must learn to express them constructively. Now that you are aware of what to anticipate, you will be better prepared to deal with any emotions you face. It will give you better control of your feelings.

Relationships and Sex

It is a popular misconception that having a baby means sex is off the table. Your sex life doesn't have to suffer because you have just entered parenthood. However, these are significant changes in life, and they might influence your sex life.

Hormonal changes, lack of time, worries about contraception, and tiredness are the main reasons why sex and intimacy become tough for new parents. If you feel like things have cooled down in the bedroom, you don't have to worry about it. Just like everything else, even this is a phase. However, if you and your partner are not on the same page about each other's sexual desires, it can become a little tricky. Things will get back on track, and all that you need to do is be patient in the meantime. After my first delivery, I felt like I would never want to have sex again. It felt like all sexual desires had merely left my body. Well, trust me, your sexual urges will return once again. It is quite common, and it can take you anywhere between 1 to 3 months to regain interest in sex. If it takes you a while longer, it is fine too.

While breastfeeding your baby, you might feel a little sensual and sexually aroused. It is because of oxytocin, a chemical released by your brain. Oxytocin helps with milk production, and it is also the reason for the sexual arousal you feel. It is quite normal. Alternatively, you might even lose all sexual interest while you are breastfeeding.

Your body will undoubtedly undergo various physical changes after you have given birth. It can take you a couple of months before you start feeling like your usual self again. In the meanwhile, you might not be happy with the way you look, and this can also cause intimacy issues. Keep in mind that most of these changes discussed in the previous section are all temporary, and will go away with time. A little exercise and a conscious diet can fast track your progress.

You might be wondering about how long it would take before you are ready for sexual intercourse once again. The answer to this question is entirely subjective and personal. It depends on you. You don't have to do anything unless you are fully ready for it. Not just physically prepared, but even mentally as well as emotionally. If you had any stitches or even difficult childbirth, you might experience pain or discomfort during sexual intercourse. Using lube can help. Consult your healthcare provider for any estrogen creams or lubricants you can use. Anxiety and self-doubt can also be the reason for this discomfort. Unless you are comfortable with your body and yourself, you might not feel confident about having sex. If that's the case, then your first priority must be self-love. As a general rule of thumb, it is advised that you wait for at least six weeks before you resume any sexual activities.

Contraception is important, even after childbirth. If you just had a baby, you might not be ready to have another one immediately. Always talk to your doctor before you decide to start having sex again.

You might not be as interested in sex as you were before the pregnancy. You might even feel worried or confused that you are no longer interested. It is especially true in the first couple of weeks following childbirth. It can make your partner feel unwanted or even rejected. These feelings are certainly not pleasant to experience, but they are natural and perfectly normal. The best thing you can do in such a situation is to have an honest conversation with your partner. If you are feeling uncertain about yourself, talk to your partner about it. Don't do anything because you feel like you're obligated to your partner. Sex is not an obligation. It is always better to express your feelings instead of suppressing them. They might end up coming out in the form of emotional outbursts, and it might cause unnecessary strain on your relationship. Encourage your partner to share his feelings with you. Don't be upset about anything he says. He might be struggling as well, so try to be empathetic towards him.

There are different ways in which you can rebuild the intimacy quotient in your relationship. After all, having a baby doesn't mean the end of your sex life. Keeping open lines of communication is the best way to go about rebuilding intimacy. As new parents, you might struggle to find some alone time together. After all, caring for your infant's needs will be your priority. However, this doesn't mean that you start neglecting each other. It can increase the stress on your relationship. It could be something as simple as having a meal together or even going out for a walk. Also, if sex isn't your priority right now, try to indulge in a little physical affection. Kissing, holding hands, and cuddling are simple things you can try.

Body Image

As mentioned in the previous sections, your body will change.

Therefore, the way you view and perceive yourself will change, too. You might look at all the other mothers who seem lean and fit even after their delivery. It might seem like they have figured it all out. I remember I stumbled upon different posts on Instagram of fit moms who looked gorgeous even after delivering a baby. I used to look at those posts and feel bad about the way I looked. This constant comparison I was subjecting myself to was wreaking havoc on my body image. I was not happy with myself and was quite miserable. I used to wonder how they had the energy to take care of an infant while hitting the gym and maintaining a healthy diet. I felt like I was pressured to return to my normal body immediately after childbirth. My inability to cope with this unnecessary stress about myself was the reason for my misery. I realized a simple truth - I am unique, and I am different from everyone else. I don't have to worry about how others look. Instead, I needed to concentrate on how I felt about myself. Here are a couple of things I realized along the way.

Most of us are usually quite hard on ourselves, and we are our worst critics. The kind of pressure we put on ourselves is unlike any pressure other can put on us. The best way to tackle this self-induced stress is through forgiveness. Understand that you have been through a lot, and you don't have to rush into anything else right away. If you feel like you're not ready to exercise right now, give yourself a break. Cut yourself some slack and forgive yourself. After my second pregnancy, I wanted to be like one of those fit mothers I kept seeing on Instagram. I purchased a specific stroller I could use for my baby while jogging. I envisioned myself going on early-morning walks with my baby. Well, this was far from reality for me. I did not have the time or the energy to do any of this. All of this made me feel more guilty. It was when I realized that I was inducing unnecessary stress on myself that I stopped. If you are feeling guilty for not exercising or not eating healthy right away, it is alright. Take all the time you need. And remember, there is no rush.

Stop comparing yourself with others. You are different, and so are they. They are not dealing with what you are dealing with right now. Therefore, what is the point comparing yourself? If you feel like you are ready to get back to your exercise routine immediately, then go for it. If you want a while longer, then take the time you need. As your infant starts to grow, you'll have more time for your usual routines. Once you get the hang of it and are comfortable taking care of your baby's needs, you will find the internal desire and motivation to concentrate on yourself.

Don't rush into it, and start slow. Take it one day at a time. Maybe you can start by slowly improving your diet before you start thinking about exercising. Even if you are exercising, stick to light cardio and don't try to bench press heavyweights immediately. Also, consult your healthcare provider before you think about exercising. While you set a healthy routine for yourself, ensure that you don't create any unrealistic goals for yourself. Setting a goal like "I will lose the pregnancy weight within ten days" is not only unrealistic, it also puts undue pressure on you. Ensure that you are realistic.

The most important step of all is acceptance. Forgive yourself and accept yourself the way you are. Once you have a baby, your priorities are bound to shift. Keep in mind that giving birth to a baby is not a simple task, and becoming a parent is never easy. Learn to accept imperfections and stop chasing the dream of perfection. Childbirth will certainly leave some scars on your body. Wear them proudly. It is nothing to be ashamed of. And don't ever let anyone body shame you. In fact, stop any negative self-talk going on in your mind about yourself. Work on feeling more comfortable with yourself before you do anything else.

Chapter 3: Parenting

Tips for New Parents

If you are entering parenthood for the first time, then you might not know what you are supposed to do. Sure, you might have received plenty of advice from others about parenting, attended childbirth classes, and so on. However, do you really know how you can thrive and enjoy your journey as a parent? In this section, I will share with you a couple of tips I wish someone had told me when I became a mom for the first time!

Being kind to yourself

Usually, most first-time parents have no experience whatsoever dealing with newborns. Yet, they expect themselves to be experts in providing baby care when they have their baby. After listening to all the advice you might have received from your mother, aunts, or any loved ones, you might start believing that you are supposed to know everything that's to be done. Turn off all the self-doubt and negative talk. Stop criticizing yourself and don't be too harsh. After all, this is the first time you have entered parenthood, and you are not expected to know everything. Even after having three kids, I still keep learning something new other every day. Parenthood is a continuous process of learning and adjusting. Therefore, be kind and compassionate to yourself.

Get some sleep

You will undoubtedly be extremely thrilled and excited to have your baby home, finally! You might have been waiting for this moment for a very long time. Now that your baby is finally here, you will want to spend every single waking moment with your little one. This is quite natural. However, don't make the mistake of exhausting yourself. The joys of parenthood are almost like a big balloon, and exhaustion can pop it quite easily. I remember there used to be days when my partner and I used to be reduced to tears because of sleep deprivation. We were like human zombies and the quality of life we were leading suffered because of sleep deprivation. Therefore, come up with a schedule and divide your responsibilities. Try to get as much sleep as you can. If you find that your baby is napping, try taking a nap as well. Sleep deprivation can make you edgy, depressed, tired, and even lead to accidents.

Trust yourself

It is quite common for new parents to experience emotional whiplash. One instance, you might be feeling like a super parent, and the next moment you might be feeling like a rookie who has no idea what to do. All this is quite common, and self-doubt can creep in if you don't keep a check on it. You must understand that you are not the only parent around. Humans have been nurturing and taking care of their young ones since the dawn of civilization. Like others before you, even you will get the hang of it. Be a little patient and kind towards yourself in the meanwhile. Time is your ally, and it will teach you everything you need to know about parenting. Stop worrying and give yourself a break. For now, stick to simple things like spending time with your baby, breastfeeding, and concentrate on giving and receiving love.

Help isn't necessarily bad

You might be tempted to do everything on your own, but don't give in to this temptation. Take all the help you can get. Trust me, you will need it. It takes a village to raise a child, and you will soon realize it. Maybe your loved ones can help you out, or you can hire some extra help. If you try to do everything on your own, you will merely end up burning yourself out. Burnout is not good for you or your child right now.

Add some flexibility

You might have specific ideas, plans, and things you want to do when it comes to parenting. Plans might work in a professional setting, but not in parenting. You can certainly stick to your core ideas and beliefs, but don't be too fixated on the plans you have made. Children are unpredictable. There might be some parenting philosophies you agree with more than the others. You might have had plenty of theories before you became a mom, but all those philosophies are bound to change once you start taking care of your child. The best thing to do is to stay flexible. If things don't turn out as planned, improvise and adapt.

Laugh it out

Learn to laugh it out. Laughing is the best stress buster. Stop chasing perfection and start rejoicing in the little joys that come your way. Let go of all thoughts of organization and maybe even a little ego. You are new at it, and you will learn. You will make mistakes, and the best thing to do is to laugh it out. Learn your lessons and move on. Stop criticizing yourself and laugh!

Mutual care

Don't forget to take care of yourself. The same applies to your partner, too. If any of your family members are taking care of your baby, you can step out for a meal together. Parenthood is not an excuse to allow your relationship to grow stagnant. The key to successful parenting is to strike a balance between all aspects of your life.

Live your life

Don't forget to live in the moment while taking care of your little one. Time does fly by. Cherish every moment that you have and stop worrying about the past or the future. Allow yourself to enjoy the simple things in life. For instance, when your baby smiles for the first time, allow yourself to smile, too.

Team Parenting

Your co-parents, teachers, coaches, grandparents, and other adults can be a part of your parenting team. Team parenting involves maintaining a productive relationship with all those adults who take an active role in caring for your baby. It is a mutual relationship based on a commitment to take care of a baby. It is about sharing certain fundamental philosophies about parenting, supporting and appreciating each other's strengths, beliefs, and efforts, being flexible, and coming up with an effective strategy to take care of the baby.

Ideally, team parenting must fulfill all the different conditions mentioned above. However, there might be certain obstacles you can run into because life is unpredictable. In this section, let us look at some basic tips you can use to optimize your efforts to team parent.

Before you start team parenting, talk about any unresolved issues you might have. Any unresolved issues between co-parents tend to affect the child's well-being. If you notice that specific arguments start cropping up based on discussions about the child's care, it is time to resolve those issues. Don't suppress any emotions and encourage the other co-parents to share their problems or concerns freely. After all, you all are adults, and it is time to start behaving like adults.

Never abdicate your responsibilities as a parent. You do have others to depend on, but this doesn't relieve you from the basic duties you have towards your child. If you have certain ideas about parenting, try implementing them. You can consult other co-parents before you make any significant decisions about your child, but the final decision must be yours. Don't just go along with what others say because you don't have the time or are uncertain about yourself.

One co-parent might assume the role of the disciplinarian while the other one can be a fun parent. Keep in mind that these roles are not set in stone. They can change from time to time. Be flexible, and don't be rigid about the rules you have assumed. You cannot always be the fun parent or play the bad cop consistently.

If you have set any specific rules about feeding, clothing, and putting the baby to sleep, then ensure consistency in implementation. The child's well-being must be the priority of all the co-parents. Inconsistency can disrupt your baby's routine. Likewise, if any of the other co-parents have come up with any different rules, stick to them. For instance, if you feed your baby at 9 AM, then ensure that others also feed your baby at 9 AM when you are not around. Routine is quite essential for a baby. It tends to give them a sense of security and comfort.

You all don't need to share the same values or beliefs about parenting. You might also have different ideas. Learn to respect each other's differing opinions. The one thing you must always agree on is the well-being of the baby. As long as this primary condition is fulfilled, you can hash out any other differences.

You and your partner might have completely different opinions about parenting. Don't think of this as a personal attack or a personal slight. Merely because you don't think alike doesn't make one of you right and the other wrong.

Towards the end of the week, set aside a specific time to discuss how the week was. Apart from this, use this time to plan any strategies for the upcoming week. If one of the co-parents wants to try a new approach, then ensure that you all support each other. Whenever a problem comes up, don't evade your responsibility, or push it on others. Take responsibility and play an active role in being a co-parent. Once all the problems have been solved, give yourself some time to talk about how the week was. Engage in a healthy conversation about any suggestions or criticisms about things that can be improved. If any issues need to be resolved, then get on them immediately. Don't put them on the backburner; resolve them at the earliest.

Single Parenting

Being a single parent means you have plenty of changes to cope with. You not only have to deal with the reality of being a single parent but also need to get accustomed to taking care of your baby. During the early days, you might experience a variety of powerful emotions. Experiencing sadness, regret, guilt, frustration, anger, fear, shame, and shock are all normal. You might also experience hope, relief, and excitement about the new life that lies ahead. Plenty of newly single parents tend to feel quite liberated from all the stress and conflict they had to deal with in previous relationships. It can be challenging, but it will get easier. It is time you take control of your life and enjoy this independence you have. In this section, I'll share with you a couple of suggestions that might come in handy to cope with life as a newly single parent.

Don't hesitate to reach out. Your family, friends, and other loved ones will be your support system. If you are not able to get the help you require from them, you can depend on others. Talk to the other people at your child's daycare center or even the local health center. Try to meet other single parents. Once you realize that you're not alone, it becomes easier. You can join online support groups as well.

It takes a while to get accustomed to any significant change in life. Don't be in a hurry, and take things slowly. Give yourself time to get used to these changes. Learn to process through every emotion you deal with. You will need some time to heal and be kind to yourself during this process.

The early days are never easy. So, stop expecting too much from yourself or even your support system for that matter. There might be a couple of decisions you don't have to make right away, so put them on the backburner. You might also have to make a couple of major choices like shifting out or finding a new house for yourself. Concentrate only on those aspects of your life that are your priority at present and forget about everything else.

There isn't much in your life that you can control. Plenty of external events that affect your life are well out of your purview of control. Learn to accept the simple reality of life. Things will get easier for you. Focus only on all the things that you can control, like how you can take care of your child. Come up with a plan of action to tackle all the things that you can control. A family routine can help make your child feel secure and looked after even when you are not around.

Cut yourself some slack and don't resort to self-blame the minute things don't turn out the way you planned. After all, you are not superhuman, and no one expects perfection from you. Therefore, stop expecting perfection from yourself. All this unnecessary stress will merely slow you down. Learn to be kind to yourself and celebrate all the progress you make.

You probably cannot change the situation you're in, but you can certainly regulate your reactions and emotions. Even if your former partner isn't well-behaved, you can behave like a mature adult. You have the choice to look after yourself and prioritize essential things in life. Choose to surround yourself with people who are supportive, as well as positive. You need as much positivity in your life right now as you possibly can get.

Start concentrating on your strengths instead of your

weaknesses. It will fill you with a renewed sense of confidence and resilience. You have survived everything that life has thrown your way. You will survive this, as well. Remind yourself that you are a confident and an independent entity. You don't need to depend on anyone else. You are your cheerleader. Remember, you have managed to cope with every single challenge that has come your way and they have all made you stronger. Therefore, think of this as a learning lesson as well. Start celebrating all the little wins that come your way. You might have finally figured out how to soothe your crying baby, so congratulate yourself.

The final thing I want you to keep in mind is to maintain a positive attitude. Allow yourself to dream and hope for a little. Even if your life isn't how you planned it would be, you have something to be grateful for - your baby.

Dad's Role

Not just new mothers, even fathers tend to experience a variety of mixed emotions. If your partner is experiencing baby blues, then don't worry. It is natural, and it too shall pass. Here are a couple of different tips that will come in handy for new dads.

First, accept a basic truth. Like you, even your partner is hoping that after pregnancy, life can get back to the way it used to be. If this is what your partner is thinking, then he needs to accept his new reality. Things will change, and once he has made his peace with it, it becomes easier. A new mom might not have the time or energy to take care of the household. So, it is time for the dads to step into the picture and take care of household responsibilities.

You and your partner need to come up with a schedule to share all the responsibilities of parenthood. You cannot take care of all the late-night feeding sessions or soothe the baby whenever he cries. Your partner needs to do the same, too. Take turns attending to your child's needs, and it will become easier. You both need to get used to the idea that your sleep is constantly interrupted. It is especially true during your child's infancy.

He needs to understand you and your emotions. You will obviously be on an emotional rollercoaster, so he needs to develop patience. It doesn't mean you use motherhood as a free pass to get out of all your responsibilities. There will be times when you need to show a little patience and others when he needs to be patient. Talk about all of this. Learn to stay level-headed even under stressful circumstances.

Keep in mind that he, too, is learning the ropes of parenthood, just like you. He might not know what you need if you don't tell him. Don't hesitate to talk to your partner about your needs. If you notice that he is experiencing postpartum withdrawal, then it is time to have an honest conversation about it.

Encourage him to take care of himself. He will not be of much use to you or your baby if he is running on fumes. The way you need a little "me" time, even your partner will need it, and do not hold it against him.

Parenting needs to be a two-person job and takes a combined team effort. Share and equally distribute your responsibilities. Talk about the expectations you have for each other. Once everything is out in the open, it becomes easier to work together.

He needs to be confident as well as patient, not just towards the baby, but even himself. Don't be too harsh on him if he makes a mistake. After all, he is learning, too, and everything is new to him the way it is to you.

Chapter 4: Back to Work?

Issues to Consider

If you were on maternity leave until now, it is time to decide whether you want to go back to work or not. I decided to become a full-time stay-at-home mom. As a new mom, you must be quite excited about your baby. You probably don't even want to take your eyes off your little one, even for a couple of seconds. Babies tend to have this effect on others. While the addition of a baby will undoubtedly enrich your life, it isn't without challenges. There will be a couple of tough decisions you will need to make. One of the toughest ones is probably to decide whether you want to go back to work or not. There are a lot of factors you must consider while making this decision. It is certainly not an easy choice, but it is quintessential. Regardless of your decision, keep in mind that there is no right or wrong decision. Every mother is different, and everyone goes through different situations of life. You might have various reasons to resume or quit work altogether. So, how do you decide which option to choose? The best way to go about making this decision is to assess your situation and consider all the tradeoffs carefully. Don't rush into this and give yourself plenty of time to think about the best option for you as well as your child. In this section, let us look at the various factors that can influence this decision of yours.

Finances

The first question you must answer is whether your family can afford it or not. Since this decision will have a significant effect on your overall life as well as your family, it is not to be treated lightly. Discuss with your partner whether your family can survive if you quit your job. To do this, make a list of all your average expenses along with all your needs. Include every little expense you can think of and add another $6000 to it (the average amount spent on a baby during the first-year).

A second paycheck certainly reduces the financial strain on your partner. However, if your family is quite comfortable, then it is entirely your decision. If you think you need additional income to maintain your current lifestyle, then you might have to reconsider going back to work. If you are willing to make a couple of sacrifices and think you can still comfortably live off one paycheck, and then maybe you can quit your job. Apart from this, there are certain personal considerations, as well. Perhaps you don't like the idea of becoming a stay-at-home mom and like to work. In such a case, resume work and see whether you still like it. If you don't, you can come up with different sources of passive income or pick up any work from home jobs. Another consideration is that you need to think about your employability quotient as well. If you take a leave from work for too long, it can become a little tricky to get back on your career track. It reduces your employability quotient. If you are fine with this, then take all the time you need.

Self-image

How do you think your decision will affect your relationship, as well as your self-image? Quitting work can influence the way you feel about yourself. After all, before pregnancy, work might have been your first priority or even your only priority. Some people cannot do away with their professional lives. Some women need a certain degree of career fulfillment to feel better about themselves. Then again, some think that being a full-time mother is the best satisfaction they can ever get in life. I was one of the latter. I don't regret my decision and am quite happy with it. So, spend some time and think about how your decision will affect your personal dynamics. Regardless of what you decide, ensure that you are honest with yourself and your partner. Do not do anything because you feel pressured into doing it. If you want to stay at home, stay at home, provided your financial conditions are not bad. If you're going to go back to work, then be honest about it as well. Don't deceive yourself or your partner. After all, you will need to live with your decision.

Child-care

Another important consideration is to determine your plans for childcare. Taking care of a baby is a full-time job. At times, you might feel the need to stay at home and look after your child until you are ready to leave him in someone else's care. You need to be emotionally prepared to resume work. After all, you are entering motherhood for the first time and it can be an overwhelming emotional experience. If you don't like the idea of leaving your baby in someone else's care, you might want to stay at home. Once again, it is a personal decision, and just because someone else is doing something doesn't mean you need to follow suit. You are the best judge of yourself. Carefully consider whether you will be fine with a decision or not. If you think you can find the right childcare support for your baby, you can resume work. However, spend sufficient time doing all the research and background work before you decide on hiring a nanny or a childcare provider.

Flexibility

Your decision about resuming or quitting work doesn't necessarily have to be a permanent one. All new moms will need some time for themselves. I personally feel that we are all entitled to it. Maybe after a couple of months of staying at home, you might want to resume work. If that's the case, then reapply! Or maybe after working for a couple of months, you might want to resign. If you aren't entirely sure about making this decision, then try both options for a while. Stick with whichever fits with your needs and requirements. Regardless of your decision, ensure that your baby's needs are well taken care of. Don't ignore your responsibility as a mother. Apart from this, ensure that you have the full support of your partner. If you aren't a single parent, having a supportive partner is quite essential.

How Can You Handle Going Back to Work?

After considering all the issues discussed in the previous section, you might have made up your mind. If you have decided to resume work, then here are a couple of tips you can use to cope with different emotions you will experience.

If you know your maternity leave is about to end in a week or maybe even a couple of days, you might be quite anxious about getting back to work. This is normal. You might be worried and afraid about another change occurring in your life. You might be anxious that your role at work will change, and you might also be worried about your ability to manage work-life with personal life. The most prominent concern you might be facing is trying to understand how you can spend time away from your baby. Instead of worrying about all this, try living in the moment. Concentrate on your maternity leave, spending time with your baby, and yourself. Stop worrying about the future or the past. You cannot control the future, but you can thoroughly enjoy the present you have. It needs to be a conscious decision on your part. Whenever you experience any anxiety or worry about your future, remind yourself that the moment you have right now is precious. After all, the time that goes by will not return.

You might be excited to resume work. This excitement might make you feel a little guilty. Well, you have nothing to feel guilty about. Before you became a mother, you had a life that was quite different from the one you have right now. By going back to work, you might be able to reclaim that lost part of your life. It is not something you need to feel guilty about. I suggest that you don't ever let anyone make you feel guilty about resuming work. As long as you learn to balance your professional and personal lives, you are doing just fine. Don't ever let anyone tell you otherwise. If you can manage to get your baby accustomed to a sleep schedule, it will be quite beneficial for you as well as your baby once you resume work. For instance, wouldn't it be quite simple if your baby sleeps through most of the afternoon while you are at work?

There are certain emotions you have to deal with after you resume work. Once you get back to work, the first week can be quite stressful and overwhelming. After all, you have been away on maternity leave until now. All those official responsibilities you forgot about are waiting for your attention now. It is a huge adjustment, and transitioning into this new role will take some time. All the emotions you experience can be a source of extreme confusion. The internal conflict going on in your mind can be a challenge, too. The separation anxiety you experience because you are away from your baby can make you feel inadequate. Apart from this, working mom guilt can also overwhelm you. If you're not careful, these emotions will quickly engulf you and weigh heavily on your heart.

The good news is that not all of these emotions are painful. Perhaps the most positive emotion you will experience is excitement and relief. Relief that you haven't lost a part of your identity and excitement to get back to doing what you used to enjoy. The relief of resuming of familiar routine can be quite comforting. Instead of worrying about all the negative emotions that keep popping up, start concentrating on the positive ones.

One month into resuming your work, you can feel quite overwhelmed. At this point, you'll be more in control of your schedule. Apart from this, you will also start to get the hang of managing your new schedule. In fact, I'm sure that you might have gained the confidence necessary to know that you can make it work for you. You can be a working mom. Learning that you don't have to compromise one aspect of your life for another one can fill you with immense self-confidence. Of course, there'll be a couple of bad days as well. After all, you can't have it all good, now can you? But now that you feel more confident and comfortable in your new life and role, you will start getting used to the routine. You might also come up with different ideas to make things easier for you and your baby.

If you are feeling overwhelmed at work, try some calming exercise. You can practice yoga or meditation. Start establishing an ideal morning routine for yourself. Maybe you can resume the routine you used to have in place before your pregnancy. Start streamlining your life, and you will feel more in control. Regardless of what you do, don't allow others' opinions to influence your decision. You need to do what is right by you. After all, you're the only one who understands what you need. All the choices you make must be in the best interest of your needs and your baby's needs. If you are not at your 100% emotionally, mentally, or even physically, you cannot cater to your baby's needs. By helping yourself, you are helping your baby. Whenever you start doubting your decisions, remind yourself of this simple mantra.

During the first year after pregnancy, you might experience postpartum depression. This is quite normal and common. You don't have to worry too much about it. As long as you start taking care of your mental and emotional needs, it will not have any drastic effects on your life. You might experience crippling anxiety at the thought of going back to work or being away from your baby. You might feel extremely tired and sad all the time. The inability to focus on your work, or anything else, is also a sign of postpartum depression. The most obvious sign of all is the inability to enjoy spending time with your baby.

If you experience any of these symptoms, it is quintessential that you reach out and seek help. Confide in your partner or any of your other loved ones. Seek therapy or counseling. Learning to deal with postpartum depression is important. You cannot overlook it or ignore it and think that it will go away. If left untreated, it can have a damaging effect on your life as well as your baby's life.

Going back to work can be quite challenging, especially for a new mom. The most obvious reason is that you don't want to be away from your baby. You might be conflicted between wanting to resume work while wishing that you could spend every minute with your baby. It can be quite confusing, as well as painful. Carefully consider your health as well. Your body needs to be mentally, physically, and emotionally prepared to resume work.

Once you know what you can expect after going back to work, it can help smooth the transition. Keep in mind that people around you will have different opinions and advice to offer. You can listen to their advice, but always make a decision based on your needs and requirements. Listen to your gut. Confide in your loved one. Another essential thing to keep in mind is that you are communicating everything with your partner. Open and honest communication is essential.

Live With Your Decision

Going back to work

If you have decided to go back to work, then you need to learn to balance your personal life with your professional responsibilities. You cannot ignore either of your duties. Juggling between these two worlds does take some practice. It can be a little tough initially, but it does get easier. Try not to carry your work back home and leave your personal life behind while at work. Focus only on the present. If you are at work, give your hundred percent at work, and if you are at home, give you 100% to your personal life. Don't try to multitask and ensure that you have sufficient support to balance these two aspects of your life. If you are scared or even worried about being a working mother, give yourself a break. You're not alone. You need about six weeks to recover after delivery fully, and after that, it is entirely up to you to decide when you want to resume work.

Don't work for more than 20 hours per week once you resume work. At least stick to this time limit during the initial stages. Your body takes six weeks to heal itself, and you will need a while longer to recover fully. Therefore, try negotiating your work hours before you resume your professional responsibilities. Apart from this, your job will be physically demanding on you. You cannot ignore the stress of professional life. Learning to balance this with the responsibility of a new baby can be quite overwhelming. Therefore, ensure that you have a proper support system in place along with a childcare plan.

Once you resume work, ensure that you have a proper routine in place. Stick to this routine, and it will get easier. Talk to your partner and come up with a list of shared responsibilities.

Staying at home

If you decided to become a full-time stay at home mom, then it is also a significant change in your life. If you are used to working in a hectic and extremely competitive, highly charged work environment, then the idea of staying at home might be a little tricky to get used to. If you enjoyed your work and loved working with your colleagues, this laid-back rhythm might take some getting used to. In your new role as a full-time mother, the amount of recognition you get for your efforts will not be much. At least, not until your baby has become a fully functioning member of society. Staying at home is not as simple and easy as a lot of other people seem to think. Just because you are home doesn't mean that you don't have any work to attend to. From taking care of household chores and responsibilities to tending to all your baby's needs, it can be quite tiring. It is a round-the-clock responsibility, and there are no coffee breaks. Learn to be open with your partner and communicate your feelings honestly. I remember I was quite scared, as well as excited, when I quit my job. You might also experience these emotions. If you do, then remind yourself that it is okay and normal to experience all this.

Balancing work and home life

Now that you have made up your mind about becoming a stay at home mom or resuming work, it is essential to learn to love your life. If you are unsatisfied with either of your decisions, then you will end up feeling frustrated. This, in turn, can take a toll on the relationship you share with your partner. Apart from this, it can also harm your self-image. Therefore, ensure that the decision you make is something you can live with. Once you have made your bed, you have to lie in it. Therefore, make sure that it is comfortable.

Part 2: Time to Regain Your Strengths, Your Shape, And Yourself

Doesn't it feel incredibly wonderful to hold your bundle of joy in your hands? As you are already aware, giving birth changes your body. Even the most confident and fit women can feel a little overwhelmed by all the changes brought about by motherhood, especially the physical changes. The postpartum body might make you miss how you used to look. However, you don't have to get bogged down by all this. All these physical changes are quite common. If you feel like you're the only one struggling with it, then you are not alone. Everyone goes through this. You are not the only one who is struggling to shed all those unwanted pregnancy pounds. Weight loss is not just a physical change, but an emotional process as well.

You not only have to take care of yourself, but your baby as well. Motherhood will change you, but it doesn't mean you need to let go of yourself. You might have changed after having a baby, but at your core, you are still the same person. Just because your priorities or lifestyle changes doesn't mean you don't enjoy the same things you used to. In this section, you will learn about different tips and strategies you can use to regain your strength, your body, and yourself in the process.

Chapter 5: Workout and Exercise after Giving Birth

There are various health benefits associated with regular exercise. Adding some form of physical activity or other to your routine not only improves your overall health but also helps with weight loss and maintenance of the weight loss. According to your needs and requirements, there are different forms of exercises available. Usually, new mothers are often hesitant about exercising after delivery. As long as you give your body sufficient time to recover and heal itself, you can start exercising. It takes a little extra effort and some motivation to include exercise in your daily routine. I know the life of a new mother can be quite hectic and tiring. You might be wondering how you are supposed to make the time for exercising when you barely have any time to sleep! Well, you don't have to start exercising immediately after delivery. Take a couple of weeks or even months if you want. Once I started exercising regularly, and noticed that my energy level was most stable, I felt better about myself. It helped me shed the pregnancy weight and made me more relaxed. There are specific exercises you can start performing right after the delivery to speed up the process of recovery.

A word of caution - always consult your healthcare provider before you decide to start exercising. If your body hasn't fully recovered after the pregnancy, any form of postnatal exercise can cause unnecessary stress on you. Apart from this, the period of recovery usually varies depending on the type of birth you had. The recovery period for a C-section is longer than the one for a vaginal birth. Apart from this, there are various other factors to determine whether you are fit to start exercising or not. Usually, it is advised that you wait for at least six weeks before you decide to exercise. Six weeks after the delivery will be your first postnatal checkup, and that's the ideal time to talk to your healthcare provider about the same.

Benefits of Exercise for Mom

It takes conscious effort, time, and energy to sculpt the perfect body you desire. The best way to get there is through exercise. If you want to shed all the pregnancy weight and get back to looking like your pre-pregnancy self, then it is time to add a little physical activity to your life. In this section, let us look at the different benefits of exercise.

Exercising helps improve your physical as well as mental well-being. Whenever you exercise, your body tends to release endorphins or feel-good hormones. It is a great way to tackle baby blues. Whenever you are feeling a little low, I suggest you go out for a jog, walk, or engage in any activity that includes physical movement. These feel-good hormones can be quite addictive, too. Once you get used to exercising regularly, it will become a part of your daily schedule, and you don't have to remind yourself constantly. So, the best way to ensure that you don't experience postpartum depression is via exercise. In this section, you'll learn about different exercise routines you can start following childbirth.

Another great thing about exercising is that it is a natural stress buster. Instead of focusing on your problems, you can channel all this energy away from your body. I usually like to go jogging whenever I feel under the weather or a little stressed out. It not only improves my mood but helps declutter my thoughts as well. Once I am calmer and more focused, I am better equipped to deal with all the challenges life throws at me.

Pregnancy tends to weaken your muscles, especially the ones in your abdominal region, pelvis, and limbs. To strengthen all these muscles, you need to start exercising. Also, exercising helps firm and tone your body.

Initially, exercising might make you feel a little tired. However, once the body gets used to it, and it becomes a part of your daily routine, you will notice that your energy levels are stabilized. Apart from this, it also improves your overall sense of well-being. This brings me to the most obvious benefit of regular exercise: weight loss. If you want to speed up the process of weight loss, then you need to concentrate on your diet and include physical activity in your daily routine. Even 30 minutes of exercising every day can have a significant effect on your overall weight loss.

When to Start?

You can start with gentle exercises like walking as soon as you feel comfortable. Start exercising only when you feel like you are ready and up to it. Remember, there is no rush. You don't have to start exercising because you see other new mothers working out piously at the gym. Some might feel comfortable exercising earlier than others. It is entirely up to you. As I have mentioned, don't forget to consult your doctor before you start exercising.

Most of the physical changes your body goes through during pregnancy start to fade away within six weeks of delivery. If you had a difficult birth, any complications during childbirth, or even a C-section, you might take a while longer. If you were not used to exercising before your pregnancy or during the pregnancy, then always start with simple exercises. Don't opt for any high-intensity exercises immediately. Take things slowly and don't be in a rush.

Pregnancy tends to weaken the muscles in your abdominal and lower back regions. So, any exercise that is too much stress on your core can cause physical discomfort. If you are not careful, you might end up injuring yourself, even while performing simple twists and stretches as well. It is because the ligaments and joints in your body have become quite pliable during pregnancy. Any physical activity that requires you to change your directions rapidly or involves high impact exercises must be avoided.

You can start performing pelvic floor exercises while engaged in other activities. For instance, you can perform Kegels while breastfeeding or even driving the car. The clenching and unclenching of pelvic muscles is quite simple and doesn't require much concentration. It is the simplest exercise to strengthen your pelvic floor.

Start including your baby whenever you exercise. If you are performing any floor exercises, you can place the baby next to you in the crib. If you want, you can also exercise along with your baby. Why don't you go for a jog and take your baby along in the stroller? It is a great idea to exercise while spending time with your little one.

You don't have to go to the gym to exercise. You can turn your living room into a gym if you want. Apart from this, there are plenty of online videos and tutorials you can follow to exercise.

Types of Postnatal Exercises

After my first pregnancy, I wasn't too happy with my postpartum body. It did lower my self-confidence. That's when I decided it was time to start exercising and get fit. However, I was not on board with the idea of doing millions of crunches. Well, then I discovered that there are different forms of exercising, and you don't necessarily have to go to the gym to exercise. In this section, I will share with you a couple of exercises that I regularly perform to keep my body fit and in shape.

Pelvic tilts

You can start performing this exercise even a week after delivery. However, if you had a C-section, then your body requires anywhere between 8 to 10 weeks to recover fully. To perform this exercise, lie down on your back on a yoga mat. Place a pillow under your knees as well as your hips. Ensure that your feet are firmly planted on the mat while your hands rest by your side. Now, take a deep breath and then slowly exhale. As you exhale, draw in your abs and slightly tuck in your pelvis. Squeeze the muscles in your pelvic region as you would by performing Kegel. Hold onto this pose to the count of five and then slowly release. Repeat this exercise 10 times. It helps develop the strength of your abdominal muscles and increase your overall stamina.

Heel slides

Lie flat on your back on the yoga mat and bend your knees. Ensure that they are placed hip-width apart. Take a deep breath, and, as you do this, draw in your abs and then flex your left foot while digging your heels into the floor. Ensure that your pelvis stays still and exhale. Inhale and exhale once again. As you breathe out, push your left heel away from your body while keeping your knee bent. Now, return to your starting position. Repeat this exercise five times with each leg.

Pelvic bridge

Lie flat on your back, and place your feet firmly planted on the floor such that your knees are bent. Now, tilt your pelvis upwords, and slowly lift your hips off the floor. You are essentially forming a bridge with your body. Hold this post to the count of five and then slowly lower yourself into the starting position. Repeat this exercise five times. It helps strengthen the muscles in your lower back, pelvis, and buttocks.

Walking

Walking might not seem like much of an exercise, but it is one of the least complicated approaches you can use to start exercising. It's not only simple but can help you shed all those extra pounds as well. Start with a simple walk. After a while, you can work your way up to a brisk walk. Even a simple stroll can do wonders for your post-pregnancy body. If you want, you can bring your child along with you. Wear a front pack to place your baby in. By carrying this extra weight, you can enhance the benefits of walking. However, before you do this, ensure that your baby is at least three months old. Also, be mindful of your position and posture whenever you are walking. You don't want your baby's arms to be flailing in the air while you are walking briskly. If you walk about 7500 steps, you can end up burning over 250 calories. It will not take you more than an hour. To increase the intensity of your workout, increase your pace and try jogging. Once again, ensure your baby's safety while doing all of this.

It might be quite challenging to stay away from your baby, even more so during the initial period. Well, the good news is, there are a couple of exercises you can do along with your baby. Before you start exercising, ensure that your healthcare provider has given you the go ahead. If you don't like the idea of letting go of your baby even for a single minute, then here are some exercises you can start doing.

Glider

Start by standing on a yoga mat and holding your baby quite close to your chest. Now, perform a forward lunge with your right leg. Keep your knees bent and ensure that your toes are aligned with your knee. Hold this position to the count of three and return to standing position. Repeat this exercise with the other leg as well. It helps strengthen the muscles in your legs, back, and your buttocks. Repeat it 7-10 times for each leg.

Infant bouncer

This exercise is quite similar to the previous one. However, there is one small variation. Instead of a forward lunge, you need to perform a side thrust. Instead of moving forward, you will move to your side and then perform a squat. Lean low and back as though you are sitting in a chair. Ensure that your knees are aligned with your ankles. Perform this 7-10 times for each leg.

Squats and twists

Stand such that your legs are spread apart. Hold your baby close to your chest. Now, perform a low squat, so that your child's feet touch the floor. As you exit the squat, move your baby closer to your chest and return to the standing position. Repeat this exercise 10-15 times.

Note: Seek your healthcare provider's advice before exercising with your baby. Also, don't perform any of these exercises before your baby is at least three months old. Stop exercising if you notice any physical discomfort. Don't overexert yourself and take sufficient breaks for recovery.

Apart from this, you can opt for light cardio, swimming, yoga, Pilates, light weight training, cycling, and low impact aerobics.

Safety Precautions

Follow any of the instructions your doctor or midwife might have suggested. Apart from this, there are certain general precautions you can follow whenever you exercise.

Ensure that you are wearing comfortable clothes. Restrictive clothing will not only make you feel uncomfortable, but it can stifle your movements as well. Wear a well-fitted sports bra. Your bra size will change after pregnancy, so ensure that you find one that fits you well.

Before you start exercising, spend some time to warm up your body. Perform a couple of full-body stretches to ensure that your body is not tense and the muscles are relaxed.

Whenever you feel any discomfort, stop exercising immediately. The exercises you opt for must not be tough and strenuous. Any pain or other unexplained symptoms are an indication that you need to take a break. If the symptoms do not go away, seek medical help immediately.

Things to Remember

You must consult your doctor or healthcare provider before following any exercise routines. If you notice any extreme physical discomfort while exercising, stop immediately, and seek medical help. Don't ignore any aches or soreness you experience. Always start with simple exercises and slowly make your way towards higher intensity workouts. Stick to the different exercise suggestions discussed in this section. Don't push yourself too hard. It is okay to want to train harder, but understand that your body is not a tireless machine. If you don't provide your body with the nutrition and rest it requires, you cannot function optimally. It might also increase the chances of accidental injuries.

While you are caring for a newborn, it can become challenging to find time to exercise. All the hormonal changes your body is subjected to can make you feel incredibly emotional. Apart from this, there will be days when you don't feel like exercising altogether. However, don't give up. Even if you don't feel like sticking to your full-fledged exercise routine, ensure that you indulge in some form of physical activity or the other. The best way to stick to an exercise plan is to include it in your daily schedule. When you set some time aside for exercising, it becomes easier to focus. Once you get used to the new routine, exercising will no longer seem like a chore. If you want to ensure that your motivation levels stay high, then start exercising with a friend or find an exercise partner. Exercising after pregnancy might not be easy, but it is doable. Trust me, it will do wonders for your overall well-being. It will revitalize your body and mind and give you the energy you need to take care of your newborn.

Chapter 6: Benefits of Baby and Mom Exercise

After the delivery, you might not even have the time to think about exercising. There will be different issues you need to deal with. It might seem a little chaotic initially, but it usually starts to get streamlined after about two months. Once your baby's natural rhythm starts developing, you can quickly establish a morning routine for yourself. Now that you have the time to think about exercising, it is time to revisit your fitness goals.

You might not want to be separated from your baby, and it might be a reason why you don't want to exercise. There are plenty of exercises you can start performing while at home! What's more, certain exercises are specifically suitable for doing with a baby. Yes, you read it right. You and your baby can start exercising together! Baby-mom exercises not only allow for physical activity, but they also strengthen the bond you share with your little one. Babies can focus, and they develop the ability to look around. They can absorb all the different stimuli in their environment and are ready to play. You can make the most of this time available to you by exercising together with your baby.

Why is it good?

In this section, let us look at the different benefits of mom-baby exercises.

It is a great way to not just spend more time with your baby, but also to step outside your house. Put your baby in a stroller and go for a walk. Get some fresh air and spend some time in the outdoors and you will feel better.

Exercising regularly helps moderate any of the changes brought about by pregnancy - physical as well as mental ones.

Postpartum depression can be easily tackled and even avoided using an exercise routine. When you go out, you have an opportunity to meet other mothers. Talking to others who are in the same situation as you are can make you feel better. You might also end up making new friends. Apart from this, shared stories, advice, and tips might give you a better perspective of motherhood. The change in scenery is an added advantage. It could act as the therapy you need to strengthen the bond with your little one. If you can exercise while your baby is playing, it will be quite lovely for the two of you.

It helps you understand that your life doesn't end because you have a baby. You don't have to worry about quitting the things you used to love doing because of motherhood. If you used to exercise regularly before childbirth, then I think it is a good idea to get back to that routine as soon as you safely can. Once you understand that you can still make time for yourself, you will feel more in control. Understanding and accepting this little fact can make you feel infinitely better.

It is also a great chance for your baby to interact with other babies! So, in a way, it helps expand the scope of his life. When your baby sees you interact with others while tending to his needs, he will understand that you are always there for him.

For a new mother, there is nothing worse than being separated from her baby. I know I couldn't bear the thought of stepping outside because I didn't want to be separated from my baby. This is known as separation anxiety. If you want to avoid it, then I suggest exercising together. You are not only getting the exercise your body needs but are also avoiding separation anxiety.

As mentioned earlier, exercising together helps strengthen the bond you share with your baby. You get more accustomed to each other's natural rhythm. Now that you are aware of the benefits it offers, I am sure you must be quite excited to start exercising with your baby.

What is happening?

The exercises you opt for are not strenuous and will not slow down the recovery process. If you exercise too hard or exert too much pressure on your body, it tends to affect milk production negatively. So, all the exercises you opt for will essentially help shape, tone, and strengthen the muscles and joints in your body. While performing the different exercises discussed in the previous section, you don't need any extra props. The only weight you will be training with is that of your baby. Yes, your baby's weight is sufficient to help strengthen your body. I am sure you will enjoy these exercises because they help you get fit while spending more time with your little one.

I know the importance of wanting to get back in shape and be fit once again. The idea of exercising is not just to improve your physical appearance, but your inner strength as well. When you notice yourself getting fitter and healthier, your self-confidence will also improve. Apart from this, it will also make you feel like you're in control of your life once again. After childbirth, it is quintessential to regain muscle flexibility. Your body has undoubtedly been through a tough time, and you need to take care of it.

Before you start exercising, spend some time and concentrate on your baby. Start with a simple body massage. Massage your baby's entire body, starting from the top of his head to the tips of his toes. Wiggle every toe and finger. Ensure that you are being gentle while doing this and aren't applying any force. Are you wondering why you need to do this? It is an easy way to energize your baby and get him involved in the process. It becomes difficult to exercise if he starts to get tired. Exposure to excessive stimuli can be tiring for a baby.

While exercising, opt for a calm environment. Get rid of all distractions and concentrate on yourself and your little one. Wear comfortable clothes and ensure that your baby is comfortable as well. If your baby is uncomfortable, then he will quickly become cranky, and you will not be able to exercise. You can sing or even talk to your baby while exercising. Play some soothing music in the background to deepen the relaxation. You can start performing aerobic moves once your baby is at least 5 to 6 months old. Since you can stop breastfeeding at that age, it becomes easier to exercise. As your baby grows, he will become heavier. So, you don't need any additional weights or dumbbells!

I love the idea of exercising with my baby. As you do this, you can come up with different ways in which you can work together. In a way, it acts as a natural stress buster. When your baby has fun with you, even you will feel better about yourself. However, if you notice any discomfort or if your baby is uncomfortable, stop exercising.

Exercise for Breastfeeding Moms

There will be a lot of lifestyle changes you need to get used to when you become a mother. Once you feel like you are ready, it is time to concentrate on your fitness and weight loss goals. Exercising while breastfeeding helps improve your physical stamina, shed the pregnancy weight, and improves your overall well-being. Apart from this, regular and consistent exercise also helps alleviate stress and baby blues. When you combine this with a healthy diet, it will undoubtedly help you lose all those extra pounds without harming the milk supply.

If you are breastfeeding and want to start exercising, then here are a couple of tips that will come in handy.

Always start out with low-intensity exercises. It could be something as simple as walking outdoors with your baby. Getting some fresh air will do you both good, and it is a great way to sneak in exercise. Regular walks improve the levels of serotonin in your body and promote positive feelings as well. Once your baby is born, your primary focus must be on caring for yourself as well as your baby. Ensure that you get sufficient sleep. Don't forget to keep your body hydrated. You can slowly start introducing cardiovascular strength-based exercises to tone your body. You might need to wait for at least two months before you can begin to do all of this. However, consult your doctor before you do anything.

It might be quite tempting to think about losing all those extra pounds rapidly. After all, who wouldn't want to shed the pregnancy weight immediately? Even if this thought is tempting, resist giving in to it. Losing more than one pound per week while lactating can increase the level of environmental toxins in the breast milk your body produces. It can also occur when your body starts burning fat rapidly.

The toxins present in your body fat will directly enter the bloodstream and breast milk. Consuming a diet that's rich in nutrients as well as calories will prevent rapid weight loss. If you do notice that you are losing weight rapidly, consult your doctor immediately.

Breastfeeding makes it easier to shed pregnancy weight. At least, this is what my experience has been. If you breastfeed your baby for anywhere between three to six months, you will find it easier to shed all the weight you piled on during pregnancy as long as you consume nutritious foods. By following a well-balanced diet, it is safe to lose weight while breastfeeding. Your daily calorie intake must be at least 1800 calories. If you don't consume nutritious meals, then the quality of breast milk produced will also suffer. Apart from this, it might also cause malnutrition.

If you are exercising as a breastfeeding mother, then keep your body hydrated. Drink plenty of water before and after exercise. Ensure that the levels of electrolytes in your body are stabilized.

You will need a high impact bra that offers plenty of support for your breasts while exercising. Your breasts will change from pregnancy, post pregnancy, and while breastfeeding as well. So, ensure that you get a bra that fits you well and supports your breasts without feeling too constrictive. Your old sports bras might not fit you like they are supposed to. I suggest that you opt for nursing sports bras with flaps over the breasts. Once you are done exercising, don't forget to remove the sports bra and change into comfortable clothing. When your breasts are full of milk, it might cause discomfort while exercising. Either feed your baby or try pumping before you start exercising.

Engaging in intensive training can increase the content of lactic acid in the breast milk. You might have also heard that exercising can turn the breast milk sour. Well, you don't have to worry about this because even after a strenuous workout, lactic acid will quickly disappear from your breast milk. Also, your baby will not be put off from breastfeeding because of this.

Exercise for C-Section

Since a C-section is major surgery, it will take at least six weeks to heal. So, I suggest that you stop pushing yourself too soon. However, there are a couple of pelvic floor exercises you can start performing as soon as you feel comfortable after childbirth. Pregnancy increases the strain and stress on your pelvic floor muscles, and therefore strengthening them must be your priority. Whenever you hold or pick up your baby, start tightening the muscles in your pelvic floor, and rectify your posture.

Because of the pregnancy, you might have gotten used to stooping or hunching. You might also do this because of the C-section stitches. Therefore, it is quite natural to feel a little vulnerable about your abdomen after such a major surgery. However, if you keep stooping, it can cause lower back troubles, and it will also push your tummy forward. So, consciously work on improving your posture.

Try to stand up as correctly as you can and do it as often as your body allows you to. It helps strengthen the muscles in your abdominal region and strengthen the ones in your back. During the two months following the C-section, avoid lifting any heavy objects. There are a couple of gentle toning exercises you can practice during the first six weeks. Pelvic bridges, pelvic tilts, and leg stretches are all suitable. These exercises were discussed in the previous section, and you can start following them. Even after a C-section, these exercises will not strain the stitches in your abdomen or damage the scar tissue. If you feel any discomfort or a slight twinge in the stitches, immediately seek medical attention.

Planks, sit-ups, straight-leg raises, or any other exercise that might cause your tummy to be pushed out must be avoided at all costs. They increase the strain on the group of muscles which were stretched because of the baby bump. Diastasis recti are the gaps that are left behind in your abdominal muscles after pregnancy. It tends to bulge out when extra pressure is applied to the abdominal region. So, any exercise that pushes your tummy out is not suitable for your recovery.

The skin surrounding the C-section scar can cause an overhanging belly. Your scar might feel tighter in this region than the skin present directly above it. To reduce this, concentrate on gradually losing those extra pounds. Pelvic floor exercises, coupled with simple and easy tummy exercises, are your best options. You might not notice any change in your physical appearance immediately, but if you keep at it for a couple of months, you will end up losing all those extra pounds. Gently flexing your abdominal muscles can help heal the scar tissue. Try to stand straight and perform gentle tummy exercises to heal this scar.

Start increasing the pace of your physical activity during the six weeks after childbirth. Maybe you can start with brisk walking for five minutes and slowly extend this timeframe. Do this only if you think you can, and your body is cooperating. If you're not sure about what the best form of exercising is, then consult your doctor or midwife.

Aerobic exercises that engage your heart and lungs can also help develop your core strength and return your body to its ideal state of fitness. Slowly work your way back into this form of exercising only after the first postnatal checkup. Only when the doctor says it is okay for you to exercise should you start exercising. After all, a stitch in time saves nine. A little precaution goes a long way. Keep in mind that taking care of your newborn must be your priority. If you are not feeling up to it yourself, you cannot care for your newborn like you're supposed to.

Swimming, cycling, or even brisk walking can help you shed some of the baby weight you gained during pregnancy. During an initial couple of days, you might not be able to exercise for more than 10 minutes at a stretch. Even if it's just 10 minutes that you can exercise for, then it is alright. Don't put unnecessary stress on yourself. After all, you are trying to reduce the burden on yourself. This kind of stress can lead to mental or emotional burnout. I remember I couldn't exercise for a couple of months after my first delivery. I was wrought with an overwhelming sense of frustration. I was frustrated with myself and my body. Now, when I look back, I know it was faulty thinking. My body needed a while to recover, and by giving myself the necessary time, I was stronger than I ever was.

Any high impact activities like running or extreme aerobics might not be possible for at least six months after the delivery. This is usually because of the effect of pregnancy hormones on your ligaments and joints. Since a pregnancy lasts for nine months, it is a good idea to give yourself nine months for recovery and healing. You can start performing exercises to strengthen your core and abdominal muscles anywhere between 4 to 6 months after childbirth. The exercises you can do include squats, downward dog pose (while you suck in your gut), and the superman pose.

Start out slow, and you can steadily increase the time and intensity of the workout. Don't forget to listen to your body. Your body knows what it needs, and if you listen to it, you will know what you need. You don't have to train yourself to exhaustion. Instead, concentrate on exercising regularly and consistently.

If you want, you can always join a postnatal exercise group or perform lower impact and gentle exercises once you have recovered. If you notice that you are unable to walk comfortably or find it difficult to perform any pelvic floor exercises, then your body isn't fully recovered yet. Apart from this, if you experience any pain even 12 weeks after the surgery, your body is not healed. If you notice any of these symptoms, don't exercise. Take a break and give yourself the time you need to recover.

If there were any complications after the surgery like an infection, consult your doctor before you start exercising. If you're working with an instructor or trainer, don't forget to mention the C-section you have had.

By keeping these simple tips and suggestions in mind, you can start working on your fitness goals. As I have already mentioned, motherhood changes your lifestyle and perspective in general. There are different ways in which you can get accustomed to these changes instead of thinking of them as challenges.

Chapter 7: Good Nutrition and Diet for New Moms

For nine months, your body supplied the fetus with all the nutrients it needed to grow and develop. Even after pregnancy, you need a diet that provides your body with all the nutrients it needs. Your body not only needs to recover, but it also needs to have sufficient strength to care for your baby. Your calorie intake in the months after the delivery should be anywhere between 1800 to 2200 calories. If you are nursing, then your body will need an additional 500 calories. The number of calories you need to consume will be significantly higher if you are underweight, nursing more than one child, or exercise for longer than 45 minutes daily. Consult your doctor to figure out the right number of calories you require. Apart from this, you might also need some supplements for a speedier recovery.

During pregnancy, most of the nutrients your body had were used to take care of the fetus. Therefore, it is obvious that your body needs to start replacing all the nutrients that are lost during pregnancy and childbirth. You no longer have to eat for two, but the food you consume has to be nutritionally dense. For every meal you consume, ensure that at least half your plate is full of fruits and vegetables. Start adding whole grains like oatmeal, brown rice and such, instead of refined ones. Apart from this, you need to concentrate on reducing the intake of any packaged processed foods and drinks, which might contain extra sugar, salt, and unhealthy saturated fats. Your body also needs protein, calcium, and iron. The best sources of protein include beans, lean meats, soy products, seafood, and eggs. Protein is essential for the recovery of your muscles after pregnancy. If you're breastfeeding, you can eat up to 7 servings of protein per day. Iron is a crucial nutrient since it enables your body to produce blood cells. It comes in handy because, after delivery, your body does lose a lot of blood. The best sources of iron include red meats, tofu, and beans.

You might be quite tempted by the idea of following a crash diet to lose all the weight you piled on during pregnancy. Most of the new mothers tend to lose up to 4 pounds per month after delivery. You can certainly speed this process up, but it is not advisable. If your daily calorie intake is lower than 1800 calories, you can be seriously malnourished. Also, rapid weight loss is never recommended. If there are any drastic fluctuations in your weight and calorie intake, there will be extreme mood swings, as well. Keep in mind that you need additional energy. Not just to recover, but also to take care of your young one. Instead of worrying about losing this weight quickly, concentrate on consuming a healthy diet and including some form of exercise in your daily routine.

Nutrition for New Mothers

Avoid crash dieting

If you truly want to attain your weight loss goals, then stay away from crash dieting. When you deprive your body of all your favorite foods, it merely increases the stress your body is under. After all, childbirth and postnatal care are quite stressful for your body. You don't need to add extra stress to all this. Once you start getting stressed out, you'll likely end up gaining more weight than losing it. Stress eating is incredibly common among new mothers, and if you don't want to fall into this trap, opt for a healthy and well-balanced diet. Eat healthily and eat only when you are truly hungry. Whenever you are stressed or bored, don't eat. If you want to shed those extra pounds, opt for a diet that's full of healthy foods. Regardless of fitness and weight loss goals, ensure that your daily calorie intake is not less than 1800 calories.

Try to understand that your body will need a while to recover from the exhaustion it underwent during labor, as well as delivery. Give yourself some rest until the six-week postpartum checkup before you start worrying about your daily calorie intake. Once this checkup is complete, and your practitioner gives you the green signal, you can start exercising. Wait for at least two months, especially if you're breastfeeding, before you think about weight loss. By dieting too soon and not giving your body the time it needs to recover, you are merely delaying the recovery process. Your body needs all the energy it can get to keep up with the demands of your newborn. If you are nursing, a poor diet can hurt your baby's health as well. Whenever you think about dieting, ensure that you are setting certain realistic weight-loss goals for yourself. Understand that you might never return to your exact pre-pregnancy shape or weight, but that is alright. You can certainly become fitter and healthier. Therefore, always have realistic expectations for yourself.

Nutritious foods

Your body will need plenty of nourishment, especially after giving birth and during the breastfeeding period. Always opt for foods that are rich in nutrients and low in empty calories. Fill yourself up with superfoods before you think about having any desserts. The best sources of Omega-3 fatty acids are olive oil and naturally fatty fish. Milk, as well as yogurt, is rich in calcium, which is quintessential for maintaining the health of your bones. Start consuming plenty of fiber and protein-rich foods. These are not only good for you but also leave your tummy feeling full longer. Opt for full-fat dairy products, and whole grains instead of processed ones if you want to speed up the process of weight loss. Making these changes is quite simple, and it helps you attain your weight loss and fitness goals. Include plenty of vegetables and fruits that are naturally fibrous and low in calories, such as apples, oranges, cherries, and different berries.

Try to add as many vegetables and fruits as you possibly can to your daily diet. Start making smoothies out of them instead of purchasing fruit juices. Try to cook as much at home as you possibly can. If you are unable to cook much, you can always ask your partner or other loved ones to help you out in the kitchen.

Foods to avoid

If you are breastfeeding, then there are a couple of foods you must avoid at all costs. Stay away from alcohol, caffeine, and certain varieties of seafood. Any drink that contains alcohol in it, such as wine, beer, hard lemonade, wine coolers, or even malt liquors, must be avoided. The toxins present in these will be absorbed by the body and transferred to your baby via your breast milk. Any stimulant like caffeine must also be avoided. Once again, it can pass through your body and into your baby via breast milk. It tends to affect your baby's growth and development. Caffeine is often found in sodas, tea, chocolate, coffee, and over-the-counter medications. Therefore, make a point to carefully read through the list of ingredients before you decide to eat anything. Avoid certain types of fish like shark, tilefish, king mackerel, and swordfish, which tend to have extremely high levels of mercury. Mercury is a toxin that can hinder your baby's brain growth. Ensure that you eat only up to 6 ounces of canned tuna in a week. Whenever you choose tuna, always opt for the light varieties instead of the dark ones.

Snacking

Always keep a couple of healthy snacks handy regardless of whether you are going out or are at home. If you have meal-prepped and everything is ready, it becomes easier to cook. Apart from this, when you replace all the junk food in your house with healthy options, the chances of eating junk food will dwindle. Start reducing the amount of processed food you consume. Convenience food is certainly an easy way out, but it is not always healthy. Instead of consuming empty carbs, especially when you're trying to lose weight, it is better to concentrate on eating nutrient-dense foods.

Prenatal vitamins

Once your baby is delivered, and you want to lose weight, always consult your doctor before you do this. Talk to your doctor about the diet and exercise plan you wish to follow. The supply of breast milk will be drastically affected if you lose weight quickly. Stay away from any diet pills, since they contain certain harmful ingredients that can be passed to your baby through breast milk. Even after your pregnancy, there might be specific prenatal vitamins you will need to consume. Talk to your doctor about these things.

Drink lots of water

Drinking plenty of water not only prevents dehydration, but it is good for your overall health as well. Apart from this, it also prevents you from giving in to your urges to snack unnecessarily. If you want, you can always add various flavorings as well as electrolytes to the water you consume. Different berries, slices of lemon, or even a handful of mint leaves can spruce up the water you are drinking.

Get sufficient sleep

Getting good sleep is almost as important as a healthy diet. If you are tired of being tired all the time, it is nothing more than sleep deprivation. Taking care of a newborn will undoubtedly take up all your time and energy. However, try to get as much sleep as you possibly can in the meanwhile. Ask your partner, parents, or any of your other loved ones to help you out with the baby while you get some sleep. When you don't get sufficient sleep, your mood also tends to suffer. The efficiency and effectiveness of your body's performance are dependent on the rest you get.

Exercise

The importance of exercising cannot be stressed enough. If you want to lose weight, then you need to exercise. It isn't easy to lose weight, and you will need to show some consistency and commitment to losing weight. The only way to attain your weight loss and fitness goals is via exercise and a well-balanced diet. As soon as you feel better, you can start exercising. Follow the different tips and suggestions given about exercise in the previous chapters.

Nutrition for Breastfeeding Mothers

There are no special dietary guidelines you need to follow if you are breastfeeding. However, it is quintessential that you consume a healthy and well-balanced diet and keep your body hydrated. While breastfeeding, stay away from any restrictive and strict weight loss regimes and diets. If you are breastfeeding, then here are a couple of suggestions you must follow to ensure that your body gets all the nutrients it needs.

Sufficient fluids

While breastfeeding, you might realize that you are thirstier than usual. Therefore, it is quite important to keep your body hydrated. Consume plenty of fruit juices, milk, and water to quench your thirst. Avoid drinking soda, or any other pre-packaged beverages that are full of processed sugars. You can consume liquids in any form, but be wary of the caffeine present in them. You don't have to drink more fluid than what your body requires. Whenever you feel thirsty, drink some water. In fact, while breastfeeding, I think it is a good idea to keep your favorite drink or even a glass of water next to you.

Variety of foods

How much do I eat? It is one question a lot of new mothers tend to worry about. Since you are breastfeeding, you need to nourish and support your body. Allow your appetite to guide you along the way. Unless you're bingeing or overeating, eat until your tummy is full. Your daily calorie intake must be anywhere between 1800 to 2500 calories. Never ignore any signs of hunger, especially during the first couple of months of breastfeeding. In fact, you might notice that you are hungrier than usual during this period. Make a couple of healthy snacks and keep them handy so that you can eat something whenever you feel extremely hungry. Make a point to consume a variety of foods. Include as many different categories of food as you can think of to your daily meals if you possibly can.

Spicy food

Spicy foods are quite common in a lot of cultures across the globe. If you consume any spicy food, it shouldn't bother your baby. Some babies tend to develop gas when their mothers consume spicy or gassy foods. Always eat in moderation. It isn't possible to categorize food into one specific group that tends to create problems for all babies. You don't have to avoid eating any particular foods, but see if you notice any adverse reaction in your baby within six hours of breastfeeding.

Vegetarian diet

Diets that are 100% vegetarian or mostly vegetarian are quite common all over the world. The quality of breast milk produced by mothers following a vegetarian diet is as nutritionally healthy as that produced by others. You don't have to drastically change your diet because you are nurturing your baby. In fact, as long as you are mindful of your protein intake and ensure that your body gets all the protein it requires, it is all good. Apart from this, you might need to take certain supplements for iron, calcium, and vitamin D during the breastfeeding period. All those new moms who follow a vegan or macrobiotic diet might need an additional supplement of B12. Since vegan diets are often deficient in vitamin B12, ask your doctor to give you the necessary supplements.

Avoid drinking caffeinated beverages, along with alcohol while breastfeeding. If you cannot let go of your caffeine intake, I suggest that you limit to two eight-ounce servings per day. Consuming excessive caffeine can make your baby jittery and irritable. Apart from this, it can also make it quite difficult for him to fall asleep. The effects of caffeine you notice in your body will be transferred to your baby, as well. Therefore, avoid consuming caffeine. Stay away from alcoholic beverages while breastfeeding. The alcohol gets directly absorbed by your body and transferred into the breast milk. It can have a lasting and damaging effect on your baby's development and growth.

Tobacco and smoking

While breastfeeding or pumping, I suggest that you stay away from smoking and the use of tobacco altogether. Nicotine, just like caffeine, can also get transferred from your body to the breast milk. Nicotine can induce restlessness, diarrhea, and even jitters in your baby. Apart from this, the use of tobacco can also reduce the quality and quantity of the milk produced by your body. Smoking is never a healthy habit, and there is no time like the present to quit. If you are breastfeeding your baby, his health needs to be your priority. Therefore, start doing everything you possibly can to ensure that your baby gets all the nourishment it requires.

Weight Loss Tips

Don't eat for two

Your calorie intake might have been rather high during pregnancy. It is time to reduce your calorie intake to the daily requirement of 1800 to 2400 calories per day, depending on your level of activity and whether you are breastfeeding or not. If you are breastfeeding, you need about 450 to 500 extra calories per day. However, this doesn't mean that you should start counting every morsel of food that you eat. It simply means that you should be mindful of what you are eating. You could always download a calorie counting app to keep track of all the calories you are consuming. If tracking every single mouthful of food sounds exhausting, you can instead concentrate on those foods that you keep eating repeatedly. Your go-to food should be tasty, healthy, easy to prepare, and nutritious. You can find plenty of recipes on the Internet.

Start controlling your cravings

During your pregnancy, your hormones had a field day, and cravings would just sneak up on you. Well, you shouldn't let this habit continue now that you have given birth. Physical exhaustion, combined with insufficient sleep, might make you crave all sorts of junk food. However, this doesn't mean that you should give in to your cravings. Eat only when you are hungry and not because of any other reason. Keep a couple of healthy snacks on hand for whenever hunger pangs strike. Pick foods that will keep you feeling fuller for longer. Foods rich in protein and fiber are great options.

Calorie intake

During your pregnancy, you were probably used to drinking smoothies, fortified fruit juices, and other protein drinks for improving your intake of calcium and other nutrients. However, these drinks are full of sugar and calories that your body no longer needs. So, cut down on their intake, and you can have healthy substitutes like skimmed milk instead of whole fat milk and yogurt instead of ice cream. Have plenty of water, especially during the day. Drinking water will not only keep your body hydrated, but it will also keep you feeling full and will reduce your craving for sugar and calorie-rich food. Add a few drops of lemon juice to your sparkling water if you feel like.

Lean protein

During your pregnancy, your body would have needed extra protein for maintaining its health. However, now that you aren't pregnant, you need to cut back on your protein intake as well. You no longer need to have fatty red meats and should instead stick to lean protein if you don't want to increase your risk of heart diseases. Your body will need about 2-3 servings of protein per day, and each of these servings shouldn't be more than 3-4 ounces.

Cut back on the extras

Adding a little butter or some heavy cream might not have been a big deal during your pregnancy, but you need to start cutting back on all those extras if you want to lose weight. Instead of saturated oils, you should opt for healthy fats like olive and canola oils.

Being mindful of your meals

It's a good idea to remind yourself that eating isn't a race. Take the time to savor what you eat and enjoy your food. You are likely to realize when you are full when you start chewing your food more. It helps in easier digestion, but along the way, you will begin to notice the different flavors in the food that might have gone unnoticed previously. Try eating with chopsticks; it will slow down your speed while eating. It might not always be possible to eat in silence, but it would be good to have some time to think and reflect. If not all your meals, make it a point of having a few meals in silence. It doesn't even have to be a meal. You can simply sit in silence and savor your favorite cup of tea. Notice all the different textures and flavors of the food you consume.

A balanced meal

Stay away from all sorts of processed foods that are rich in harmful sugars, unhealthy fats, and carbs. Instead, you should opt for healthy foods that are rich in fiber, nutrients, and other important macros. Healthy food will help to nourish your body and will leave you feeling energetic. Unhealthy foods like chocolates or chips can be replaced with a fruit or a handful of nuts. Start having complex carbohydrates like whole grains and leafy vegetables instead of starch like bread, pasta, or pizza. Stay away from all processed foods and instead opt for healthy treats like kale chips, nuts, fruits, or anything that isn't full of saturated fats and trans fats. Replace sugary drinks with water (sparkling or still).

Eat the rainbow

Here is the list of foods that you should include in your diet according to their colors.

- Red: red peppers, tomatoes, apples, cherries, grapes, strawberries, raspberries, and watermelon.
- Orange: carrots, pumpkin, peppers, oranges, tangerines, nectarines, sweet potatoes, and yams are good for your eyes.
- Yellow: peppers, cantaloupe, beans, zucchini, squash, grapefruit, lemon, and papayas.
- Green: green leafy vegetables and anything that's green in color.
- Blue and purple: blueberries, nightshades like eggplant and peppers, red cabbage, and grapes.
- White: cauliflower, garlic, peas, potatoes, bananas, and pears contain selenium and allicin that are good for the

heart.

Add physical activity

It might seem quite difficult to motivate yourself to exercise when your belly was weighing you down. Now that you aren't as heavy as you were, you can start exercising again. You should always consult with your doctor before you start exercising. Depending on the method of childbirth, the recovery period differs as well. You can start with simple Kegels and other stretches before moving on to intensive exercises.

Chapter 8: Your Intimate Relationship with Your Husband/Partner

During your pregnancy, you might have been worried about the effect the new baby would have on your sex life. Postpartum sex is something a lot of women worry about, and if you're one of them, you are not alone. You probably used to wonder how the baby would affect your body, mind, and the equation with your partner. The good news is, even if pregnancy causes significant changes in your life, your sex life doesn't have to suffer. There are a couple of things you can keep in mind to ease yourself back into your sex life and try to make it even better than it ever was. Sex is an incredibly important aspect of your life, as well as a relationship with your partner. Engaging in sexual activities not only increases the intimacy you share but also strengthens the relationship you have. All couples need to engage in healthy discussions about their likes and dislikes. These conversations help spice things up in the bedroom.

Barriers to Intimacy

It is not uncommon for women to experience fear and anxiety at the thought of resuming their normal sex life after pregnancy. Maybe the pain you experienced during labor is still quite fresh in your mind, or perhaps the hormones that regulate your sensuality have not yet regained their equilibrium. There could be different reasons why you don't feel at your sensual best after pregnancy. In fact, you might be so focused on the role of a new mother that you might have forgotten that you do have a partner to look after as well. Or it could be something as simple as the fact that sex is not on your mind as often as it used to be in the past. It is quite easy to overlook one's sex life, but it will undoubtedly harm the personal relationship with your partner.

It's not just you; even your partner might have certain anxieties about his sex life. Prolonged inactivity can induce severe anxiety. If your partner was with you during the birth of your baby, he might have also developed an irrational fear that any sexual activity might end up hurting you. After all, it is quite difficult to see someone you love experience pain of any kind. So, in his bid to not inflict any harm on you, he might abstain from engaging in any sexual activities with you. My husband was with me during the birth of our first child, and I think it scared him a little. Even when I was okay with the idea of resuming our normal sex life, he was a little skeptical. Yes, as surprising as it might seem to you, even your partner will have his share of reservations about it. There are different physical, psychological, emotional, and even environmental factors that tend to hinder your sex life after pregnancy. Before we start discussing different tips you can use to kickstart your sex life, let us analyze the different barriers to intimacy.

Perhaps the greatest barrier to intimacy is exhaustion. It is quite difficult to feel even slightly romantic or sexual when you are utterly exhausted. This is especially true during the early months of your baby's life. Most of your time and energy will be directed towards taking care of your little one. It is during this time that you are learning the ropes of motherhood. The lack of sleep, coupled with all the work involved in taking care of a newborn, can leave you tired to the bone. When you barely have the time to sleep for more than three to four hours a day, I am sure sex will not be high on your list of priorities. It stands true for your partner, as well.

The lack of privacy can also affect your sex life. You may no longer have the bedroom to yourself as you used to in the past. Maybe you decided to allow the baby to sleep with you. Three is certainly a crowd, especially when it comes to intimacy between partners. The new phase of parenthood can mean a lack of privacy.

Any fluctuations in your hormone levels or that of your partner can also lead to a reduction in one's sexual appetite. When this is combined with all the postpartum changes that take place in your body, it can have a direct effect on your level of sexual desire. For instance, these hormonal changes can reduce vaginal secretions that can leave your vagina feeling dry and incredibly sensitive to any source of pain or abrasions. Your sexual desires, as well as natural lubrication, will start to dry up while you are nursing your newborn. However, it is believed that mothers who opt to breastfeed their babies tend to enjoy sex sooner than mothers who bottle-feed their babies. So, this is another reason why you should start breastfeeding your baby.

All the physical changes you undergo during pregnancy might hurt your body image. If you don't feel sexy yourself, your sexual appetite will reduce. You might also start thinking that your partner no longer finds you desirable. These factors will certainly ruin any intimacy in a relationship.

Experiencing mild or severe cases of postpartum depression can also inhibit your sexual desires. When your emotions are all over the place and you are feeling quite low all the time, it is highly unlikely that you'll want to engage in any sexual activity. If you notice any signs of postpartum depression, I suggest that you seek medical help immediately. It is not a condition to be treated lightly, and it certainly must not be overlooked.

There is plenty of anxiety as well as fear associated with postpartum sex. You might be worried about how you would perform or even start questioning your ability to have sex again. You might also worry that engaging in sexual activities might end up physically hurting you.

As a new mother, it is quite obvious that you would want to spend a lot of time with your baby. Most of your time and energy would be devoted to taking care of your baby's needs. If you don't spend sufficient time with your partner, it might also be a reason for unnecessary jealousy. He might begin to envy the baby because you no longer pay attention to his needs. Most of the barriers to intimacy can be easily resolved with open communication. Once you start talking about your desires, feelings, expectations, anxieties, and worries, things will get easier.

Engaging in sexual intercourse within a couple of months of childbirth can be painful for a woman. This pain continues until the perineum is fully healed. It is often bruised, stretch, and at times even taunt during delivery. If there is any reduction in the natural lubrication produced by the vagina, it can add to the discomfort you experience. If the pain is too much, stop immediately, and seek medical attention. Also, consider using lubricants to make things easier for yourself as well as your partner.

It can be quite difficult to stop thinking about your baby during the initial couple of months. You might be so focused on taking care of your little one that you might not be able to think about anything else. It becomes even more difficult if your baby sleeps in the same room. If so much of your energy, as well as emotions, are directed towards a baby, you might not have any attention left to give to your partner.

If you are your partner don't have similar priorities, it can also affect your sex life. For instance, if sex is not on your list of priorities, you will obviously not think about it. In fact, you might be eager to catch up on some sleep or maybe take a leisurely bath when you have the time. Likewise, if your partner also feels the same, sex can certainly take the back seat for a while. If you want to rekindle the intimacy in your relationship, then you and your partner need to make sex a priority. Unless you make a conscious effort to rectify this situation, it will not change and might even worsen.

Your attitude or maybe that of your partner might have changed entirely towards sex after pregnancy and childbirth. The way you or your partner view your body might have completely transformed. Once you see your baby suckle at your bosom for nourishment, the way you and your partner view your breasts will change. This change in attitude can also hinder your sex life. It might make you both quite conscious of your bodies, too.

Sex and Co-Sleeping

Co-sleeping must not hurt your sex life. You can maintain a healthy and passionate sex life even if your baby is sharing the room with you. After all, there are no rules that sex needs to be restricted to the bedroom alone. Get a little creative; there are no fixed places to have sex. So, don't be too bothered by co-sleeping arrangements. There are different rooms in the house you can use, and you can engage in sexual activities whenever your little one is napping. Unless you also need a nap, I think you can easily have a quickie before the baby wakes up. Once you start to become more creative and spontaneous, the intimacy you share will certainly improve. If you want to wait until bedtime, then there is a solution to that situation as well. Allow your baby to fall asleep in another room, and then you can bring him back to your room once you are done! All this sneaking around certainly adds a little extra excitement to your sex life.

Tips to Rebuild Intimacy

I know, having a baby means you'll be running short on time. You might be tired, sleep-deprived, and even irritable because of all these things. However, if you don't pay any attention to it, your sex life is bound to suffer. Sex is not just pleasurable, but it is good for you in various ways. It helps strengthen your immune system by increasing the production of antibodies. It reduces and regulates your blood pressure and alleviates the levels of estrogen. This, in turn, helps reduce the overall risk of heart diseases. Since you will be engaging the pelvic floor muscles while engaging in sexual intercourse, it reduces the risk of incontinence. Apart from this, it is a great stress buster and produces a sleep-inducing hormone that enables you to sleep better at night. Sex is a great painkiller, as well. Not to mention an incredible way to exercise. You and your partner stand to gain all these benefits by engaging in sex. However, I know sex might not be the first thing on your mind, especially after you just had a baby.

Once your body has had the time to heal, and you feel ready, you can start having sex. Usually, you need to wait for at least six weeks after delivery. Always consult your healthcare provider before you start having sex. Here are a couple of tips you can use to rekindle the flame in your romance.

Keep in mind that you don't have to rush into it. This is an incredibly important point to remember. You don't have to do anything that you don't want to. Ensure that you are physically as well as mentally ready to resume sexual intercourse. If you start having sex before you are ready, you'll end up hurting yourself and even your relationship in the process. If you feel sore, consult your healthcare provider immediately. If you are feeling insecure about your body, remind yourself that you are sexy the way you are. Regardless of whatever the reason is, take things slowly and gently ease your way back into being intimate with your partner.

There are a lot of misconceptions about contraceptives after childbirth. Just because you delivered a baby a while ago doesn't mean you cannot get pregnant. You can still get pregnant even if your menstrual cycle hasn't started. Therefore, get some birth control immediately. Talk to a gynecologist about it and ensure that you always use contraception while having sex.

There are a couple of different things you can do to rebuild intimacy in your relationship. You can start with something as simple as a sensual bubble bath. Once you have put your baby to sleep, draw a warm bubble bath. You and your partner can soak in the luxurious bath and unwind. It is a great way to add some intimacy to your relationship.

It is always quality over quantity when it comes to sex. It doesn't matter how frequently you have sex, but the quality of it matters a lot. You don't necessarily have to do it twice a day if you don't want to. Ensure that you and your partner are both comfortable with each other and are happy while engaging in any sexual activities.

Learn to be spontaneous. I know you might not always have the privacy you hoped for, but don't let that stop you. You don't have to limit sexual activities to the bedroom alone. Whenever the mood strikes you or your partner, get started. Do you remember the initial phases of your relationship, when you and your partner couldn't keep your hands off each other? Well, it is time to relive those memories.

Make a conscious effort to spend more time together. Having a baby will certainly take up every ounce of your attention, but this doesn't mean you both start ignoring each other. I'm sure you like having your partner's attention. Likewise, even your partner desires the same. You don't necessarily have to start having sex to improve your sex life. Even something as simple as cuddling together can make you and your partner feel much better about each other. Cuddling is quite romantic and intimate.

Lubrication will come in handy. If you need a little extra help, don't hesitate to get some lube. Ensure that the lube you are using doesn't trigger any allergic reactions. When in doubt, always consult a healthcare practitioner before you start using anything.

It's not just you who needs to adjust to all the new changes that come along your way. Even your partner needs to get accustomed to all these changes. Being a parent is an entirely new ballgame, and it takes some time to get used to it. Spend some time and get to know each other all over again. Rediscover yourself and your relationship. You can set up a weekly date night or any such one on one activity.

If you are worried about anything, then talk about it. Don't suppress any fears or worries you have, and instead, start discussing them with your partner. This is the only way in which your partner can understand you. Neither you nor your partner are mind readers, so communication is the only way in which you can understand each other better. Good communication can significantly improve your sex life. It also strengthens the connection you both share. Learn to let go of all your inhibitions and talk freely to your partner. Encourage your partner to do the same.

If you don't feel like engaging in any sexual activity, all that you need to do is say no. If you're not ready for it, be honest about it with your partner. You don't have to push yourself to do anything merely to please your partner. If your relationship is strong enough, then your partner can handle a no. You don't have to please him by making yourself uncomfortable. The same applies to your partner, as well. I think the best way to fix this situation is by communicating with each other. I cannot stress enough the importance of communication in relationships.

If you feel like you're up to it, then maybe you can spend some time and dress up sexily. It will be a pleasant change for you as well as your partner. Get out of those boring mom clothes and buy some sexy lingerie. Try seducing your partner. Wear something that you know will drive your partner crazy. It will make you feel more comfortable and confident about your body. Trust me, your efforts will pay off!

I have tried all these tips, and I know they work! You might not feel like ever having sex again after delivering a baby, but this opinion will change eventually. When it does, and you feel ready, it is time to get to work.

Things to Avoid

Communication is essential, but it might not always be easy. Any difficulties you and your partner have related to communication can easily make their way to your bedroom. If you don't have the time to talk before your baby goes to sleep, then it is highly likely that all unresolved issues and problems would creep into bed with you. Your bedroom isn't meant for negotiations, at least not when you are trying to rekindle the fire in your relationship. Learn to leave all the problems outside.

If you feel that neither of you has any time left, then try setting aside a specific time slot to talk about other things. Once all the conflicts are resolved and any misunderstandings cleared up, it certainly becomes easier to concentrate on your sex life. When you and your partner are happy with each other, and in a good place, intimacy will improve. It certainly isn't sexy to talk about finances while things start heating up in the bedroom. Keep in mind that there is a time and place for every conversation, so tread accordingly.

You and your partner need to be empathetic and sensitive towards each other's emotions. If your partner feels unloved and unworthy, then instead of scolding him, be a little tender and loving towards him. If you feel like you need some extra love, don't hesitate and convey the same to your partner as well. Don't hold onto any petty issues and laugh it out. Laughter is the best way to strengthen the bond you share with your partner as you both wade through the waters of parenthood. Think of laughter as the buoy that enables you to stay afloat. Your life might not turn out the way you have planned. After the birth of our third child, we finally managed to wiggle out some time from our hectic lives and scheduled a date night. Everything was in place; a family member was to look after our kids so that my husband and I could go out on a date. As if on cue, just as we were heading out the door, my toddler came running to me asking for her favorite blanket. When the blanket couldn't be located, she threw a tantrum unlike any before. Well, that was the end of our date night. The romantic dinner we looked forward to had turned into a treasure hunt to locate the precious blanket. It was a little disappointing, but we did have a little fun together.

In the end, all that matters is your attitude. If you learn to laugh at such frustrating instances, you will have plenty of humorous incidents to talk about in the future.

Feeling Sexy and Confident

Losing weight

You don't have to rush into it and take things one day at a time. If you forcefully abstain from eating, it is not a good idea. Ensure that your body gets all the nutrients and vitamins it requires to maintain your health and give you the energy to take care of your infant. By breastfeeding your baby, you can increase your body's calorie expenditure as well. It is not only good for your baby's health, but it is good for your health, too. Exercising is the best way to lose weight. If you don't have time to exercise, at least make time to indulge in sex. Sex helps burn plenty of calories and also strengthens the relationship you share with your partner.

Makeup

After pregnancy, you might not have much time to take care of yourself. When you become a mother, you will barely have any time to follow your usual makeup and skincare routine. It might come to a stage where you no longer recognize the tired reflection you see in the mirror. If you're tired of all this, it is time to regain your self-confidence. Learn some basic makeup techniques to mask the tiredness to make yourself look fresh. Using a good CC or BB cream coupled with some tinted moisturizer will make your face look fresher and cleaner. Try your hand at a little contouring, add some color using blush, and wear lipstick! This makeup routine barely takes longer than 5 minutes, and it will certainly make you feel like a million bucks.

Hair care

Washing your hair at night will certainly save you a couple of minutes the next morning. All that you need to do is style and maybe set your hair the way you want to. For a quick updo, you can use a donut hair band or a hair ring. Start using a sea salt spray on your bedhead to get rid of the tangles and give it a naturally bouncy and wavy look. Hair care doesn't take much effort. Once you start taking care of your mane, you will feel better about yourself.

Your style

Start wearing clothes you feel good in. You don't necessarily have to follow any of the latest trends or attempt any looks that don't suit you. Start investing in some great quality and well-fitting body shapers and lingerie. Your bra size has most likely changed now, so get yourself professionally measured at a retail outlet before you buy any new undergarments. If you think you will not be able to manage the cost of a new wardrobe, then invest in some accessories that can help jazz up your regular outfits. Learn to embrace your new shape and your body. Once you are comfortable within your own skin, you will be more confident. And confidence is perhaps the sexiest accessory you can ever wear.

Dress up

Picking the right outfit matters a lot. Start looking for a little inspiration before you get started. Go through various magazines, websites, and catalogs to find someone you can draw inspiration from. You can start wearing the most basic of outfits and still manage to look good. You don't necessarily have to dress up in designer wear to feel better about yourself. If you start feeling conscious of your post-baby belly, wear a well-stitched jacket over it. Start clearing and opt for light layers instead of thick ones. Good posture is important, as well. Don't ever stop believing in yourself. Whenever you feel unsure of yourself, learn to replace these thoughts with the ones that inspire self-confidence. Keep in mind that no two individuals are ever alike. You are a unique person, so stop comparing yourself with others. You are perfect and beautiful the way you are. Unless you learn to accept yourself, you will be riddled with self-doubt and body image issues. You are perfect and beautiful the way you are. Unless you learn to accept yourself, you will be riddled with self-doubt and body image issues.

Pamper yourself

Get to know yourself once again, and learn to pamper yourself. Head over to a salon or spa and get pampered. If you start to feel better about yourself, you will start feeling better about everything else in your life as well.

Nursing

Every once in a while, take a break from breastfeeding. Buy a breast pump, fill up a feeding bottle or two with breast milk, and handover the duty of feeding the baby to someone else. Breastfeeding constantly will certainly eat away at the sexy self-image you have. So, take a break and enjoy yourself.

Eat right

It might sound very simple. You have been through a lot, mentally as well as physically. Your body needs extra vitamins and minerals for replenishing all the nutrient stores that were depleted. Start eating healthy foods, drink plenty of water, and take the necessary supplements. If you feel energetic, you will have more time to concentrate on yourself.

"Me" time

It might seem impossible to schedule some "me" time, especially during the initial weeks after delivery. It is quite easy to forget about yourself and dedicate all your time and energy to your little one. It is okay if you don't immediately fold the laundry. While your baby is sleeping, make the most of it. You can take a nap, read a book, soak up in the bathtub, watch your favorite sitcom, or do something that you enjoy. Make sure that you get some "me" time. Also, head out of the house once a week. Let your partner or anyone else you trust take care of your baby for an hour or two. Don't forget to take care of yourself just because you need to care for your baby. Any activity that makes you happy and forget all about stress is a hobby. From singing to dancing or even painting, there are different hobbies. If you have any hobbies, then there is no time like the present to start enjoying them. If you don't have any hobbies, it's time you try your hand at different things.

Give yourself a break

Try to understand that your body managed to accomplish something quite astounding by not just making and growing, but also giving birth to a new human. You are possibly your own worst critic. Learn to let go of all unnecessary criticism and start rejoicing in motherhood. Give yourself a break; you deserve it.

Chapter 9: When to Have another Child?

I think the question about having another child is trickier than deciding to have the first one. It is undoubtedly more complicated than asking yourself, "Do we want another child, and do we have sufficient money for it? If yes, then let's go ahead." Having another baby is like recreating your family. If you are thinking about having another child, then here are a couple of things you must take into consideration.

If I'm honest, this is not an easy decision to make. However, a lot of people are entirely unfazed by this question. Either they already know how many children they want to have, or go ahead and have as many kids as they want to. If that works for you, then go for it. I am sure your brain might be running various permutations and combinations to determine how your life would be if you have another child. For instance, your age, financial situation, existing family dynamics, and your outlook towards life are some of the primary considerations which help determine whether you are ready to have another child or not. So, let us carefully analyze each of these factors to put an end to the internal tug of war going on between your heart and mind.

Family Dynamics

Having your first baby might have turned your world upside down. My partner and I spent months figuring out how we would deal with our new roles as parents before the delivery. However, everything was quite different from what we had imagined. It took us quite some time to get the hang of parenthood. After a while, the three of us were a cohesive family unit. We were both used to being parents by now. At this point, we started considering the idea of having another child. I was extremely keen on having a second child because I wanted a big family. I loved the idea of the house being filled with happy children. Since I already knew what I wanted, all that was left to do was talk to my partner about the ideas I had.

You can certainly sit down and start making a list of the pros and cons of having another child. However, this is one decision wherein your heart's opinion matters more than your brain's rationality. So go ahead and listen to what your heart says. If you want another baby, and your partner does, too, then you have your answer. In fact, there is no time like the present, and make the most of it. As long as you know you will be able to take care of yourself, your child, your partner, and the baby you plan to have, there is no reason not to.

Adding another baby to your existing family will undoubtedly change the dynamics once again. You not only have to take care of the child you have right now but also prepare yourself for another one. It means more responsibilities and duties, but even more love and happiness. So, are you ready to take on all these responsibilities? Do you think your family can handle this change?

All the existing relationships as well as routines you have tried to establish will change with every pregnancy. I felt like I won the figurative baby lottery when my firstborn turned out to be a well-adjusted, happy child. Therefore, having another one just felt like a natural decision for me. I was a little skeptical about all the changes that were soon to follow, but I was quite happy about it. Now that you already have a child at home, you might have figured out a couple of things about parenthood. Now, you are better equipped to deal with a pregnancy, childbirth, and the aftermath of it. All this experience will certainly come in handy if you decide to have another child.

Time and Effort

On the flip side, if your child is rather fussy and takes up all your time and attention, you might not be too keen on having another child immediately. After all, you would not be interested in adding more stress to your life than what already exists. All this will have an effect on your life as well as the equation you share with your partner. Obviously, having two children means double the effort, double the time that's required, and double everything. However, adding more children to your family will certainly make you happier. All happiness will also multiply.

Another critical factor you need to consider is the number of children you plan to have and the ones you already have at home. After all, you are a parent, and you will be responsible for their well-being. As a parent of three kids, I know the effort that goes into raising them. I always wanted a big family, so this did not seem like much of an effort to me. However, it is an entirely personal decision, and unless you feel like you're up to it, you don't have to go ahead. In the end, you and your partner need to decide because you will be the ones dealing with the responsibilities.

Health

Consider the timing as well as your health before you think about having another child. Childbirth and pregnancy are naturally stressful for mothers, even when everything goes along smoothly. If you had any competitions during your previous pregnancy or painful childbirth, then you might have some doubts about having another child. Apart from this, your age also matters. If you're older than 35, the risks associated with pregnancy also increase. Therefore, talk to your medical practitioner about all your worries and then see whether having another child is the right option for you. Your body needs to be physically capable of carrying a pregnancy to term.

Not just that, but there are other mental and emotional implications of pregnancy you need to deal with as well. Dealing with a pregnancy at the age of 20 is quite different from being pregnant when you're 30. Therefore, ensure that you have considered all these factors before you and your partner start trying for another child.

Timing

You will need anywhere between 1 to 2 years to feel like your old self. If you don't want to put yourself through everything you went through during the previous pregnancy, then maybe it was not the right time to have a child. If you are hesitant about having another child, then put it on hold. You don't have to rush into anything. Take all the time you need to ensure that you are mentally and physically prepared for it. Not just you, even your partner needs to be ready for it. What if you want to have a child and your partner is not yet prepared for it? In such a situation, give your partner the time he needs. After all, parenting a child is a shared responsibility. Ensure that you give yourself at least one and a half to 2 years between each pregnancy.

Financial Aspect

Don't forget to consider the financial implications of pregnancy. The way you planned for your first child, you will need to repeat the same steps for the second child as well.

Financial aspects of pregnancy cannot be overlooked. If you were planning on resuming work after your first child, then you might be a little skeptical about conceiving again. If you don't want your career to suffer, then you and your partner need to have an honest conversation about having another child. If you think that the financial situation at home is not as stable as you would want it to be, then take some more time until you both are financially prepared to accept all the responsibilities of a second child. From saving for school to college and probably their wedding, there are different funds that you will need to start accumulating. Your personal opinion about your career also matters. I know money is not everything, but it certainly comes in handy when you're trying to raise a family. Your monthly budget and finances need to have sufficient space to accommodate a second child while taking care of the one you already have. A lot of women find it difficult to keep up with a full-time or part-time job once the second or third child comes along. If you think you can afford to quit, then it might be quite easy to take care of a second child. Childcare is expensive, so write out your finances.

Routines

Do you have a nice routine that you have established with your partner and your child? Do you have a proper childcare system in place? Is everyone finally able to get a good night's rest without any interruptions? Maybe you have finally reached a point where you and your partner once again have time for each other. Perhaps you resumed work, and you love working. These are all important aspects you must consider before you think about having another child. Remember, having a baby will once again recapture all the time and energy you spend on other things right now.

I'm sure you would have talked to different people about this. You might have heard different answers from them. Keep in mind that they are all just opinions and suggestions. Don't allow others to dictate your decision. In the end, you and your partner need to decide what is the best course of action for your family.

I know it is certainly a lot to consider. While thinking about having another child, you will certainly face all the doubts you did before you had your first one — all the different what-ifs and maybes can be quite overwhelming. If you're not sure what to do, then take some time and carefully reconsider your life. How would you react if you discovered that you are pregnant today? Talk to your partner about it, and sit together and discuss all these considerations. In the end, the decision needs to be yours. You and your partner need to be on board with the idea of having another child. What might be right for someone might not necessarily be the right fit for you. After all, the idea of a family is quite subjective, and there is no universal one size fits all kind of answer. It is a personal decision, so always allow your heart to guide you.

Conclusion

I want to thank you once again for choosing this book. I hope it proved to be an informative, insightful, and engaging read.

Parenthood is bound to change your life in several unexpected ways. From undergoing physical to mental and emotional changes, your lifestyle will also change. Change is the keyword here. Learning to accept and deal with these changes is the first step towards parenthood. After the long wait of nine months, when you finally hold your bundle of joy in your arms, nothing else will matter. The love you feel for your baby is unlike any other. Whenever you feel a little worried or anxious, take a look at your baby, and all your worries will melt away.

Accepting, loving, and caring for yourself need to be on your list of priorities. Your baby's needs will certainly take precedence over everything else. It doesn't mean you ignore everything else — concentrate on your overall well-being as well as your partner's, too. The relationship you share with your partner will change. However, it doesn't mean the end of romance. You and your partner need to actively come up with new and exciting ways to strengthen your relationship.

Anticipating all the different ways in which your life can change is the best way to accept and deal with those changes. The different tips and tricks given in this book will help you deal with the physical, emotional, and other lifestyle changes brought about by parenthood.

Learning to take care of yourself is important. If you have any worries or concerns, share them with your partner. Work together, spend more time together, start trusting yourself, and have a little faith in your skills as a parent. Keep in mind that you are new to all this, and you are learning. Learning takes a conscious effort, consistency, and plenty of time. So, be patient and kind to yourself in the meantime.

The decision about resuming work after pregnancy is a personal one. It is entirely up to you to decide what you want to do. Consider your financial situation, career consequences, and the childcare plan you have in place. Once you are happy with your solution to all these considerations, you will have your answer. You don't have to do what others say; go with what you want to do. After all, it is your life.

One of the most obvious changes associated with pregnancy is weight gain. Now that you are holding your bundle of joy in your arms, it is time to refocus on your fitness and weight loss goals. Start by setting certain realistic goals for yourself. Accept your body for the way it is and don't indulge in body shaming or any negative self-talk. There are different exercises you can start performing within six weeks of your pregnancy — concentrate on strengthening your muscles and joints. By consuming healthy and wholesome meals, you can ensure that you meet your weight loss goals as well. Your health and well-being must be your priority. After all, it takes plenty of energy to care for a newborn.

If you don't like the thought of being away from your baby, then there are different exercises you can perform together. These exercises not only help you meet your fitness goals, but also strengthen the bond you share with your baby. Good nutrition is quintessential for a new mother. If you have decided to breastfeed your baby, then you need to concentrate on the food you consume. A well-balanced meal helps your body produce sufficient milk for your baby and gives up the nourishment it requires. If you don't start taking care of yourself right now, you might not be able to take good care of your baby. Get sufficient rest, avoid stressful activities, and start adding a little exercise to your daily routine.

Once you have done all of this, it is time to concentrate on the relationship you share with your partner. Rekindling the romance in your relationship is very important, especially after pregnancy. All the physical and emotional changes associated with pregnancy can take a toll on your relationship if you're not careful. Therefore, some consistent and conscious effort to rekindle the spark is in order. The best way to get started is by having an open and honest conversation about what you both feel and expect from each other. Once everything is out in the open, it becomes easier to deal with any emotions. Regardless of what it is, ensure that the channels of communication between you and your partner are always open. Don't hesitate to talk about anything with your partner. You are free to share all your worries and anxieties with him.

In this book, you were given all the information you require to prepare yourself for parenthood. Preparation is not just about understanding what lies ahead, but it is also about coming up with the necessary mental and emotional strength to keep going. Once you know what to expect, you will be in a better position to handle everything that comes your way. This, in turn, will make you feel more in control. Change is never easy, but you can certainly take steps to make the transition easier. Parenthood will bring about immense joy and satisfaction to your life. With the right attitude and mindset, you can tackle any challenge that life throws at you.

The one thing you must always keep in mind is to prepare yourself for the unexpected. Life doesn't always turn out the way you might have planned. Likewise, you cannot plan for every little detail of your life as a new parent. Learn to be flexible and adapt according to your situations. You might have spent hours and days together making plans on how to parent your child. However, nothing can ever truly prepare you for the experience you are about to have! So, I suggest that you buckle your seatbelts and get ready for an adventure of a lifetime! Being a parent is one of the most joyous aspects of life. Your child will be the source of immense happiness, and nothing can take this away from you. Learn to deal with all the stresses and obstacles that come along your way. Embrace parenthood with open and loving arms. Have a little faith in yourself, and everything will be fine.

Thank you, and all the best!

References Section 3

Adjusting to Motherhood - La Leche League GB. Retrieved from https://www.laleche.org.uk/adjusting-to-motherhood/#emotional

Becoming a dad: adjusting to fatherhood. (2019). Retrieved from https://raisingchildren.net.au/grown-ups/fathers/early-days/becoming-a-dad

Becoming a Father (for Parents) - Nemours KidsHealth. Retrieved from https://kidshealth.org/en/parents/father.html

beyondblue - Healthy Families. (2019). Retrieved from https://healthyfamilies.beyondblue.org.au/pregnancy-and-new-parents/becoming-a-parent-what-to-expect/adjusting-to-parenthood

Dunlop, J. (2019). Science confirms you are a different person after giving birth. Retrieved from https://www.mother.ly/life/how-becoming-a-mom-changes-you

Hamady, J. (2013). The Truth About Becoming A Parent. Retrieved from https://www.psychologytoday.com/us/blog/finding-your-voice/201312/the-truth-about-becoming-parent

Pinola, M. (2015). Everything You Need to Consider Before

Having Another Child. Retrieved from https://lifehacker.com/everything-you-need-to-consider-before-having-another-c-1692577488

Redrick, M., & Oz, L. (2019). How does one feel after becoming a mother? | Parenting. Retrieved from https://www.sharecare.com/health/parenting/how-feel-after-becoming-mother

Sarah, R. (2019). https://www.parents.com. Retrieved from https://www.parents.com/parenting/dynamics/single-parenting/surviving-and-thriving-as-a-single-mom/

Single parent? Tips for raising a child alone. Retrieved from https://www.mayoclinic.org/healthy-lifestyle/childrens-health/in-depth/single-parent/art-20046774

Single parents: the early days after separation. Retrieved from https://raisingchildren.net.au/grown-ups/family-diversity/single-parents/single-parents-early-days

Smith, M. The Ten Truths About Becoming a First Time Dad - The Good Men Project. Retrieved from https://goodmenproject.com/families/the-ten-truths-about-becoming-a-first-time-dad-wat/

Strebe, S. (2019). A First-Time Mom Shares the Truth About Life After Baby. Retrieved from https://www.mydomaine.com/first-time-mom-confessions

The Breastfeeding Mom's Best Exercise Guide | Medela.

(2019). Retrieved from http://www.medelabreastfeedingus.com/article/135/the-breastfeeding-mom's-best-exercise-guide

Tommy's - When and how to exercise after a c-section. Retrieved from https://www.tommys.org/pregnancy-information/labour-birth/caesarean-section/when-and-how-exercise-after-c-section

Made in the USA
Monee, IL
02 December 2020